T0202526

Lecture Notes in Artificial Intelligence   13549

Subseries of Lecture Notes in Computer Science

Series Editors

Randy Goebel
University of Alberta, Edmonton, Canada

Wolfgang Wahlster
DFKI, Berlin, Germany

Zhi-Hua Zhou
Nanjing University, Nanjing, China

Founding Editor

Jörg Siekmann
DFKI and Saarland University, Saarbrücken, Germany

More information about this subseries at https://link.springer.com/bookseries/1244

Nirav Ajmeri · Andreasa Morris Martin ·
Bastin Tony Roy Savarimuthu (Eds.)

Coordination, Organizations, Institutions, Norms, and Ethics for Governance of Multi-Agent Systems XV

International Workshop, COINE 2022
Virtual Event, May 9, 2022
Revised Selected Papers

Springer

Editors
Nirav Ajmeri
University of Bristol
Bristol, UK

Andreasa Morris Martin
University of Bath
Bath, UK

Bastin Tony Roy Savarimuthu
University of Otago
Dunedin, New Zealand

ISSN 0302-9743 ISSN 1611-3349 (electronic)
Lecture Notes in Artificial Intelligence
ISBN 978-3-031-20844-7 ISBN 978-3-031-20845-4 (eBook)
https://doi.org/10.1007/978-3-031-20845-4

LNCS Sublibrary: SL7 – Artificial Intelligence

This Springer imprint is published by the registered company Springer Nature Switzerland AG
The registered company address is: Gewerbestrasse 11, 6330 Cham, Switzerland

Preface

Coordination, organizations, institutions, norms and ethics (COINE) are five key governance elements that regulate the functioning of open multi-agent systems. The goal of the COINE workshop series that began in 2006 is to bring together researchers in autonomous agents and multi-agent systems (MAS) working on these five topics. The workshop focuses on both scientific and technological aspects of social coordination, organizational theory, artificial (electronic) institutions, normative and ethical MAS.

This edition of the COINE workshop, co-located with the 21st International Conference on Autonomous Agents and Multi-Agent Systems (AAMAS), was held virtually (through Zoom) due to the COVID-19, on May 9, 2022. A total of 15 papers were submitted to the workshop and 14 were accepted after peer review (11 full and three short). These papers were reviewed by three Program Committee members using a single-blind review method.

The papers were presented in three sessions. About 30 participants attended the workshop. This workshop also featured an invited talk on "Consent as a Foundation for Responsible Autonomy" from Munindar P. Singh, North Carolina State University, USA. The abstract of the talk is included in this volume.

This volume contains extended and revised versions of the 14 papers accepted to the workshop. The revisions made to the papers were reviewed by one reviewer, and this formed the second round of peer review. We are confident this process has resulted in high-quality papers.

The workshop could not have taken place without the contribution of many people. We are very grateful to our invited speaker as well as to all the COINE 2022 participants who took part in the discussions. We thank all the members of the Program Committee for their hard work (who are listed after this preface), and the guidance offered by the COIN(E) Champions. We also thank EasyChair for the use of their conference management system. Thanks also goes to the Springer for publishing the post-proceedings.

September 2022

Nirav Ajmeri
Andreasa Morris Martin
Bastin Tony Roy Savarimuthu

Organization

Chairs

Nirav Ajmeri	University of Bristol, UK
Andreasa Morris Martin	University of Bath, UK
Bastin Tony Roy Savarimuthu	University of Otago, New Zealand

Program Committee

Huib Aldewereld	HU University of Applied Sciences, Netherlands
Natasha Alechina	Utrecht University, Netherlands
Stefania Costantini	University of L'Aquila, Italy
Marina De Vos	University of Bath, UK
Nicoletta Fornara	Università della Svizzera italiana, Switzerland
Christopher Frantz	Norwegian University of Science and Technology, Norway
Benjamin Kuipers	University of Michigan, USA
Maite López-Sánchez	University of Barcelona, Spain
Eric Matson	Purdue University, USA
Juan Carlos Nieves	Umeä University, Sweden
Pablo Noriega	IIIA-CSIC, Spain
Julian Padget	University of Bath, UK
Luís Moniz Pereira	Universidade Nova de Lisboa, Portugal
Jaime Simão Sichman	Universidade de São Paulo, Brazil
M. Birna van Riemsdijk	University of Twente, Netherlands
Harko Verhagen	Stockholm University, Sweden
Pınar Yolum	Utrecht University, Netherlands

Consent as a Foundation for Responsible Autonomy (Abstracts)

Munindar P. Singh

North Carolina State University, Raleigh NC 27695, USA
mpsingh@ncsu.edu

Abstract. This talk focuses on a dynamic aspect of responsible autonomy, namely, to make intelligent agents act responsibly at run time. That is, it considers settings where decision making by agents impinges upon the outcomes perceived by other agents. For an agent to act responsibly, it must accommodate the desires and other attitudes of its users and, through other agents, of their users.

The contribution of this talk is twofold. First, it provides a conceptual analysis of consent, its benefits and misuses, and how understanding consent can help achieve responsible autonomy. Second, it outlines challenges for AI (in particular, for agents and multiagent systems) that merit investigation to form a basis for modeling consent in multiagent systems and applying consent to achieve responsible autonomy.

Contents

Designing International Humanitarian Law into Military Autonomous Devices

Jonathan Kwik[1], Tomasz Zurek[2]([⊠]), and Tom van Engers[3]

[1] Faculty of Law, University of Amsterdam, Amsterdam, The Netherlands
h.c.j.kwik@uva.nl
[2] T.M.C. Asser Institute, R.J. Schimmelpennincklaan 20-22, 2517 JN The Hague,
The Netherlands
t.zurek@asser.nl
[3] Complex Cyber Infrastructure, Informatics Institute, University of Amsterdam,
Amsterdam, The Netherlands
T.M.vanEngers@uva.nl

Abstract. This position paper presents a discussion on the problem of implementing the rules of International Humanitarian Law in AI-driven military autonomous devices. We introduce a structure of a hybrid data- and knowledge-driven computational framework of a hypothetical targeting system built from the ground up with IHL compliance in mind. We provide a model and a discussion of necessary legal tests and variables.

Keywords: Military AI · International Humanitarian Law · Autonomous devices · Autonomous weapon

1 Introduction

The application of artificial intelligence (AI) in weapon systems has become a major point of contention in the past decade. While many States have embraced the potential that AI brings for increasing precision and speed, improving their warfighting capacity, and reducing unneeded casualties [30,46], a significant opposition group has also formed which contests whether AI can ever be used in military contexts in a lawful and ethical manner [44].

One point which is not in debate is the applicability of international humanitarian law (IHL), the body of international law which governs the conduct of parties to an armed conflict. In particular, IHL [2] provides that belligerents do not have full freedom in their choice of means of warfare, i.e., the weapons they deploy. Any new weapon adopted by belligerents must be in compliance to IHL, and any new technology introduced must conform itself to these existing rules [25]. This includes AI. States [6,48], international organisations and NGOs [24,34] and commentators [39,46] universally agree that any weapon system which incorporates AI must uphold IHL.

Tomasz Zurek received funding from the Dutch Research Council (NWO) Platform for Responsible Innovation (NWO-MVI) as part of the DILEMA Project on Designing International Law and Ethics into Military Artificial Intelligence.

N. Ajmeri et al. (Eds.): COINE 2022, LNAI 13549, pp. 1–18, 2022.
https://doi.org/10.1007/978-3-031-20845-4_1

In light of this universal point of departure, there has been disagreement whether AI can actually be designed to comply with the legal rules. Many have expressed doubt that this can be done, arguing that AI will never be able to replace humans in this regard [42]. Those that elaborate usually point to the many (subjective) variables involved in IHL decisions and that these legal evaluations can only practically be effectuated by humans, not by the narrow AI of today [9]. In particular, the principles of distinction and proportionality in IHL are frequently cited as examples of rules which would be impossible to implement through AI [43]. Indeed, if a system is unable to properly execute these tests but is deployed regardless for tasks which would require it to conduct such legal assessments, it would be deployed unlawfully.

In this article, we counterbalance this perspective by proposing a structure of a hypothetical system which is constructed from the ground up with IHL rules in mind. The basic structure of the system is based on a commander's targeting cycle. During this process, commanders rigorously conduct several evaluations derived from IHL, and it is one of the primary mechanisms which ensure that principles such as distinction and proportionality are upheld in the field [8]. By translating this process into an equivalent in AI form, we provide one potential way IHL can be designed directly into an AI weapon system, and demonstrate that the demands for an IHL-compliant AI weapon system can theoretically be met. Our proposal aims at filling the gap between legal research on IHL and research on AI-driven autonomous decision-making systems.

Our system is deliberately built optimistically, in the sense that we capture all relevant legal tests required during targeting directly into one system. This includes target selection and sorting, distinction, proportionality calculation, and harm minimisation. It reflects what some define as a (fully) autonomous weapon system [38], i.e., where AI takes over all the functions of a commander. However, not all AI-controlled weapon systems will *necessarily* perform all of the steps described in our framework. A decision-making aid might only need the target sorting and collateral damage calculation functions, while a smart missile might only execute the proportionality calculation functionality. We make no statements on how, in detail, particular modules would be built in practice and the feasibility of such a system [30]. Rather, our main aim is explorative, i.e., to demonstrate that purely from a programming perspective, such a task can be undertaken. Another reason for including all legal tests into one framework is that variables such as military advantage and harm reduction are utilised throughout the various steps of the cycle. By capturing the entire targeting process at once, we are able to illustrate how different legal tests interlink and draw from the same variables and inputs.

Another distinctive feature of our framework is its hybrid nature which combines knowledge-driven and data-driven reasoning. One major dilemma often raised in the debate concerning AI and weapons is the dual problem that, on the one hand, the complexity and dynamicity of the modern battlefield practically requires resort to data-driven techniques such as deep neural networks for adaptability [12,41], while on the other hand, a level of decision-making transparency is required in IHL for the purposes of predictability and accountability

[20,27]. Through the use of a hybrid system, we draw on the strengths of both techniques while addressing both these challenges.

While we focus exclusively on the legal duties in IHL as the basis for our framework, it should be noted that in practice, many other factors - such as political and ethical perspectives - will also be important when defining the system's design requirements. [7,11,16,21,33] provide useful overviews of such considerations in the field of AI and weapon systems. We do not integrate these factors into our system at this point to maintain the framework's generality, as each State and military organisation will have different policies in force. By focusing primarily on the legal requirements, which are universal and non-derogable, we present a framework that is at a minimum IHL-compliant, after which organisations can adopt additional ethical, organisational and political requirements in accordance with their respective preferences and policies.

This paper proceeds as follows. We begin with a brief comment on the law applicable to military systems and the targeting cycle in general. We then explore, in depth, the military targeting cycle upon which our system's framework was built. This includes two aspects. First, we discuss the formal steps of the targeting process and how these are implemented during military operations. Second, we discuss what IHL principles are relevant for the targeting stage and their respective timings. We then integrate the law into the targeting process and present formalisations of specific rules of IHL, such as proportionality and minimisation, thereby also highlighting the variables which are the most important as inputs for these tests. On this basis, we subsequently introduce the framework of our system, briefly discuss the necessary functionalities of the system, its structure, and required data.

2 The Law and the Operational Framework

Limitations on the use of particular weapons are among the oldest provisions in the law of war and are inextricably woven into the fabric of modern IHL [50]. While there have been specific conventions restricting or prohibiting particular weapons such as chemical weapons or landmines, IHL also contains general principles such as the principle of distinction and proportionality which apply as a matter of customary international law [19]. For our framework, we will primarily rely the latter for two reasons. First, there evidently is no specialised normative convention as of yet for AI weapons, as the matter is still under discussion before the CCW Conferences in Geneva at the time of writing. Second, even if such a convention would exist, it is highly unlikely that all States would accede to it [51]. It is therefore in any situation relevant to consider more general IHL as a unifying normative standard applicable to all States.

As referenced in the introduction, there is little doubt that IHL applies to AI weapons. While modern IHL was born in the twentieth century and many new technologies have been introduced since then (e.g. precision weapons, cyber-weapons, AI), any new weapon is to conform itself to the applicable rules, and not vice versa [25]. IHL is applicable "without regard to the kind of technology in question" [17]. This is confirmed consistently throughout the debate on AI weapons. While there is some contention on whether existing IHL is necessarily *sufficient* to regulate all challenges that arise from AI in weapon systems [24], it is uncontroversial that IHL continues to apply for the use of military AI [18]. We echo Canada's [6] position that ensuring the lawfulness of AI weapons should be "constant reference points" for any discussion on the matter.

The ability of weapons to fulfil IHL requirements must be tested as early as the development, testing and adoption stages [23]. For parties to Additional Protocol I (API), this is explicitly provided in the form of a duty to conduct an 'Article 36' legal review [2]. Nevertheless, in our discussion, we will focus more on the operational half of the weapon's lifecycle. The reason for this is that reviews are conducted with respect to the *envisaged* tasks and circumstances of use for that particular weapon, and not *in abstracto* [37]. An example can be drawn from legacy weapons. During the Gulf War, Iraq was broadly condemned for the use of SCUD missiles, which had rudimentary guidance systems (i.e., a low accuracy rate), against Israeli population centres. However, such a weapon might validly pass a legal review if it was designed to be deployed only in civilian-free locations [40]. Similarly, an AI weapon with a very low specificity rate for distinguishing between military and civilian objects is not necessarily indiscriminate if, for instance, it is designed to operate underwater [46]. We argue, for this reason, that it is of particular importance to highlight the deployment phase of an AI weapon, i.e., the law that applies to military operations. Any generalised conclusions that may be drawn for the purposes of legal review (e.g. accuracy rates) can subsequently be drawn from the principles applicable to operations.

When we speak of the *operational* half of a weapon's lifecycle (i.e., deployment and use), the targeting cycle becomes our primary reference point. The aim of this process is to synchronise the choice of weapon, target and operational constraints to obtain the desired military effect [10]. Crucially, this effect must be achieved *while* ensuring compliance with IHL [8]. For this reason, militaries directly integrate legal tests into the targeting process to ensure that any weapon that is being considered meets the standards required for lawful use. Unfortunately, this operational perspective has not garnered the attention it deserves: Ekelhof [15] notes that much of the discussion on AI in weapon systems fails to properly take into account the military targeting process. We will therefore place greater scrutiny on this military art of targeting and the way IHL principles are implemented in practice during concrete operational circumstances.

2.1 The Targeting Cycle

In this section, we summarise the key steps of the targeting cycle based on the US military and NATO standard. While specific details and protocols may differ between military organisations, there the six steps explained below are generally applicable to most military operations.[1]

---

[1] The following overview is drawn from [13, 15, 32, 35].

(1) **Goal analysis** involves the commander analysing the broader goals previously set at the strategic or operational levels. For instance, in the NATO context, goals, target sets and guidance are generally provided by the Joint Force Commander. The commander considers the desired end state described by the broader goals and how to best achieve it.

(2) **Target analysis**, also called target development, involves the identification and specification of eligible targets. From this analysis, a general calculus is made of the action, time, and resources required to engage this target, to what extent this would contribute toward achieving the goals determined in Step (1), and whether there is a risk of collateral damage in view of its location, function, or characteristics.

(3) **Capability analysis** involves an assessment of the means and methods of warfare available to the commander [8]. It is during this phase that a weapon or weapons mix is selected which would best achieve the desired effects in light of details of the potential targets identified in Step (2). The art of comparing different alternatives and assigning the optimal combination, quantity and delivery of weapons (systems) to minimise collateral damage to the furthest extent possible while still achieving the desired objective is frequently referred to as *weaponeering* [44].

(4) **Capability assignment** features the definitive matching of the chosen capability mix to the targets. If necessary, the commander can order additional operational safeguards or considerations to be implemented. The assigned order is then forwarded to component commanders for final planning and execution.

(5) **Execution** takes place at the tactical level and features the operation being carried out based on the considerations made during all previous phases. A miniature version of the targeting cycle is performed here by the component commander. At some point, a decision to use force is made that cannot be undone, such as the drawing of the trigger on a sniper rifle or the launching of a weapon that cannot be recalled [35]. This is called the *execution moment*.

(6) **Assessment** is a crucial element in the iterative targeting procedure. Any change in the environment as a result of Step (5) is assessed, noted, and reported back to determine the impact of the use of force both in terms of achieving the desired military effect and damage to civilians. From this new information, the operational goals are re-assessed and the process begins anew in Step (1) until the desired military objective is achieved [22]. Additionally, even if no new engagements are planned, results from Step (6) are still recorded for the purposes of general after-action reviews and lessons learnt, both important processes for preventing the repetition of mistakes in future operations [32].

A graphical representation of this process can be found in Fig. 1.

2.2   Integrating the Law into the Cycle

Certain obligations in IHL are considered to be inextricably linked to the targeting process. These requirements are for a major part to be found in Article 57

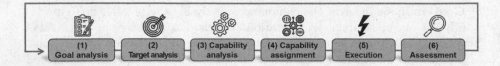

Fig. 1. Graphical illustration of the targeting cycle

of API. For instance, the UK Ministry of Defence [47] notes that "any system, before an attack is made, must verify that targets are military entities, take all feasible precautions to minimise civilian losses and ensure that attacks do not cause disproportionate incidental losses". In Thurnher's [45] view, targeting requires "examination of three key requirements of the law of armed conflict: distinction, proportionality, and precautions in the attack". A summation of these obligations, however, does not provide us with an indication of when and how they are exactly applied within the operational context. For this reason, we take a closer look at how militaries implement these legal tests when executing the targeting cycle.

As with the individual steps of the targeting cycle itself, there is no universal template to fall back upon, but there is usually an efficient order adopted by most militaries. Some authors, such as Corn [8] and Ducheine and Gill [14], have proposed flowcharts to this effect as shown in Fig. 2. Corn's approach is more akin to a decision tree, while Ducheine and Gill's approach better illustrates how individual legal tests are timed within the 6 steps illustrated in Fig. 1. The latter also demonstrates well the effects of different variables such as collateral damage and military advantage and that the process can skip tests or loop around, depending on the applicable inputs.

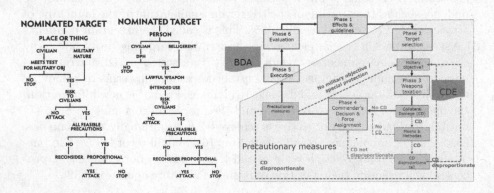

Fig. 2. Proposed flowcharts by Corn [8] and Ducheine and Gill [14]

While such flowcharts are useful for human commanders, for our hypothetical AI system, we need to extract more clearly the specific legal tests, how they are executed, and what inputs are required for each. We expand on this now.

3   Timing and Application of Legal Tests

No particular legal test is applied during **(1) Goal analysis**. However, the goal and rationale of the operation itself may have ramifications in terms of defining the importance of particular objectives or targets, i.e., the military advantage that can be gained. We will thus refer back to these goals in later phases when their legal relevance becomes more apparent.

(2) Target analysis features several important legal requirements. First, the principle of distinction (API Art.48) requires the collection of information and intelligence to ensure that the envisaged target(s) are indeed valid objectives. IHL asks attackers to "verify that the objectives to be attacked are neither civilians nor civilian objects and are not subject to special protection but are military objectives" (API Art.57(2)(a)(i)). Step (2) is usually deemed the ideal moment to apply this test [14]. Militaries also conduct collateral damage estimation at this phase, i.e., whether there is risk of incidental civilian harm tied to the target [32,44].

A specific form of precautions found in **API Art.57(3)**, and our first main legal test, can be applied at this stage [35]. This paragraph requires the following: "When a choice is possible between several military objectives for obtaining a similar military advantage, the objective to be selected shall be that the attack on which may be expected to cause the least danger to civilian lives and to civilian objects". This test involves two variables: military advantage and collateral damage, both of which can be derived from Step (1) and Step (2) respectively. While both variables are complex to quantify, the rule itself is relatively straightforward. If by $D = \{D_1, D_2, ...\}$ we denote a set of possible Decisions (*in casu*, attacking a particular target), and we define the Military Advantage gained from decision D_t as MA_t and the collateral damage involved from decision D_t as IH_t (from 'Incidental Harm'), then in a binary situation between D_1 and D_2, we could formalise the rule as follows:

$$\text{if } \exists_{D_x \in D} \forall_{D_y \in D \setminus D_x} s.t. MA_x \approx MA_y \wedge IH_x < IH_y \text{ then select } D_x \qquad (1)$$

(3) Capability analysis is the most involved step in terms of legal tests. The two most important principles addressed at this stage concern proportionality and minimisation, which both relate to collateral damage. First, **proportionality** prohibits any Decision (i.e., a combination of a target, capability and method of delivery) which causes incidental civilian harm excessively disproportionate to the concrete military advantage anticipated (API Art.57(2)(a)(iii)). As with the test in Art.57(3) above, this involves a comparison between military advantage and collateral damage. Multiple options can be considered 'proportionate' as long as the threshold of excessiveness is not exceeded [31]; in other words, proportionality effectively sets a maximum threshold of how much collateral damage remains acceptable vis-à-vis the anticipated military advantage. If we define this threshold as p, we can formalise[2] the rule as:

---

[2] A similar approach to the modeling of proportionality rule can be found in [52].

$$\textbf{if } \exists_{D_x \in D} \text{ s.t. } \frac{IH_x}{MA_x} \leq p \textbf{ then } status(D_x) = legal \textbf{ else } status(D_x) = illegal$$

$$(2)$$

It is not sufficient to only look at proportionality. IHL also mandates that incidental harm to civilians must be *minimised* to the furthest extent feasible (API Art.57(2)(a)(ii)). Essentially, "[i]f there is a choice of weapons or methods of attack available, a commander should select those which are most likely to avoid, or at least minimize, incidental damage" [26]. This obligation involves comparing different options in terms of capabilities, operational constraints and methods of delivery. For instance, applying this test may result in less accurate weapons being discarded, altering the timing of attack, or selecting a less destructive damage mechanism [37]. Commanders are not expected to do the impossible: the corollary of *feasibility* empowers commanders to take into consideration all relevant circumstances, including those relevant to the success of military operations [37]. If too much military advantage is lost due to a particular minimisation measure, they are permitted to select a more reasonable option that better balances the humanitarian and military considerations in play [40]. In a binary comparison therefore, this rule would be formulated:

$$\textbf{if } \exists_{D_y \in D} \forall_{D_x \in D \backslash D_y} : \frac{IH_y}{MA_y} < \frac{IH_x}{MA_x} \textbf{ then } select D_y \qquad (3)$$

It must also be emphasised that because proportionality and minimisation are both concerned with the variable of collateral damage (IH), the tests can be disregarded in cases where this variable does not factor [14]. If the weapon is projected to function only in a military-exclusive environment, for example, these tests may be skipped.

Finally, there is one additional requirement that must be mentioned at this stage related to weapons which are *inherently illegal*. Customary law generally recognises two aspects which make a weapon unlawful per se: that of causing unnecessary suffering and of being inherently indiscriminate [37,45]. In addition, *weapons treaties* may be in force for the belligerent which limit the use of certain weapons beyond what customary law requires [4]. While these are important legal restrictions, it is irregular for these weapons to reach the targeting stage: It is the role of weapons reviewers to filter out such weapons during development and adoption [23,48]. Nevertheless, it cannot be ruled out that a weapon fulfilling such criteria actually reaches the front lines at some point. To guard against this possibility and maintain IHL-compliance, we add this function to allow the AI to deny its own use if its deployment would be unnecessarily injurious, inherently indiscriminate or prohibited by treaty.

During **(4) Capability assignment** up to the **execution moment**, a series of final precautionary measures are enacted. In part these involve continuous *re-tests* of all previous obligations on a more detailed level [35]. The reason for this is to ensure that all input assumptions related to the classification of the target, its military worth and the collateral damage estimations underlying the previous decisions remain applicable. Related to this, IHL also requires *cancelling* the ordered attack if it becomes known throughout this period that any of these assumptions are no longer valid (API Art.57(2)(b)). In addition, advance *warning* must be provided in cases where civilians can be affected (API Art.57(2)(c)), although this duty only applies in cases where this is reasonable, i.e., where it would not compromise the success of the attack [37].

Finally, during **(6) Assessment**, a legal obligation that could be relevant is the duty to *suppress and repress*. It is part of the broader obligation to respect and ensure respect for IHL at all times [1], and involves both general measures to prevent and address violations of IHL ('suppression') and, in case a serious breach has occurred, that the persons responsible for such violations be held criminally responsible ('repression') [1]. Thus, requirements related to foreseeability, understandability, traceability and the keeping of digital records may become relevant at this stage [27].

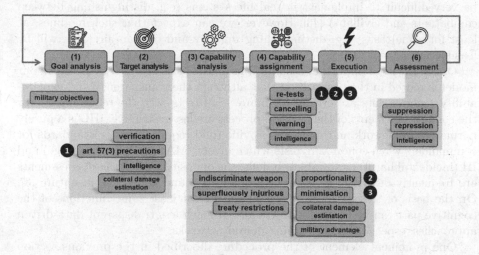

Fig. 3. Overview of legal tests and inputs during the targeting cycle

A graphical summary of targeting phases and the corresponding legal tests, in addition to supporting actions that contribute toward the fulfilment of these legal obligations, are depicted in Fig. 3. Legal tests are represented by orange boxes, important inputs by purple boxes, and the formulae described above by black circles. The framework is intended to be function-agnostic, but whether each test is to be applied by a human or an AI will depend on the specific AI under consideration. If the execution of a particular phase is left to an AI, then it must be demonstrated that the AI in question is capable of executing the legal tests necessary for that phase [4].

4 The General Framework of the Autonomous Targeting System

In the previous section, we described the general targeting sequence and the legal tests that must be applied during each step for lawful use of force. In this section, we are going to present the general structure of our autonomous targeting system which incorporates these legal tests into its functionality. Note that we will not discuss any particular targeting scenario, but rather introduce a general (function agnostic) framework which is IHL-compliant. Moreover, we will not discuss the technical details of the machinery which can be used to implement the targeting system, but only propose a structure and possible techniques which may allow for creation of a targeting system which can observe the legal requirements identified in Sect. 2. Further technical details of this system will be discussed in future papers. We realize that some functionalities may still be very difficult to implement in real life systems (e.g. distinguishing between combatants and civilians) [43]. However, we can expect that such modules, at least for some tasks (e.g. distinguishing military and civilian aircraft), will be feasible in the near future.

One of the most important assumptions on the basis of which we designed our model is rooted in the observation that although the transparency and explainability requirements are crucial for many legal tests [27], the requirements for the cognitive elements of the decision process are less restrictive. IHL is a purely normative framework and does not provide rigid requirements or standards for commanders when conducting tests which involve MA (military advantage) and IH (incidental harm) as variables. In fact, the opposite is true: these assessments are frequently described as eminently qualitative and subjective in nature [3]. On the basis of the above, we can assume that at least some functions of the cognitive part can be created with the use of much less transparent data-driven approaches, especially deep learning neural networks.

One prominent element of the procedure described in the previous section is the comparison between anticipated military advantage and anticipated incidental harm. Obviously, while making his decision, a human commander does not represent either variable in a quantifiable form. An autonomous AI-driven model, however, requires not only a quantifiable representation, but also a representation which allows for their formal comparison [5].

We will use values as a central concept allowing for representation of both military advantage and incidental harm. Values we understand as an abstract (trans-situational) concept which allows for the estimation of a particular action or a state of affairs and which influences one's behavior. Consequently, on the basis of such a definition, we assume that particular values can be satisfied to a certain degree [53]. Such a definition of value can be seen as a kind of abstraction of concrete results of an action, and allows us to use them as a central concept in our model where they play an important role as an intermediate concept representing an abstraction of a targeting situation.

On the basis of the above, we provide a discussion of how, from a technical viewpoint, the requirements of each stage of the targeting process can be fulfilled.

Since this is a position paper presenting the overall structure of the system, we will not enter into the technical details of particular functions used in the model, unless it is necessary to make the model understandable or when it constitutes a key element of the discussion. More detailed presentations of the technical nuances will be included in future work.

A battlefield is a multiagent environment par excellence featuring many allied, neutral and adversarial agents which the system must be able to understand and account for [36]. In our framework, we present all functions as if they are fulfilled by a single agent for simplicity. In actual systems, it is possible that several agents are involved which contribute together toward the execution of the framework's different functions, or that particular functions are performed by distinct agents working together. Additionally, input data such as signal intelligence may be obtained from an allied agent, which can either be a human observer or another AI unit such as a reconnaissance drone [49]; similarly, the final decision resulting from our framework can be effectuated by an agent on the frontlines such as a human squad or combat robot. These permutations do not affect the viability of our framework as long as all functions are executed correctly by the agents involved and, in the case of collaborating agents, all necessary tests take into consideration all involved agents. With regard to adversarial agents, sufficient robustness and adaptability against opponents' efforts to disrupt the system's proper functioning must be made into important design requirements [12].

5 The Structure of the System

In this section we introduce the general structure of the proposed system.

5.1 The Basics of the Model

Firstly, we discuss the basics:

- **Introduction of goals.** In the first stage of the targeting process, the commander performs the analysis of the desired state on the strategic and operational levels. Since such an analysis is performed from a broader perspective, taking into account the general goals of military operations, we argue that for the autonomous device, such a goal can be represented as a set of thresholds of a group of values which constitute a more general value *military advantage*.
- **Input data.** In order to perform all required tests and to decide which decision should be made, some necessary data has to be prepared. Firstly, the agent should distinguish a set of available actions with their anticipated results and evaluate them in the light of MA and IH. In order to fulfill this stage, a set of preparatory tasks should be performed:
  - Generation, on the basis of signal intelligence and the general circumstances of the case (denoted by S), of the set of decisions which can possibly be made in given circumstances. By D we denote a set of available decisions.

- Prediction of the result of every decision from the set. Note that for the tests described in the previous section, the levels of MA and IH relate to the *anticipated* results of decisions, which means that they are by nature uncertain. Let R be a set of all possible results of actions (decisions from set D) and let PR be a set of conditional probabilities of those results, given a particular situation and decision.
- Evaluation of the decision results in the light of the set of relevant values. Suppose a set of decision results R and a set of functions Φ_V which returns the level of satisfaction of a particular value v_x by result r_y. By VR we denote a set of levels of satisfaction of all values by the results of all available decisions.

  Since function Φ has a crucial character for our model, we briefly present here how it can be obtained. The goal is to find a function which for every possible result ($r \in R$) can predict the level of satisfaction of every value (the level to which a predicted result of a decision would satisfy the relevant value, e.g. *military advantage*, *life of civilians*, etc.). Suppose that every result from set R (possible results of actions) will be evaluated and labelled by human annotators in the light of every value (by assigning a number representing the level of satisfaction of a given value). On the basis of such data and a ML-based regression mechanism, a regression function can be trained which can predict the level of satisfaction of a given value on the basis of a particular result. A more detailed analysis and discussion of this approach will be presented in future work.
- Calculation of the expected level of satisfaction of a particular value (it can be calculated on the basis of probabilities of results PR and evaluation of the decisions' results VR.) By EV we denote a set of levels of satisfaction of all values by all available decisions.

5.2   The Structure

In this section we present the structure of the proposed system:

- *Extraction of available decisions* is responsible for obtaining a set of available decisions (S is an input, D is an output of the module).
- *Result prediction module* is responsible for predicting results of decisions with their probabilities (D and S are inputs to the module, while PR and R are outputs).
- *Evaluation module* is responsible for performing function ϕ (G, S, and R are inputs to the module, VR is an output).
- *Parameters' extraction module* is the module which returns the set of parameters of decisions. By the parameters of a decision we understand details of a decision such as type of weapon, timing, etc. D is an input, PAR is an output of the module.
- *Expected evaluation module* is responsible for calculating the expected evaluation of decisions in the light of values (VR and PR are an input, EV is an output of the module).

- *Treaties fulfillment module* is responsible for performing function filtering decisions which do not fulfill treaties (PAR and $FPAR$ are inputs, DTR is an output of the module). If by $FPAR$ we denote the set of requirements imposed by treaties, then the module can work as a logic-based reasoning mechanism.
- *Goals fulfillment module* is responsible for performing function filtering decisions which do not fulfill the commander's goals (G and EV is an input, DG is an output of the module). If by a goal we understand the minimal acceptable levels of values' satisfaction (see [53]), then a given decision will fulfill the goal if the expected level of satisfaction of relevant values will be above the thresholds assumed in G.
- *Harm minimization filter* is responsible for the process of minimization of incidental harm (EV is an input, DMH is an output). A given decision will pass the test if for this decision formula 3 will be fulfilled.
- *Proportionality test* is responsible for performing the proportionality test (EV is an input, DP is an output). A given decision will pass the test if for this decision formula 2 will be fulfilled.
- *Article 57(3) Filter* is responsible for the process of filtering decisions which for the same military advantage causes greater harm to civilians (Article 57(3), EV is an input, DT is an output). A given decision will pass the test if for this decision formula 1 will be fulfilled.
- *Fulfillment of requirements* is responsible for joining together results of the above tests (DT, DP, DMH, DG, and DTR are inputs and DAV is an output). A given decision will fulfill this requirement if all tests have been passed.
- *Decisions ordering* is responsible for ordering available decisions (those fulfilling the above tests) on the basis of the level of satisfaction of Military Advantage (DAV and VR is an input, *Decisions* is an output of the module).

The structure of the proposed model is presented in Fig. 4. The model features a clear distinction between (1) the cognitive part of the decision process, including functions extracting available decisions, their results, and evaluation (the upper part of the scheme) and (2) the reasoning part of the decision process, including legal tests, goal test, treaties test, etc. (lower part of the scheme). This distinction between the parts of the decision process is a notable strength of the framework we propose because it provides some degree of transparency and explainability. These attributes have been identified as crucial both for the lawful use of AI weapon systems and upholding the responsibility of its users [27].

As such, the structure we propose relies on the conviction that for the sake of transparency, legal tests should be performed in an explainable way, i.e. the system should explicitly check whether a given decision passes all necessary tests, while the other elements of the decision process can utilize data-driven approaches. Such an approach is compliant with the general approach regarding hybrid systems, in which the data-driven part is used for extraction of the input data for a knowledge-based system, and generally allows for filling the so-called semantic gap between data and knowledge [29].

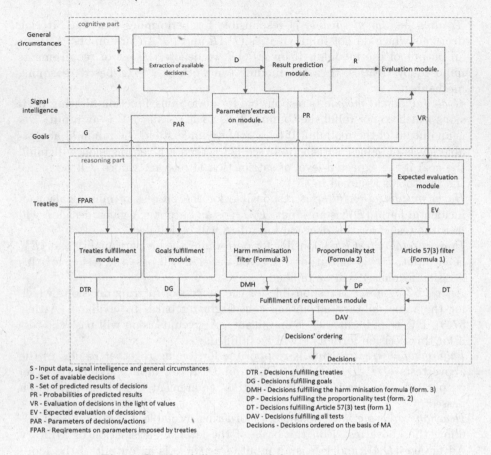

S - Input data, signal intelligence and general circumstances
D - Set of avaiable decisions
R - Set of predicted results of decisions
PR - Probabilities of predicted results
VR - Evaluation of decisions in the light of values
EV - Expected evaluation of decissions
PAR - Parameters of decisions/actions
FPAR - Reqirements on parameters imposed by treaties

DTR - Decisions fulfilling treaties
DG - Decisions fulfilling goals
DMH - Decisions fulfilling the harm minisation formula (form. 3)
DP - Decisions fulfilling the proportionality test (form. 2)
DT - Decisions fulfilling Article 57(3) test (form 1)
DAV - Decisions fulfilling all tests
Decisions - Decisions ordered on the basis of MA

Fig. 4. Graphical illustration of the system's structure

6   Discussion and Conclusions

The paper introduces a framework for creating an AI-based hybrid targeting system for military autonomous agents capable of operating within the bounds of IHL. The main goal was to present a way how IHL can be integrated from the ground up into a military AI system in order to better guarantee IHL-compliance. We present the main stages of the targeting process, identify which legal requirements are imposed by IHL and what variables and elements these tests encompass, and introduce a mechanism which allows for the development of a system fulfilling those requirements.

To achieve this, we introduced a model of a hybrid system which combines data-driven parts (possibly created with the use of deep learning neural networks) and knowledge-driven parts. This type of system composition allows us to draw from the advantages of both AI paradigms, while also compensating for at least part of their respective disadvantages. In particular, one major disadvantage of data-driven AI, lack of transparency, is overcome to some extent, which is a boon for IHL compliance.

Further development of our framework requires the verification of the model. Since this paper presents a general model of the decision-making process only, we cannot introduce here a fully-fledged, technical verification of our proposal. Instead we briefly sketch how the verification of the model can be performed.

Since our framework consists of two parts - cognitive and reasoning ones - the verification should be performed twofold:

– The cognitive part should be verified on the basis of statistical quality of all modules. For example, the quality of sensors, the accuracy of predictions and evaluations, etc. The verification of this part is task-dependent. For example, signal intelligence should be verified in the light of accuracy of object detection related to the specific sensors: cameras, recorded sound, satellite pictures etc.; the prediction module should be evaluated in the light of accuracy of predictions made; etc. Every module should be verified in the context of the concrete intended purpose for which the device is designed [28].
– The reasoning part requires formal and legal verification of all tests (see Sect. 3 where we discuss some legal aspects concerning the model) and the whole reasoning process and the formal and experimental analysis of the reasoning machinery used to performing necessary tests, which will be presented in our future works.

Our hypothetical framework was developed with the aim of identifying and elaborating the functionalities which would be necessary for AI-driven systems to conform to IHL. We make no practical pronouncements concerning technical implementation or in what type of weapon this framework would be incorporated, as these details would depend on the military organisation's specific needs. In addition, it is possible that comparable systems are currently under development by militaries. These systems are likely to remain confidential and thus, it is difficult for us to test our framework vis-à-vis those systems. Our proposal nevertheless can be used as a reference or guideline for both current and future constructors intending to build systems with IHL compliance in mind.

References

1. Geneva Convention for the Amelioration of the Condition of the Wounded and Sick in Armed Forces in the Field (adopted 12 August 1949, entered into force 21 October 1950) 75 UNTS 31
2. Protocol Additional to the Geneva Conventions of 12 August 1949, and relating to the Protection of Victims of International Armed Conflicts (adopted 8 June 1977, entered into force 7 December 1978) 1125 UNTS 3 (1977)
3. Anderson, K., Waxman, M.C.: Law and ethics for autonomous weapon systems: why a ban won't work and how the laws of war can (2013)
4. Boothby, W.H.: Regulating new weapon technologies. In: Boothby, W.H. (ed.) New Technologies and the Law of War and Peace, pp. 16–42. Cambridge University Press, Cambridge (2019)

5. Boulanin, V.: Mapping the development of autonomy in weapon systems: a primer on autonomy. Stockholm International Peace Research Institute, Stockholm (2016)
6. Canada: Opening Statement by Canada at Second Meeting of the Group of Governmental Experts on Lethal Autonomous Weapons Systems (LAWS), 9–13 April 2018. Technical report (2018)
7. Chavannes, E., Arkhipov-Goyal, A.: Towards Responsible Autonomy: The Ethics of Robotic and Autonomous Systems in a Military Context. The Hague Centre for Strategic Studies, The Hague (2019)
8. Corn, G.S.: War, law, and the oft overlooked value of process as a precautionary measure. Pepperdine Law Rev. **42**, 419–466 (2014)
9. Crootof, R.: The killer robots are here: legal and policy implications. Cardozo Law Rev. **36**, 1837–1915 (2015)
10. Curtis E. Lemay Center: Air Force Doctrine Publication 3–60 - Targeting (2019). https://www.doctrine.af.mil/Doctrine-Publications/AFDP-3-60-Targeting
11. Dahlmann, A., Dickow, M.: Preventive regulation of autonomous weapon systems. Technical report. Stiftung Wissenschaft und Politik Research Paper 2019/RP 03, Berlin (2019). https://doi.org/10.18449/2019RP03
12. Defense Innovation Board: AI principles: recommendations on the ethical use of artificial intelligence by the department of defense defense innovation board. Technical report, Department of Defense (2019). https://media.defense.gov/2019/Oct/31/2002204458/-1/-1/0/DIB_AI_PRINCIPLES_PRIMARY_DOCUMENT.PDF
13. Department of the Army: The Operations Process (2019)
14. Ducheine, P., Gill, T.: From cyber operations to effects: some targeting issues. Militair Rechtelijk Tijdschrift **111**(3), 37–41 (2018)
15. Ekelhof, M.: Human control in the targeting process. In: Autonomous Weapon Systems: Implications of Increasing Autonomy in the Critical Functions of Weapons, pp. 53–56. ICRC, Versoix (2016)
16. Eklund, A.M.: Meaningful Human Control of Autonomous Weapon Systems: Definitions and Key Elements in the Light of International Humanitarian Law and International Human Rights Law. Totalförsvarets forskningsinstitut, Stockholm (2020)
17. Geiß, R., Lahmann, H.: Autonomous weapons systems: a paradigm shift for the law of armed conflict? In: Ohlin, J.D. (ed.) Research Handbook on Remote Warfare, pp. 371–404. Edward Elgar, Cheltenham (2017)
18. Group of Governmental Experts on Lethal Autonomous Weapons Systems (GGE on LAWS): Report of the 2019 session of the Group of Governmental Experts on Emerging Technologies in the Area of Lethal Autonomous Weapons Systems, UN document CCW/GGE.1/2019/3, 25 September 2019. Technical report, Geneva (2019)
19. Henckaerts, J.M., Doswald-Beck, L.: Customary International Humanitarian Law, Volume I - Rules. ICRC, Geneva (2005)
20. Holland Michel, A.: The black box, unlocked: predictability and understandability in Military AI. Technical report, United Nations Institute for Disarmament Research, Geneva, Switzerland, September 2020. https://doi.org/10.37559/SecTec/20/AI1. https://unidir.org/black-box-unlocked
21. House of Lords: Select committee on artificial intelligence, report of session 2017–19, AI in the UK: Ready, willing, and able? Technical report, HL Paper 100, 16 April 2018 (2018)
22. Huffman, W.B.: Margin of error: potential pitfalls of the ruling in the prosecutor v. Ante Gotovina. Military Law Rev. **211**, 1–56 (2012). https://hdl.handle.net/10601/2104

23. International Committee of the Red Cross: A Guide to the Legal Review of New Weapons, Means and Methods of Warfare: Measures to Implement Article 36 of Additional Protocol I of 1977. ICRC, Geneva (2006)
24. International Committee of the Red Cross: Report of the ICRC Expert Meeting on Autonomous weapon systems: technical, military, legal and humanitarian aspects, 26–28 March 2014, Geneva. Technical report (2014)
25. International Court of Justice: Legality of the Threat or Use of Nuclear Weapons (1996)
26. International Criminal Tribunal for the Former Yugoslavia: Final Report to the Prosecutor by the Committee Established to Review the NATO Bombing Campaign Against the Federal Republic of Yugoslavia. Technical report (2001). https://www.icty.org/en/press/final-report-prosecutor-committee-established-review-nato-bombing-campaign-against-federal
27. Kwik, J., Van Engers, T.: Algorithmic fog of war: when lack of transparency violates the law of armed conflict. J. Future Robot Life, 1–24 (2021). https://doi.org/10.3233/FRL-200019
28. Meier, M.W.: Lethal autonomous weapons systems. In: Complex Battlespaces, pp. 289–316. Oxford University Press, Oxford, January 2019. https://doi.org/10.1093/oso/9780190915360.003.0010
29. Meyer-Vitali, A., et al.: Hybrid AI white paper. Technical report, TNO (2019). tNO 2019 R11941
30. Ministère des Armées (France): L'intelligence artificielle au service de la défense. Technical report, Ministère des Armées, Paris (2019)
31. Neuman, N.: Applying the rule of proportionality: force protection and cumulative assessment in international law and morality. Yearb. Int. Hum. Law **7**, 79–112 (2004). https://doi.org/10.1017/S1389135904000790
32. North Atlantic Treaty Organisation: Allied Joint Doctrine for Joint Targeting, Edition A Version 1 (April 2016) AJP-3.9 (2016)
33. Office of the Assistant Secretary of Defense for Research and Engineering: Technical Assessment: Autonomy. US Department of Defense, Washington, D.C. (2015)
34. Roff, H.M.: Meaningful human control or appropriate human judgment? The necessary limits on autonomous weapons (2016)
35. Roorda, M.: NATO's targeting process: ensuring human control over (and lawful use of) 'autonomous' weapons. In: Williams, A.P., Scharre, P.D. (eds.) Autonomous Systems: Issues for Defence Policymakers, pp. 152–168. NATO, The Hague (2015)
36. Russell, S.J., Norvig, P.: Artificial Intelligence: A Modern Approach, 3rd edn. Pearson, New Jersey (2010)
37. Sandoz, Y., Swinarski, C., Zimmerman, B.: Commentary on the Additional Protocols of 8 June 1977 to the Geneva Conventions of 12 August 1949. Martinus Nijhoff (1987)
38. Scharre, P., Horowitz, M.C.: An introduction to autonomy in weapon systems. Technical report, Center for a New American Security (2015)
39. Scharre, P.D.: The opportunity and challenge of autonomous systems. In: Williams, A.P., Scharre, P.D. (eds.) Autonomous Systems: Issues for Defence Policymakers, pp. 3–26. NATO, The Hague (2015)
40. Schmitt, M.N., Garraway, C.H., Dinstein, Y.: The Manual on the Law of Non-international Armed Conflict, With Commentary. International Institute of Humanitarian Law, San Remo (2006)
41. Schuller, A.: At the crossroads of control: the intersection of artificial intelligence in autonomous weapon systems with international humanitarian law. Harv. Natl. Secur. J. **8**, 379 (2017)

42. Sharkey, N.E.: Towards a Principle for the Human Supervisory Control of Robot Weapons. Politica Società **3**, 305 (2014)

43. Szpak, A.: Legality of use and challenges of new technologies in warfare - the use of autonomous weapons in contemporary or future wars. Eur. Rev. **28**(1), 118–131 (2020). https://doi.org/10.1017/S1062798719000310

44. Thorne, J.G.: Warriors and war algorithms: leveraging artificial intelligence to enable ethical targeting. Technical report, Naval War College (2020). https://apps.dtic.mil/sti/citations/AD1104171

45. Thurnher, J.S.: Examining autonomous weapon systems from a law of armed conflict perspective. In: Nasu, H., McLaughlin, R. (eds.) New Technologies and the Law of Armed Conflict, pp. 213–228. T.M.C. Asser Press, The Hague (2014)

46. Thurnher, J.S.: Feasible precautions in attack and autonomous weapons. In: Heintschel von Heinegg, W., Frau, R., Singer, T. (eds.) Dehumanization of Warfare, pp. 99–117. Springer, Cham (2018). https://doi.org/10.1007/978-3-319-67266-3_6

47. UK Ministry of Defence: The UK approach to unmanned aircraft systems: joint doctrine note 2/11. Technical report, United Kingdom Ministry of Defence (2011)

48. United States Office of General Counsel of the Department of Defense: Law of War Manual, Updated December 2016. Technical report, Department of Defense (2015)

49. U.S. Air Force Office of the Chief Scientist: Autonomous horizons: system autonomy in the air force a path to the future, volume I: human-autonomy teaming. Technical Report, AF/ST TR 15–01 (2015)

50. Wallace, D.: Cyber weapon reviews under international humanitarian law: a critical analysis, Tallinn paper no 11. Technical report (2018)

51. Wilson, C.: Artificial intelligence and warfare. In: Martellini, M., Trapp, R. (eds.) 21st Century Prometheus, pp. 125–140. Springer, Cham (2020). https://doi.org/10.1007/978-3-030-28285-1_7

52. Zurek, T., Woodcock, T., Pacholska, M., van Engers, T.: Computational modelling of the proportionality analysis under international humanitarian law for military decision-support systems, January 2022. https://ssrn.com/abstract=4008946

53. Zurek, T.: Goals, values, and reasoning. Expert Syst. Appl. **71**, 442–456 (2017). https://doi.org/10.1016/j.eswa.2016.11.008

Epistemic Diversity and Explanatory Adequacy in Distributed Information Processing

Asimina Mertzani[1]([⊠]) [iD], Jeremy Pitt[1,2], Andrzej Nowak[2,3], and Tomasz Michalak[4]

[1] Department of Electrical and Electronic Engineering, Imperial College London, London, UK
asimina.mertzani20@imperial.ac.uk
[2] Robert B. Zajonc Institute for Social Studies, University of Warsaw, Warsaw, Poland
[3] Department of Psychology, Florida Atlantic University, Boca Raton, FL 33431, USA
[4] Institute of Informatics, University of Warsaw, Warsaw, Poland

Abstract. A common problem facing an organisation of autonomous agents is to track the dynamic value of a signal, by aggregating their individual (and possibly inaccurate or biased) observations (sensor readings) into a commonly agreed result. A meta-problem is to *explain* the observation of the value: to say what rules produced the signal value that has been observed. In this paper, we use the Regulatory Theory of Social Influence and self-organising multi-agent systems to simulate a Distributed Information Processing unit (DIP) trying to solve such a meta-problem. Specifically, we examine what configuration of initial conditions on the DIP produce what type of epistemic condition for the collective, and determine the *explanatory adequacy* of this condition, i.e. to what extent does the DIP's explanation of the rules match the actual rules. The results offer some further insight into the need for epistemic diversity for self-improvement in dynamic self-organising systems.

Keywords: Distributed information processing · Explanatory adequacy · Knowledge processing · Social influence · Multi-agent systems

1 Introduction

A commonly recurring problem confronting an organisation, composed of autonomous agents connected by a (social) network but lacking a central authority, is to map a set of individual measurements, judgements, votes, opinions or preferences into a single collective output. This problem is typically encountered in social systems (e.g. jury trials, deliberative assemblies, etc.) as well as cyber-physical systems (e.g. cybernetic systems, sensor networks, etc.)

An instance of this general problem is truth tracking, when the task of an organisation of autonomous agents is to track the dynamic value of a signal, by aggregating their individual (and possibly inaccurate or biased) observations (sensor readings) into a commonly agreed result. In this sense, the organisation can be seen as a *Distributed Information Processing* (DIP) unit. However, such a DIP can also face a meta-problem: to *explain* the observation of the value – i.e. to say what rules produced the signal value that has been observed. In this case, the DIP is not trying to pool its diverse opinions to order to produce a social choice, but to pool its diverse knowledge to produce a 'plausible' explanation.

N. Ajmeri et al. (Eds.): COINE 2022, LNAI 13549, pp. 19–37, 2022.
https://doi.org/10.1007/978-3-031-20845-4_2

This paper investigates a solution to this problem using the Regulatory Theory of Social Influence (RTSI) [12]. RTSI is chosen because it has two unique propositions: firstly, that social influence is bilateral, i.e. that as well as sources seeking targets to influence, targets are seeking sources by whom to be influenced; and secondly that in addition to exchanging opinions, people also exchange information processing rules. Both of these propositions are essential for addressing the problem: the first because we want experts or 'specialists' to emerge, because they know more and are better at solving the problem; and the second because we want their knowledge (of the rules) to flow over the social network.

Therefore, we implement an algorithmic model of RTSI within a self-organising multi-agent systems' to simulate a DIP trying to solve such a meta-problem by proposing (collectively) a set of rules to explain the observed value that may (or may not) match the actual rules that produce the value. Specifically, we experimentally investigate what configuration of initial conditions on the DIP produce what type of epistemic condition of the DIP.

We then want to evaluate the *explanatory adequacy* of the DIP's solution. The term 'explanatory adequacy' is used in linguistics to describe an analysis which provides a 'reasonable' account of a linguistic phenomenon [18]. We want to know if the DIP can produce a 'reasonable' or 'plausible' explanation, based on the extent to which its collective explanation matches the actual cause (i.e. the *ground truth*). We measure the difference using a suitable metric (cosine similarity) and use that as an indicator of explanatory adequacy.

Accordingly, this paper is structured as follows. Section 2 establishes the background of DIP and RTSI, and gives a formal specification of the problem. Section 3 describes the experimental design, Sect. 4 defines the multi-agent simulation, and Sect. 5 presents a set of experimental results. After a consideration of related and further work in Sect. 6, Sect. 7 concludes that these results offer some further insight into the need for epistemic diversity for self-improvement in dynamic self-organising systems.

2   Background: DIP, RTSI and Plato's Cave

In this section we review the background to this work: organisations as distributed information processing units (DIP), a theory of social influence in such units, the Regulatory Theory of Social Influence (RTSI), and a specification of the problem we are trying to solve, which has similarities, at an abstract level, to the problem posed in the allegory of Plato's Cave (see http://classics.mit.edu/Plato/republic.mb.txt).

2.1   Distributed Information Processing Units (DIPs)

Many organisations, in the form of complex cyber-physical, socio-technical or social systems, often have to function as *Distributed Information Processing* units (DIPs), i.e., although composed of many different autonomous components, the components have to act as a collective to transform a set of data inputs into a single output. Although, depending on the context, the precise definition differs (cf. [23] vs. [12]), in this paper the term DIP refers to an organisation of autonomous, (socially) networked agents encountering a requirement to self-manage their diverse, dispersed, and potentially incomplete and inconsistent knowledge.

In general, successful knowledge management enables a DIP to make correct decisions, identify expertise, maintain collective memory, provide education, spark innovation and even accumulate "wisdom". A more mundane function, perhaps, is to converge on a *ground truth* from a set of observations that may have been influenced by environmental or community bias (cf. [20]). Here, though, rather than converging on the truth, we want to study how a DIP can produce *explanatory adequacy*: can the DIP converge on the rules that produced that truth, rather than the truth itself. In this situation, we need a theory which considers social influence not just in terms of the exchange of opinions, but also in the exchange of processing rules. The theory we use is the Regulatory Theory of Social Influence.

2.2 Regulatory Theory of Social Influence (RTSI)

RTSI is a psychological theory proposed by Nowak [12] that focuses on the target's perspective of social influence, and specifically, examines how the targets look for sources by whom to be influenced. This theory emphasises a target's intentions and strategies, and posits that targets actively monitor others' opinions and behaviours, and are fully engaged in the controlling the influence process.

In this way, a target tries to optimise its decision-making and conserve its own resources by delegating the tasks of information gathering and/or information processing to individuals that they credit for the such tasks. This enables targets to leverage others' network, processing capacity or knowledge, maximising their access to information and information processing rules. Therefore, social influence becomes an instrument of targets to maximise their individual cognitive efficiency and quality of their outcomes, which are reflected by improvements in individual and collective performance over time.

2.3 Problem Specification

In this study, the situation to be addressed by a DIP, using RTSI, is illustrated in Fig. 1. The DIP is embedded in an environment, in which there is a process $\mathcal{P}$ that converts some set of inputs into an output. The process $\mathcal{P}$ is parameterised by a set of n processing rules, each with an associated weight in [0..1]. This set of rules, denoted by $\mathcal{K}$, is the *ground truth knowledge* given by:

$$\mathcal{K} = \{(r_i, w_i) \mid i \in [1..n] \wedge \Sigma_{i=1}^{n} w_i = 1.0\}$$

We denote by $\mathcal{K}_r$ the set of rules in $\mathcal{K}$ (without the weights).

Each agent a in the DIP 'knows' $\mathcal{K}^a$, which is some subset of m rules of $\mathcal{K}_r$, $m \leq n$. Each agent associates a random weight with each of its rules, with the weights normalised to sum to 1.0, so that the knowledge of agent a is:

$$\mathcal{K}^a = \{(r_1, w_1), \ldots, (r_m, w_m)\} \quad \text{such that} \quad \forall i, 0 \leq i \leq m, r_i \in \mathcal{K}_r$$

Note, that if $i = 0$, then the agent knows nothing.

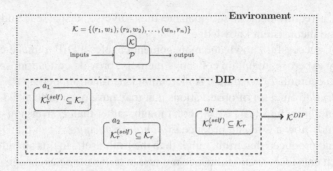

Fig. 1. The Problem: Is $\mathcal{K}^{DIP}$ an 'adequate explanation' for output of $\mathcal{P}(\mathcal{K})$?

The problem for the $\mathcal{N}$ agents comprising the DIP is to use their partial and distributed knowledge to 'explain' the solution to process $\mathcal{P}$ as parameterised by $\mathcal{K}$. This is done by each agent offering its own explanation $\mathcal{K}^a$ for parameters to process $\mathcal{P}$, and these are 'aggregated' into a collective explanation $\mathcal{K}^{DIP}$. In addressing this task, the agents have three 'tools' at their disposal:

- *sharing*: using RTSI, an agent can ask one of the neighbouring agents in its social network, for a processing rule (or rules) that it (the neighbouring agent) used in its 'explanation' of $\mathcal{K}$.
- *feedback*: each agent receives feedback from the environment on the quality of the collective knowledge and their own contribution, which is used to update 'attitudes' to itself and a neighbouring agent (if it asked one); and
- *'discovery'*: new agents joining the system may bring new knowledge to the system, which may then be shared as above, using RTSI.

Given this context, we investigate:

- what different initial conditions of the DIP, including population variation (e.g. static, dynamic), rate of social learning, and rate of 'discovery', . . .
- . . .produce what different epistemic condition on the individual knowledge bases, i.e. the similarity of $\{\mathcal{K}^a \mid a \in \mathcal{N}\}$, which we identify as either diversity, incongruence, or stagnation, and. . .
- . . .evaluate explanatory adequacy of $\mathcal{K}^{DIP}$, i.e. the (dis)similarity of $\mathcal{K}^{DIP}$ to $\mathcal{K}$.

In passing, we note that this problem can be seen, at its most abstract, as a form of Plato's Cave, wherein a group of people in a cave try to derive the true nature of an object from the shadow it casts on the cave wall. Note, though, there are three perspectives on knowledge: $\mathcal{K}$, the ground truth knowledge, $\mathcal{K}^{DIP}$, the aggregated knowledge of the DIP, and the "knowledge potential" $\mathcal{K}^{\cup}$, which is an epistemological limit on what it is possible for an agent to know, because this knowledge exists somewhere in the DIP.

However, as in Plato's Cave, this is not a once-off, one-shot problem. The overall situation is as illustrated in Fig. 2, where it can be seen that the DIP composition is

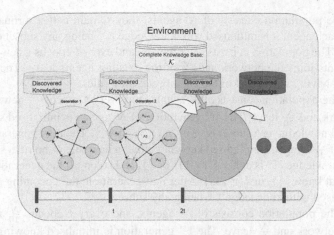

Fig. 2. The DIP unit and knowledge changing over time

dynamic (agents may leave and join), and the knowledge made available ("discovered", or introduced along with new agents) also varies.

Therefore, "expertise" in the group is also temporary, and knowledgeable agents who may be good at the task may also be lost to the group. As such, there are two perspectives on the collective: one being a functional perspective as a DIP, where the collective pool knowledge and identify expertise in order to accomplish a common goal (cf. [1]), and the other being a societal perspective, where the group is using social influence as a way to persuade and change attitudes about a common problem (cf. [13]). Accordingly, we will use the terms 'experts' or 'specialists' in the DIP and the sources of influence in RTSI inter-changeably, and equate knowledge with the processing rules; likewise the terms DIP, community and collective are all inter-changeable.

3   Experimental Design

To address the problem defined in the previous section, this section details the experimental design, firstly specifying the initial conditions on the DIP, (i.e. the independent variables), and secondly specifying a metric for computing the DIP's epistemic condition and explanatory adequacy (i.e. the dependent variables).

3.1   Initial Conditions for the DIP (Independent Variables)

For specifying the initial conditions on the DIP, we define two independent experimental variables, $\mathcal{F}$ and $\mathcal{R}$. The former determines the rate of change of the population and rate of change of knowledge. The latter defines a constraint on the RTSI algorithm which affects how the agents communicate the processing rules and how they influence one another.

The DIP will operate in a succession of T *epochs*, and every $t < T$ epochs (except in the *static* condition) some new agents are added and some are removed. In each epoch the DIP will produce and evaluate $\mathcal{K}^{DIP}$ against $\mathcal{K}$, so $\mathcal{F}$ can have one of eight values:

- *static:* The population consists of $\mathcal{N}$ agents, they remain active throughout all T epochs. Each agent a is initialised with knowledge $\mathcal{K}^a$ being any subset of $\mathcal{K}$.
- *dynamic:* The population consists of $\mathcal{N}$ agents, and every t epochs a new generation of $\frac{\mathcal{N}}{10}$ agents joins the network and $\frac{\mathcal{N}}{10}$ of the existing agents leave. The agents are initialised having any subset of the eight processing rules.
- *restart:* The population consists of $\mathcal{N}$ agents, and every t epochs $\frac{\mathcal{N}}{10}$ new agents join the network and $\frac{\mathcal{N}}{10}$ leave. The 1st generation of $\mathcal{N}$ agents is initialised so that each agent's a knowledge is a subset of $\{(r_1, w_1), (r_2, w_2)\}$. The next generation, which consists of $\frac{\mathcal{N}}{10}$ agents, is initialised knowing either a new rule or no rule, so each new agent's knowledge $\mathcal{K}^a$ is either $\{(r_3, 1)\}$ or $\{\}$, and so on till the generation the generation that knows $\{\}$, or $\{(r_8, 1)\}$. After that generation, the upcoming generations are initialised with knowledge $\mathcal{K}^a$ being any subset of $\mathcal{K}$.
- *iterate:* The population consists of $\mathcal{N}$ agents, and every t epochs $\frac{\mathcal{N}}{10}$ new agents join the network and $\frac{\mathcal{N}}{10}$ leave. The 1st generation is initialised knowing $\{(r_1, 1)\}$, the next knows a new rule, so their knowledge is $\{(r_2, 1)\}$, and so on, so every new generation knows only a new processing rule and the only way to access past knowledge is to interact with others.
- *add rapid:* The population consists of $\mathcal{N}$ agents, and every t epochs $\frac{\mathcal{N}}{10}$ new agents join and $\frac{\mathcal{N}}{10}$ leave. The 1st generation of $\mathcal{N}$ agents is initialised so that each agent's a knowledge is a subset of $\{(r_1, w_1), (r_2, w_2)\}$. The next generation knows what their ancestors knew and a new processing rule, so the knowledge of each new agent a is a subset of the rules $\{(r_1, w_1), (r_2, w_2), (r_3, w_3)\}$, and so on. So, new knowledge is progressively added to the population through the new generations.
- *add slow:* The is scenario is similar with *add rapid*, but, in this setting, the new generations are added every $t * 1.6$ epochs instead of t.
- *add rapid/slow long:* New generations are added every $t/t * 1.6$ epochs as per *add rapid/slow*, but the simulator runs for $T * 2$ epochs.

Additionally, for each of the different values of $\mathcal{F}$ we specify two ways of communicating the processing rules $\mathcal{R}$:

- *max*: The sources can only share only one processing rule, therefore they select the rule with greatest weight, which corresponds to the rule that they perceive as the most important piece of knowledge.
- *all*: The sources share their knowledge base, so the target gains access to all the rules that the source knows.

3.2   Epistemic Condition and Explanatory Adequacy

To 'measure' the epistemic condition and the explanatory adequacy of the DIP under different initial conditions, we require a metric to measure diversity in two dimensions:

- the epistemic diversity, i.e. how different the agents' knowledge bases are from each other, given by $\sum_{i=1}^{N} \sum_{j=1}^{N} \mathbf{diff}(i, j)$; and
- the explanatory adequacy, i.e. the divergence of the DIP's knowledge from the ground truth knowledge, given by $\mathbf{diff}(\mathcal{K}^{DIP}, \mathcal{K})$.

For the **diff** function, there are many metrics to measure diversity, such as Euclidean Distance, Manhattan Distance, KL divergence etc. We use cosine similarity, because we want to identify the variations between the vectors of weights on processing rules – which represent agents' knowledge and ground truth of the environment – and therefore need a metric that focuses on the orientation rather than the magnitude.

Cosine similarity is a metric used for the comparison of the similarity between two non zero vectors $\mathbf{A}$ and $\mathbf{B}$ in $\mathbb{R}^n$. Specifically, it measures the cosine of the angle between the two vectors, and its value is given by Eq. 1:

$$cos\_sim(\mathbf{A}, \mathbf{B}) = \cos(\theta) = \frac{\mathbf{A} \cdot \mathbf{B}}{\|\mathbf{A}\|\|\mathbf{B}\|} = \frac{\sum_{i=1}^{n} A_i B_i}{\sqrt{\sum_{i=1}^{n} A_i^2}\sqrt{\sum_{i=1}^{n} B_i^2}} \tag{1}$$

After defining the metric for evaluating the performance of the collective and the individuals, we need then to define the two groups of the population being observed. The first group is the *participants* which refers to all the agents that have been randomly selected to participate to the next epoch. The other group, who are the 'specialists', is a subset of the *participants* and identifies the sources of processing rules. In particular, in this context, if agent i asks for processing rules agent j, and j asks agent k, then specialist is considered the agent k which constitute the actual source of influence. These agents don't have any notion of expertise, but they are the ones credited by their network.

In the beginning of the experiments, all the agents give equal credence for processing rules to all the agents of their network, they are initialised with different knowledge, and consequently, they give different processing rules to the agents that ask them, and the credence that others give to them is adjusted overtime based on the utility of the information that they offer.

Aiming to identify the capability of the agents to adequately explain the environment (explanatory adequacy), we computed the cosine similarity of the knowledge bases $\mathcal{K}^a$ of agents with the ground truth $\mathcal{K}$, which we denote with $\mathcal{CE}_1$ as well as the cosine similarity of the knowledge bases $\mathcal{K}^a$ of specialists with the ground truth $\mathcal{K}$, which we denote with $\mathcal{CS}_1$. Moreover, to observe knowledge distribution and diversity through the exchange of processing rules (epistemic diversity), we measured the difference between the pairwise comparison of the cosine similarity of the knowledge bases $\mathcal{K}^a$ of the agents and the number of participants divided by the difference between the square of the number of participants and the number of participants which we denote by $\mathcal{CE}_2$, and difference between the pairwise comparison of the cosine similarity of the knowledge bases $\mathcal{K}^a$ of the specialists and the number of specialists divided by the difference between the square of the specialists and the number of specialists, which we denote by $\mathcal{CS}_2$. Moreover, the calculation of $\mathcal{CE}_1$ and $\mathcal{CE}_2$ is given by Eqs. 2 and 3 respectively, and the calculation of $\mathcal{CS}_1$ and $\mathcal{CS}_2$ can be computed by substituting *participants* with *specialists* on those equations.

$$\mathcal{CE}_1 = \frac{\sum_{i=1}^{participants} cos\_sim(\mathcal{K}^i, \mathcal{K})}{\sum_{i=1}^{participants} i} \tag{2}$$

$$\mathcal{CE}_2 = \frac{\sum_{i=1}^{participants,} \sum_{j=1}^{participants, j \neq i} cos\_sim(\mathcal{K}^i, \mathcal{K}^j) - \sum_{i=1}^{participants} i}{\left(\sum_{i=1}^{participants} i\right)^2 - \sum_{i=1}^{participants} i} \tag{3}$$

4 Formal Specification

This section provides the formal specification of the multi-agent model. This section defines the agents of the system, the environment in which they exist as well as the RTSI algorithm for knowledge processing based on which the agents act in this environment.

4.1 The Environment

The environment $\mathcal{E}$ consists of a network of agents which try to identify the complete knowledge base $\mathcal{K}$ corresponding to the ground truth. The agents are connected through a network $\mathcal{G}(\mathcal{N}, \text{m}, \mu)$ which is a Klemm-Eguiluz network [8] with $\mathcal{N}$ nodes (where each node is a agent), m the number of fully connected agents used for the generation of the network and characterised as "active", and μ the probability of a new agent to be attached to one of the "active" agents (otherwise the agents attaches to an inactive agent and becomes active, substituting a randomly selected agent from the active agents) as described in [17]. This network type was selected because it combines all three properties of many "real world" irregular network, that is high clustering coefficient, short average path length, and scale-free degree distribution.

4.2 Agent Specification

The autonomous networked units of the population are described by the term "agents". The specification of the agents is based on the specification in [15], and is given by the 6-tuple defined in Eq. 4:

$$i = \langle SN, \mathcal{K}^i, sc_i, TN_i, a, b \rangle \qquad (4)$$

where SN_i is its social network (connected neighbours), $\mathcal{K}^i$ its knowledge, which is a subset of the knowledge in the environment $\mathcal{K}$ (possibly with different weights), sc_i is a measure of self-confidence of its knowledge (relative to its neighbours), in whom it also gives credence $\tau_{i,j}$ for each agent $j \in SN_i$ (cf. [3]). These values are stored in an ordered list of credence to neighbours TN_i, and are updated each time agent i asks a neighbour j for knowledge (i.e. for a processing rule or rules) depending on how well (similarly) this neighbour approximates the complete knowledge of the environment $\mathcal{K}$. Each agent orders its neighbours in descending order of credence. Each agent has also two reinforcement coefficients a, b which define the rate of change of self-confidence and credence to the network after each epoch.

4.3 Algorithm

The algorithm is an iterative process of T epochs, and in every epoch each participating agent goes through the steps described in Algorithm 1. Therefore, in every epoch, a subset of agents $\mathcal{A}$ is randomly selected to participate in the next epoch *participants* $\subset$ $\mathcal{A}$. The aim of the agents is to manage to produce a good approximation of the complete knowledge base of the environment $\mathcal{K}$, while they are only given only a subset of this knowledge.

Throughout the epochs each agent looks for sources in the DIP that can provide the processing rules that produce the best approximation of the complete knowledge $\mathcal{K}$. The knowledge of the DIP can be accessed by asking a neighbouring agent. Therefore, in each epoch, each agent iterates over its social network SN_i according to the order of credence TN_i, to find the source to ask. The neighbour selected j is questioned how similar is its knowledge with the complete knowledge base $\mathcal{S}^{\cup}$ and also the agent asking computes the similarity of its own knowledge with the ground truth $\mathcal{S}^{(self)}$. If the neighbour asked can offer a better approximation of the ground truth than the agent asking has, then the agent proceeds in asking the neighbour for processing rules. Depending on the value of the independent variable $\mathcal{R}$, the agent that asked for processing rules (target) either receives as a reply a processing rule with a weight (which is the processing rule of the neighbour j that has the greatest weight for j), if $\mathcal{R} = max$, otherwise it receives all the processing rules and their weights. Then, i is integrating this knowledge $\mathcal{K}^{\cup}$ to its knowledge $\mathcal{K}^i$. After that follows the process of reflection, in which each agent updates its credence to the neighbour selected τ_{ij} and its self-confidence sc_i depending on whether it can more adequately explain the environmental knowledge than its neighbour.

$$w_{r_i avg} = \frac{\sum_{j=1}^{participants} w_{r_{ij}}}{\sum_{j=1}^{participants} j} \quad (5) \qquad\qquad w_{r_i c} = \frac{w_{r_i avg}}{\sum_{i=1}^{n} w_{r_i avg}} \quad (6)$$

In this way, the collective forms a knowledge $\mathcal{K}^{DIP}$ which is the outcome of the aggregation of the participating agents' knowledge and normalising the weights, as shown in 5 and 6. The collective/DIP knowledge is defined as in 7.

$$\mathcal{K}^{DIP} = \{(r_1, w_{r_1 c}), ..., (r_r, w_{r_r c})\} \qquad\qquad (7)$$

Algorithm 1: RTSI for knowledge seeking: for each agent i

$j = selected\ neighbour\ from\ network$;
$\mathcal{S}^{(self)} = cos\_sim(\mathcal{K}^{(self)}, \mathcal{K})$;
$\mathcal{S}^{\cup} = cos\_sim(\mathcal{K}^{\cup}, \mathcal{K})$;
if $\mathcal{S}^{(self)} < \mathcal{S}^{\cup}$ **then**
    if $\mathcal{R} = max$ **then**
        $\mathcal{K}^{\cup} = \{(r_x, w_{r_x}) | (r_x, w_{r_x}) \in \mathcal{K}^j \wedge \neg\exists(r_y, w_{r_y}) \in \mathcal{K}^j.w_{r_y} > w_{r_x}\}$;
    else
        $\mathcal{K}^{\cup} = \mathcal{K}^j$;
    end
end
if $\mathcal{S}_i^{(self)} > \mathcal{S}^{\cup}$ **then**
    $sc_i = sc_i + a * (1 - sc_i)$;
    $\tau_{i,j} = \tau_{i,j} - b * \tau_{i,j}$;
end
if $\mathcal{S}^{(self)} < \mathcal{S}^{\cup}$ **then**
    $sc_i = sc_i - b * sc_i$;
    $\tau_{i,j} = \tau_{i,j} + a * (1 - \tau_{i,j})$;
end

According to this formal specification, a multi-agent simulator has been implemented in Python3, which is an extension of the system presented in [14] to include the exchange of processing rules. This simulator was used to run a series of experiments, the results of which are present in Sect. 5.

Table 1 presents the simulator parameters for the agents and the RTSI algorithm. This specifies either a fixed representative value used in the experiments (e.g. the number or agents, reinforcement coefficients, etc.) or a range of values for those that are randomly assigned (e.g. the individual agent knowledge bases). Other experiments could examine different combinations of initialisation of these variables, e.g. to look for effects of scale, but this is left for further work.

Table 1. Simulator Parameters and Variables

Symbol	Description: factor of agent i	Initial Condition/Range
$\mathcal{N}$	Network of agents	100
m	Total number of edges	$\frac{\mathcal{N}}{10}$
μ	Number of edges to 'active' agents	0.75
$participants$	Agents participating in the next epoch	$\frac{\mathcal{N}}{2}$
$\mathcal{K}^i$	Individual knowledge base	$\{(r_1, w_1), \ldots, (r_m, w_m)\}, \forall i, 0 \leq i \leq m.r_i \in \mathcal{K}_r$
r_k	Processing rule k	$k = \{1,2,...,r\}$
w_{r_k}	Weight of rule r_k	$0 \leq w_{r_k} \leq 1$
sc_i	Self-confidence for similarity of knowledge	0.5
a, b	Self-confidence & credence reinforcement coefficients	0.1, 0.1
SN_i	Social network	1 to $\mathcal{N}$ agents
TN_i	Ordered list of credence to social network	list length from 1 to $\mathcal{N}$
τ_{ij}	Credence to agent j	$0 \leq \tau_{ij} \leq 1$
$\mathcal{S}^{(self)}$	cos_sim between self and environmental knowledge	$0 \leq \mathcal{S}^{(self)} \leq 1$
$\mathcal{S}^{\cup}$	cos_sim between knowledge of agent (neighbour) asked and ground truth	$0 \leq \mathcal{S}^{\cup} \leq 1$
$r_{\cup}$	Rule proposal of (neighbour) agent asked	$r_k. \in \mathcal{K}_r$
$w_{\cup}$	Weight proposal of (neighbour) agent asked	$0 \leq w_{\cup} \leq 1$
$\mathcal{K}^{\cup}$	Knowledge proposal of (neighbour) agent asked	$\{(r_1, w_1), \ldots, (r_m, w_m)\}, \forall i, 0 \leq i \leq m.r_i \in \mathcal{K}_r$
$\mathcal{K}^{DIP}$	Collective knowledge	$\{(r_1, w_1), \ldots, (r_m, w_m)\}, \forall i, 0 \leq i \leq m.r_i \in \mathcal{K}_r$
$w_{r_i avg}$	Average weight of rule r_i	$0 \leq w_{r_i avg} \leq \frac{\mathcal{N}}{2}$
$w_{r_i c}$	Normalised average weight of rule r_i	$0 \leq w_{r_i c} \leq 1$

5   Experimental Results

This section describes three experiments which investigate what initial conditions on the DIP produce what type of epistemic condition, and how 'adequately' does that epistemic condition explain the ground truth knowledge. The experiments range over the variables $\mathcal{F}$ and $\mathcal{R}$ of Sect. 3.1 under the initial conditions specified in Table 1, with $T = 5000, t = 300$:

- Experiment 1: Static population of agents, with complete fixed knowledge, and dynamic population with complete fixed knowledge (all the knowledge is available from the first epoch of the simulation).

– Experiment 2: Dynamic population with progressive addition of new knowledge but non-persistence of 'discovered' knowledge.
– Experiment 3: Dynamic population with progressive addition of new knowledge and with persistence of already 'discovered' knowledge.

The following subsections describe the results of each experiment in turn, before discussing some over-arching results in Sect. 5.4.

5.1 Experiment 1: Static and Dynamic Populations

In the first set of experiments, we explore the dynamics of the system for $\mathcal{F}$ being set to *static* and *dynamic*, and agents are initialised with any combination of the available processing rules.

Figure 3 illustrates the evolution of common and specialists knowledge for the different settings. Specifically, the 1st column illustrates the results for *static* and the 2nd for *dynamic* for $\mathcal{R}$ being *max* and *all*. The black line is calculated according to $\mathcal{CE}_1$, the red based on $\mathcal{CS}_1$, the green according to $\mathcal{CE}_2$, and, finally, the blue line based on $\mathcal{CS}_2$.

Therefore, the black line indicates how 'adequately' the DIP identifies the ground truth $\mathcal{K}$, while the red line indicates whether how 'adequately' the specialists identify the ground truth $\mathcal{K}$. The green and blue lines demonstrate the diversity of knowledge within the collective and within the specialists, showing the (dis)similarity between the knowledge of each group.

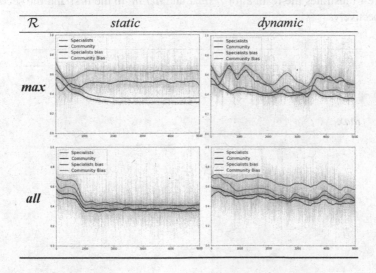

Fig. 3. Exp. 1: Knowledge dynamics for static and dynamic population.

Starting with the *static* condition, when $\mathcal{R} = max$, the similarity between the processing rules of the agents is high, since the group as a whole is influenced by the specialists to promote a single rule. By contrast, when the sources share all their knowledge ($\mathcal{R} = all$), the community and the specialists similarity is decreased. However, the lines corresponding to how well do specialists and community track the environmental knowledge (red and black) remain low in both cases. This is because the population is static, therefore the community is prone to ask the sources credited during the first epochs, regardless of whether they maintained their knowledge. Static populations are stable but also stagnant and agent don't increase significantly their processing capacity although they could (since all the knowledge is discovered).

With the *dynamic* condition, for both *max* and *all*, the agents can better explain the environmental knowledge. In the former case, the knowledge of the specialists and the community is continuously modified as illustrated by the fluctuating green and blue lines. This demonstrates that different *epistemes* are generated in this condition, and the system could be characterised as quasi-stable and moving from one temporary equilibrium to another with different values for its control variables (cf. [16]). In the latter case, the specialists are well-identified and have significantly higher similarity with the environmental knowledge than the community; however it seems that the other agents cannot assimilate this knowledge and the DIP knowledge seems stagnant.

5.2   Dynamic Population, Progressive Addition, non-Persistence

In this experiment, we observe how the system works with a dynamic population (in which the specialist sources are not so easily identified), there is progressive addition of new knowledge brought by joining agents, but knowledge is non-persistent (i.e. new agents only bring new 'discovered' knowledge).

Figure 4 illustrates the results for *restart* and *iterate* in the first and the second column respectively.

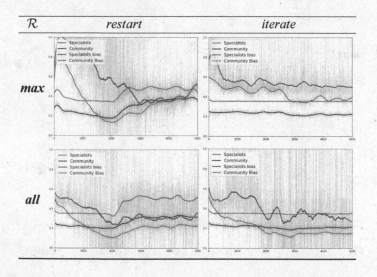

Fig. 4. Exp. 2: Knowledge dynamics for DIP with non-persistent knowledge

In the *restart* condition, the first generation is initialised with two rules available, the next joins with the third rule, and so on until the 8th generation that has all the rules available (as defined in Sect. 3.1). For $\mathcal{R} = max$, the similarity of processing rules within the community is high since agents are given only one rule from the sources. This phenomenon is less striking for $\mathcal{R} = all$, where agents quickly assimilate new knowledge. Note that when new generations possess only one processing rule (only the new piece of knowledge), agents consider that they cannot learn from others, and their knowledge remains narrow (low similarity with the environmental knowledge). However, after epoch 2100, when all the processing rules are made available for the new generations, there is a significant increase in the community and specialists' knowledge because agents have different levels of knowledge (i.e. different similarity with environmental knowledge) and they seek sources to provide them with missing bits of knowledge.

The phenomenon of agents not asking for processing rules because they perceive others as having similar knowledge is even clearer under the *iterate* condition. Particularly, in both *max* and *all*, most agents seem to have equal knowledge (i.e. equal similarity of own processing rules and environmental processing rules), due to the fact that they all have either zero or one processing rule, and consequently only agents having an empty knowledge base ask for knowledge. This variation between the empty knowledge base and the knowledge base containing one processing rule generates the difference in the similarity of the knowledge of the sources and the community (red and green lines), with the specialists. Additionally, the fluctuation of the intrinsic similarity of the collective as well as the group of specialists is caused by the randomness in the selection of agents to leave and join the network.

5.3 Dynamic Population, Progressive Addition, Persistence

In this experiment, we observe the behaviour of the system under progressive addition of knowledge, but new agents may bring any discovered knowledge. Figure 5 demon-

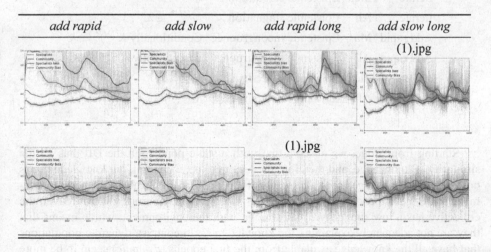

Fig. 5. Exp. 3: Knowledge dynamics for progressively added knowledge.

strates $\mathcal{CE}_1$, $\mathcal{CS}_1$, $\mathcal{CE}_2$, and $\mathcal{CS}_2$ for the *add rapid/slow (long)* scenarios, for $\mathcal{R}$ *max* in the first row and *all* in the second.

The rapid progressive addition of knowledge allows minor improvement both in short-term and long-term (*add rapid* and *add rapid long*). Particularly, in both *max* and *all*, the specialists and community knowledge remains low (red and black lines) because new rules cannot be assimilated. By contrast, the slow addition fosters epistemic improvement (*add slow* and *add slow long*). Moreover, in all these scenarios, when $\mathcal{R} = max$ different *epistemes* are produced because sources share parts of their knowledge and both the community and the sources develop different beliefs over time.

5.4   Summary of Experiments

To conclude this section, Table 2 summarises what configuration of initial conditions for the DIP produces what type of epistemic condition of the DIP, and assesses the capability of the DIP to explain adequately the environment.

Table 2. Summary of experimental results

$\mathcal{F}$	$\mathcal{R}$	Epistemic condition	Explanatory adequacy
Static	Max	Epistemic stagnation	$\mathcal{K}^{DIP} \not\cong \mathcal{K}$
Static	All	Epistemic stagnation	$\mathcal{K}^{DIP} \not\cong \mathcal{K}$
Dynamic	Max	Epistemic incongruence	Conditionally $\mathcal{K}^{DIP} \cong \mathcal{K}$
Dynamic	All	Epistemic incongruence	Conditionally $\mathcal{K}^{DIP} \cong \mathcal{K}$
Restart	Max	Epistemic diversity	$\mathcal{K}^{DIP} \cong \mathcal{K}$
Restart	All	Epistemic diversity	$\mathcal{K}^{DIP} \cong \mathcal{K}$
Iterate	Max	Epistemic stagnation	$\mathcal{K}^{DIP} \not\cong \mathcal{K}$
Iterate	All	Epistemic stagnation	$\mathcal{K}^{DIP} \not\cong \mathcal{K}$
Add rapid	Max	Epistemic incongruence	Conditionally $\mathcal{K}^{DIP} \cong \mathcal{K}$
Add rapid	All	Epistemic incongruence	conditionally $\mathcal{K}^{DIP} \cong \mathcal{K}$
Add slow	Max	Epistemic diversity	$\mathcal{K}^{DIP} \cong \mathcal{K}$
Add slow	All	Epistemic diversity	$\mathcal{K}^{DIP} \cong \mathcal{K}$

Starting from *static*, we observe that with a static population the DIP has a high similarity of knowledge, and therefore they seem to be congruent, but knowledge does not seem to be exchanged over the social network. This does not allow further improvement in the system and potential adaptation to a dynamic environment. Moreover, the collective has a low similarity of knowledge with the environment, which means that they are not adequately explaining the knowledge $\mathcal{K}$. In contrast, dynamic populations that have all the knowledge available from the first epochs (*dynamic*) seem to be more diverse, and they transition from a status of higher to lower congruence and vice-versa.

Although for certain periods of time they manage to accurately explain the environment, there are other periods that they do not succeed in identifying the ground truth.

Moreover, when agents perceive their knowledge to be similar to others knowledge, they do not ask for processing rules and the collective knowledge stagnates. Specifically, in the *restart* condition, during the first epochs where they are given only one processing rule, agents do not communicate their knowledge. This is also the case for the *iterate* condition, where knowledge remains stagnant while the collective is fragmented. Therefore, we argue that knowledge remains static and the agents do not manage to model the phenomenon which they observe in the environment, when they consider that others are incapable of helping them (perceiving their knowledge similar with their own knowledge), although they might have different knowledge that is useful for them.

This would suggest that systemic evolution and epistemic diversity require both knowledge differentiation and the capability of agents to perceive this differentiation. However, in *restart*, when all the knowledge becomes available (after 2500 epochs), the agents quickly increase the utility of the collective knowledge with respect to explanatory adequacy and they produce a collective knowledge that is a better approximation of the knowledge situated in the environment. It is worth noting that the sources seem to 'emerge', i.e. to increase the utility of their knowledge, significantly more than the community, which shows that the ones identified by the collective as specialists are also more likely to assimilate new knowledge.

Furthermore, the rapid addition of new processing rules fosters diversity, but the agents do not have enough time to adapt and assimilate new knowledge; therefore they can be congruent in the short term but incongruent in the long-term. This cannot guarantee that the DIP will manage to produce an adequate explanation of the environmental knowledge for an extended period. In this case, we observe different *epistemes* being generated, which could be considered a demonstration of Foucault's Theory of Knowledge & Power in cyber-physical systems. However, when agents share all their knowledge (*all*) the population becomes more congruent with the environment and has the potential to evolve since it can provide an adequate explanation of the environment.

6   Related and Further Research

Related research has extensively studied issues of consensus formation in complex systems [11]. More specifically, previous work has focused on the conditions which lead to the alignment of the network [4], as well as the division of it into multiple opinions [7]. Much effort has also been made to identify the probability of forming a majority depending on the network topology [5].

A baseline for using RTSI as a model of distributed information processing, proposing the exchange of subjective opinions for the formation of a collective decision and the self-organisation have been established in [15]. This work extends this model of RTSI in a different direction, and specifically proposes the communication of processing rules not for forming a collective opinion but for developing a collective knowledge and social explanations. Lopez-Sanchez and Müller [10] suggest that social influence in the form of hate speech can propagate through the whole virtual community and propose countermeasures such as education, deferring hateful content and cyber activism as mechanisms for altering it. In this research, we argue that social influence can be also used as an instrument for spreading knowledge and providing explanations instead of propagating hate and negative opinions.

Additionally, there is a substantial body of literature in topics of information sharing and norm emergence. Villatoro et al. [22] proposed the use of social instruments to facilitate norm convergence and proved that the subconventions delay global convergence and jeopardise stability. Incremental social instruments and creating ties between agents has also provided a mechanism for dissolving self-reinforcing structures and facilitating global norm emergence [9]. Norm or convention emergence can be also achieved though social learning [19], and under various topologies [2]. Although these works offer deep insight into the emergence of a collective property (socially-constructed behaviours) from local interactions, our approach differs by proposing RTSI as a mechanism for producing 'adequate' collective explanations for external properties from local interactions.

Further research could establish a set of evaluation criteria and metrics for multi-agent populations that face problems of producing social and environmental explanations. Additionally, further work on different conditions in the population such as agents having personalities or intentionally sharing only that part of their knowledge they want to, in order to direct opinions and thoughts, or more advanced methods for developing self-confidence and credence to the network, such as models of costly signaling or block-based approaches. Moreover, future research could extend the communication of the network and allow not only the exchange of processing rules but also the exchange of the reasons for selecting these processing rules.

Furthermore, the present setting could be modified so that not only can the community adapt its knowledge but also the environmental knowledge can change, towards or away from to the knowledge of the collective. Moving towards the might cause a loss of expertise that becomes critical when the environmental knowledge moves away from the DIP knowledge. Finally, a really ambitious step is to move from explanation to innovation, how knowledge of the rules can be used to shape the environment for purposes of self-improvement.

7   Summary and Conclusion

In summary, the contributions of this paper are:

- We have specified a problem of explanatory adequacy for self-organising multi-agent systems, as disparate agents use their social network to aggregate their possibly incomplete and inconsistent knowledge bases to 'explain' some observed phenomenon;
- We have implemented an algorithm based on the Regulatory Theory of Social Influence (RTSI), which includes bilateral influence between targets and sources and the exchange of information processing rules, and implemented it in a simulator for a Distributed Information Processing unit (DIP); and
- We have run three experiments to explore what initial conditions of the DIP and the RTSI algorithm lead to what type of epistemic condition for the collective, and

use a similarity metric to determine how well these conditions do indeed provide explanatory adequacy.

In conclusion, these experiments point to the following postulates that will be explored in further work, but we regard as crucial for developing DIP for socio-technical and cyber-physical systems embedded in dynamic environments. These postulates are that systemic self-improvement through epistemic evolution requires diversity, a willingness to learn, and having good intentions.

Primarily, we argue that systemic self-improvement epistemic evolution requires *diversity*. We observed that DIP composed of almost identical agents, in terms of having the same knowledge, could not improve their explanatory adequacy. It is also important that knowledge should be preserved somewhere in the network, because this knowledge might yet be relevant and useful at a later time. Moreover, not only should the knowledge of the agents be diverse, but *the agents should be capable of understanding the diversity of knowledge sources*, and be able to identify from whom or where they can reliably acquire or consult expertise.

Secondly, systemic evolution requires each individual to be *willing to learn*. Epistemic evolution requires agents who are, in the first place, willing to make the effort to ask and to answer, but are also willing to make the effort to assimilate the answer. Both of these are assumptions made by the RTSI algorithm, and factoring in obdurate agents (who will not ask) or intentionally disruptive agents (who block or break communication chains) are scenarios that require further experimentation.

Finally, two further requirements for RTSI to enable a DIP to solve the explanatory adequacy problem are that both sources and targets must have *good intentions* against a background of *popular legitimacy*. For example, the DIP might have to deal with intentionally deceptive agents: for example, a single knowledge source, which is responsible for transferring knowledge, should not try to manipulate a target, or worse, to perturb the value of $\mathcal{K}^{DIP}$ for its own interests rather than the collective (public) interest; or, for another example, 'denialist' cliques, in the form of a group of mutually self-supporting agents whose inaccurate knowledge is altered by neither evidence nor argument but whose 'noisy' presence has a detrimental impact on effective overall performance. These situations require rules, which implies both institutions capable of constraining behaviour and popular legitimacy (i.e. general acceptance of those institutions and their rules and punishments) [21].

To highlight the importance of good intentions and popular legitimacy, from the source's side, we note that all the experiments implicitly share a common characteristic: the strong relationship between knowledge and power. In particular, under all conditions, the DIP does manage to identify the 'specialist' individuals (who are best, or least bad, at the task) and credits them for sharing their knowledge. Consequently, the most knowledgeable agents are also the ones who could, in effect control and manipulate common knowledge and public opinion. This way, these agents can not only occupy the prosocial role of knowledge gatekeeper, but could also become an antisocial 'knowledge dictator'. This dynamic is clearly illustrated in Foucault's [6] observation that power is based on and reproduces knowledge, while knowledge in turn begets power. Therefore, if the sources have other motives for sharing their knowledge, the expertise of the network can degenerate into an oligarchy (a 'knowligarchy').

Acknowledgements. We are particularly grateful to the three anonymous reviewers whose many insightful comments helped to revise and improve the presentation of this work.

References

1. Afshar, M., Asadpour, M.: Opinion formation by informed agents. J. Artif. Soc. Soc. Simul. **13**(4), 5 (2010)
2. Airiau, St., Sen, S., Villatoro, D.: Emergence of conventions through social learning. Auton. Agents Multi-Agent **28**(5), 779–804 (2014)
3. Asch, S.E.: Studies of independence and conformity: I. A minority of one against a unanimous majority. Psychol. Monogr. Gen. Appl. **70**(9), 1–70 (1956)
4. Chacoma, A., Zanette, D.H.: Opinion formation by social influence: from experiments to modeling. PLoS One **10**(10), e0140406 (2015)
5. Fadda, E., He J., Tessone, Cl., Barucca, P.: Consensus formation on heterogeneous networks. CoRR abs/2111.11949 (2021)
6. Foucault, M.: Power/Knowledge: Selected Interviews & Other Writings. Colin Gordon (1980)
7. Hegselmann, R., Krause, U.: Opinion formation by social influence: opinion dynamics and bounded confidence: models, analysis and simulation. J. Artif. Soc. Soc. Simul. **5**(3) (2002)
8. Klemm, K., Eguiluz, V.M.: Growing scale-free networks with small-world behavior. Phys. Rev. E **65**(5), 057102 (2002)
9. Liu, Y., et al.: From local to global norm emergence: dissolving self-reinforcing substructures with incremental social instruments. In: International Conference on Machine Learning (PMLR), pp. 6871–6881 (2021)
10. Lopez-Sanchez M., Müller A.: On simulating the propagation and countermeasures of hate speech in social networks. Appl. Sci. **11**(24), 12003 (2021)
11. Medo, M., Mariani, M.S. and Lü, L.: The fragility of opinion formation in a complex world. Commun. Phys. **4**(75), 1–10 (2021)
12. Nowak, A., Vallacher, R., Rychwalska, A., Roszczyńska-Kurasińska, M., Ziembowicz, K., Biesaga, M., Kacprzyk-Murawska, M.: Target in Control. SC, Springer, Cham (2019). https://doi.org/10.1007/978-3-030-30622-9
13. Cacioppo, J.T., Petty, R.E.: The elaboration likelihood model of persuasion. In: Kinnear, T. (ed.) NA - Advances in Consumer Research 11:673–675, Association for Consumer Research (1984)
14. Pitt, J., Nowak, A., Michalak, T., Borkowski, W., Vallacher, R.: Knowing what the bits know: social influence as the source of collective knowledge. In: Second International Workshop on Agent-Based Modelling of Human Behaviour (ABMHuB) (2020). http://abmhub.cs.ucl.ac.uk/2020/papers/Pitt.pdf
15. Pitt, J.: interactional justice and self-governance of open self-organising systems. In: 11th IEEE International Conference on Self-Adaptive and Self-Organizing Systems (SASO), pp. 31–40 (2017)
16. Pitt, J. and Ober, J.: Democracy by design: basic democracy and the self-organisation of collective governance. In: 12th IEEE International Conference on Self-Adaptive and Self-Organizing Systems (SASO), pp. 20–29 (2018)
17. Prettejohn, B., Berryman, M., Mcdonnell, M.: Methods for generating complex networks with selected structural properties for simulations: a review and tutorial for neuroscientists. Front. Comput. Neurosc. **5** (2011). https://doi.org/10.3389/fncom.2011.00011. ISSN 1662-5188
18. Rizzi, L.: The concept of explanatory adequacy. In: Roberts, I. (ed.) The Oxford Handbook of Universal Grammar, Oxford University Press, Oxford (2016)

19. Sen, S., Airiau, St.: Emergence of norms through social learning. In: 20th International Joint Conference on Artificial Intelligence (IJCAI), vol. 1507, pp. 1507–1512 (2007)
20. Sîrbu, A., Pedreschi, D., Giannotti, F., Kertész, J.: Algorithmic bias amplifies opinion fragmentation and polarization: a bounded confidence model. PLoS ONE **14**(3), e0213246 (2019)
21. Trebilcock, M., Daniels, R.: Rule of Law Reform and Development: Charting the Fragile Path of Progress. Edward Elgar, Cheltenham, UK (2008)
22. Villatoro, D., Sabater-Mir, J., Sen, S.: Social instruments for robust convention emergence. In: 22nd International Joint Conference on Artificial Intelligence (IJCAI), pp. 420–425 (2011)
23. Wiggins, R.E.: Distributed information processing: trends and implications. In: Aslib Proceedings, vol. 37, no. 2, pp. 73–90 (1985)

The Complexity of Norm Synthesis and Revision

Davide Dell'Anna[1]([✉])(iD), Natasha Alechina[2](iD), Fabiano Dalpiaz[2](iD),
Mehdi Dastani[2](iD), Maarten Löffler[2], and Brian Logan[2,3](iD)

[1] Delft University of Technology, Delft, The Netherlands
d.dellanna@tudelft.nl
[2] Utrecht University, Utrecht, The Netherlands
{n.a.alechina,f.dalpiaz,m.m.dastani,m.loffler,b.s.logan}@uu.nl
[3] University of Aberdeen, Aberdeen, Scotland

Abstract. Norms have been widely proposed as a way of coordinating and controlling the activities of agents in a multi-agent system (MAS). A norm specifies the behaviour an agent should follow in order to achieve the objective of the MAS. However, designing norms to achieve a particular system objective can be difficult, particularly when there is no direct link between the language in which the system objective is stated and the language in which the norms can be expressed. In this paper, we consider the problem of synthesising a norm from traces of agent behaviour, where each trace is labelled with whether the behaviour satisfies the system objective. We show that the norm synthesis problem and several related problems are NP-complete.

1 Introduction

There has been a considerable amount of work on using norms to coordinate the activities of agents in a multi-agent system (MAS) [11]. Norms can be viewed as standards of behaviour which specify that certain states or sequences of actions in a MAS should occur (obligations) or should not occur (prohibitions) in order for the objective of the MAS to be realized [9]. We focus on conditional norms with deadlines which express behavioral properties [35]. Conditional norms are triggered (detached) in certain states of the MAS and have a temporal dimension specified by a deadline, which is also a state property. The satisfaction or violation of a detached norm depends on whether the behaviour of the agent brings about a specified state before a state in which the deadline condition is true. Conditional norms are implemented in a MAS through enforcement. That is, violation of a norm results in either the behaviour being pre-empted (regimented, [5]), or in the violating agent incurring a sanction, e.g., a fine. See, e.g., [14] for how to determine an appropriate level of sanction.

For many applications it is assumed that the MAS developer will design an appropriate norm to realise the system objective. However, this can be difficult, particularly when the internals of the agents are unknown, e.g., in the case of open MAS [6], and when there is no direct connection between the language in which the system objective is stated and the language in which norms can be expressed. For example, one objective of a traffic system may be to avoid traffic collisions, but 'not colliding' is not a property under direct agent control, and prohibition of collisions cannot be stated as a norm.

N. Ajmeri et al. (Eds.): COINE 2022, LNAI 13549, pp. 38–53, 2022.
https://doi.org/10.1007/978-3-031-20845-4_3

A poorly designed norm may fail to achieve the system objective, or have undesirable side effects, e.g., the objective is achieved, but the autonomy of the agents is restricted unnecessarily.

The increasing availability of large amounts of system behaviour data [1,23] introduces the possibility of a new approach to the design of norms, namely the synthesis of norms directly from data collected during the execution of the system. For example, data may show that collisions always happen when an agent's speed is very high, allowing us to state a norm prohibiting agents from speeding too much. In this paper, we consider the problem of synthesising conditional norms with deadlines from traces of agent behaviour, where each trace is labelled with whether the behaviour satisfies the system objective.

The contributions of this paper are the following.

- We show that synthesising a conditional norm with deadline (i.e., an obligation or a prohibition) that correctly classifies the traces (i.e., the norm is violated on traces where the behaviour does not satisfy the system objective, and is not violated on other traces) is an NP-complete problem.
- We show that analogous complexity results (NP-completeness) also hold for the problem of the synthesis of sets of conditional norms with deadlines.
- We also consider the problem of synthesizing a norm that is "close" to a target norm. This problem is relevant where there is an existing norm that does not achieve the system objective, but which is accepted, e.g., by human users of a system, and we wish a minimal modification that does achieve the objective. We show that the minimal norm revision problem is also NP-complete.

This paper is organized as follows. Section 2 provides the necessary formal background on conditional norms and on traces of agent behaviours. Section 3 discusses the complexity of the problem of synthesising a single conditional norm. Section 4 discusses the complexity of synthesising a set of conditional norms. Section 5 discusses the complexity of the minimal norm revision. Section 6 discusses related work and Sect. 7 presents conclusions and future work.

2   Preliminaries

In this section we give formal definitions of the behaviour of agents in the MAS and of conditional norms.

We assume a finite propositional language L that contains propositions corresponding to properties of states of the MAS. A *state* of the MAS is a propositional assignment. A conjunction of all literals (propositions or their negations) in a state s will be referred to as a *state description* of s. For example, for $L = \{p, q, r\}$, a possible state description is $p \wedge \neg q \wedge r$ (a state where p is true, q is false, and r is true).

A propositional formula is a boolean combination of propositional variables. The definition of a propositional formula ϕ being true in a state s ($s \models \phi$) is the standard classical one. We use $\top$ for a formula that is true in all states and $\bot$ for the formula which is false in all states.

A *trace* is a finite sequence of states. We use the notation $\rho = (s_1, \ldots, s_k)$ for a trace consisting of states $s_1, \ldots, s_k$. For example, a trace could be generated by the actions of all vehicles involved in a traffic accident. We denote the i-th state in a trace ρ by $\rho[i]$. We assume that the behaviour exhibited by the agents in the MAS is represented by a set of finite traces Γ. We denote by $S(\Gamma)$ or simply by S the set of states occurring in traces in Γ. Each subset X of $S(\Gamma)$ is definable by a propositional formula ϕ_X (a disjunction of state descriptions of states in X). Note that the size of ϕ_X is linear in the size of X (the sum of sizes of state descriptions of states in X). For example, if $X = \{s_1, s_2\}$ where $s_1 = p \wedge q \wedge r$ and $s_2 = \neg p \wedge \neg q \wedge \neg r$, the description of X is $(p \wedge q \wedge r) \vee (\neg p \wedge \neg q \wedge \neg r)$. Γ is partitioned into two sets Γ_T ('good', or positive, traces) and Γ_F ('bad', or negative, traces). The partition is performed with respect to the system objective, which typically does not correspond directly to the properties expressible in L. We note that the assumption that each trace describing the behavior of the agents can be labeled as either good or bad is realistic in several contexts and for different kinds of MAS objectives. For example, instances of a process can be deemed as compliant or non-compliant w.r.t. a model [24]; in the traffic domain, traces can be labeled individually w.r.t. the expected travel time or emissions, or based on the occurrence of a collision.

The problem we wish to solve is how to generate a conditional norm which is expressed using propositions from L, and that is obeyed on traces in Γ_T and violated on traces in Γ_F.

Definition 1 (Conditional Norm). *A conditional norm (over L) is a tuple $(\phi_C, Z(\phi_Z), \phi_D)$, where ϕ_C, ϕ_Z and ϕ_D are propositional formulas over L, and $Z \in \{P, O\}$ indicates whether the norm is a prohibition (P) or an obligation (O).*

We refer to ϕ_C as the (detachment) condition of the norm, and ϕ_D as the deadline. ϕ_Z characterizes a state that is prohibited (resp. obligated) to occur after a state where the condition of the norm ϕ_C holds, and before a state where the deadline of the norm ϕ_D holds. We define the conditions for violation of norms formally below.

Definition 2 (Violation of Prohibition). *A conditional prohibition $(\phi_C, P(\phi_P), \phi_D)$ is violated on a trace $(s_1, s_2, \ldots, s_m)$ if there are i, j with $1 \le i \le j \le m$ such that ϕ_C is true at s_i, ϕ_P is true at s_j, and there is no k with $i < k < j$ such that ϕ_D is true at s_k.*

In other words, a conditional prohibition is violated on a trace if the states in the trace exhibit a pattern of the following type: a state where the norm is detached (orange in Fig. 1) is followed by a number of states (possibly none) where neither the prohibition is violated nor the deadline is reached (the yellow states), after which there is a state where the deadline is still not reached but the prohibition is violated (the blue state). Note that the state where the prohibition is violated may be the same state where the norm is detached (not shown in Fig. 1, which considers the case where the three types of states are distinct).

Definition 3 (Violation of Obligation). *A conditional obligation $(\phi_C, O(\phi_O), \phi_D)$ is violated on a trace $(s_1, s_2, \ldots, s_m)$ if there are i, j with $1 \le i \le j \le m$ such that ϕ_C*

... | $\phi_C, \neg\phi_D, \neg\phi_P$ | $\neg\phi_D, \neg\phi_P$ | ... | $\neg\phi_D, \neg\phi_P$ | $\neg\phi_D, \phi_P$ | ...

Fig. 1. Example of violation of a prohibition (Color figure online)

is true at s_i, ϕ_D is true at s_m, and there is no k with $i \leq k \leq j$ such that ϕ_O is true at s_k.

In other words, a conditional obligation is violated on a trace if the states in the trace exhibit a pattern of the following type: a state where the norm is detached (light blue in Fig. 2) is followed by a number of states (possibly none) where neither the obligation is satisfied nor the deadline is reached (the pink states), after which there is a state where the obligation is still not satisfied but the deadline is reached (the gray state). Note that, as in the case of conditional prohibitions, the state where the obligation is violated (the gray state) may be the same state where the norm is detached (not shown in Fig. 2, which considers the case where the three types of states are distinct).

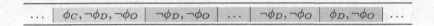

... | $\phi_C, \neg\phi_D, \neg\phi_O$ | $\neg\phi_D, \neg\phi_O$ | ... | $\neg\phi_D, \neg\phi_O$ | $\phi_D, \neg\phi_O$ | ...

Fig. 2. Example of violation of an obligation (Color figure online)

Note that the violation of a conditional prohibition or obligation does not distinguish between a single or multiple violations, i.e., a trace violates a norm if at least one violation occurs.

A conditional norm is obeyed on a trace if it is not violated on that trace. Violation conditions of conditional norms can be expressed in Linear Time Temporal Logic (LTL) and evaluated on finite traces in linear time [4].

Example 1. Consider the following simple example. Let $L = \{p, q, r\}$ be a language where p means that a vehicle is on a particular stretch of a street, q means that it is a large goods vehicle, and r means that its speed exceeds 15 mph. The p stretch is a steep incline with a blind corner, and heavy vehicles sometimes crash into a barrier at the bottom of the street. The system objective is that such crashes are avoided. An example set of positive and negative traces is given below.

$$\Gamma_T = \{\; \rho_1 = (s_1 = p \wedge q \wedge \neg r,\; s_1 = p \wedge q \wedge \neg r, s_2 = \neg p \wedge q \wedge \neg r),$$
$$\rho_2 = (s_3 = \neg p \wedge \neg q \wedge \neg r,\; s_4 = p \wedge \neg q \wedge r,\; s_4 = p \wedge \neg q \wedge r),$$
$$\rho_3 = (s_5 = \neg p \wedge q \wedge r,\; s_5 = \neg p \wedge q \wedge r)\;\}$$

$$\Gamma_F = \{\; \rho_4 = (s_1 = p \wedge q \wedge \neg r,\; s_6 = p \wedge q \wedge r, s_2 = \neg p \wedge q \wedge \neg r),$$
$$\rho_5 = (s_1 = p \wedge q \wedge \neg r,\; s_6 = p \wedge q \wedge r)\;\}$$

Intuitively, positive traces involve only slowly driving trucks when p is true, and arbitrary speeds otherwise. The following conditional prohibition is violated on all negative traces: $(p \wedge q, P(p \wedge q \wedge r), \neg p)$.[1]

3 Complexity of Norm Synthesis

Given a set of agent behaviour traces Γ partitioned into Γ_T and Γ_F, we wish to synthesize a norm that correctly classifies each trace (that is, the norm is violated on all traces in Γ_F, and is not violated on any trace in Γ_T). Clearly, this is not always possible; two sets of traces may not be distinguishable by a single conditional norm (or even by a set of conditional norms). For example:

$$\Gamma_T = \{(s_1, s_2, s_3)\}, \; \Gamma_F = \{(s_1, s_1, s_2, s_3)\}$$

cannot be distinguished by a conditional norm.

3.1 Prohibition Synthesis

We first define formally the decision problem we call *prohibition synthesis*.

Definition 4. *The* prohibition synthesis problem *is the following decision problem:*

Instance *A finite set of propositions L; a finite set of finite traces Γ partitioned into Γ_T and Γ_F, each trace given as a sequence of state descriptions over L.*
Question *Are there three propositional formulas ϕ_C, ϕ_P, and ϕ_D over L such that*
   Neg *every trace in Γ_F violates $(\phi_C, P(\phi_P), \phi_D)$*
   Pos *no trace in Γ_T violates $(\phi_C, P(\phi_P), \phi_D)$*

The correspondence between sets of states and formulas over L allows us to restate the prohibition synthesis problem as follows: given a set of positive traces Γ_T and negative traces Γ_F, find three sets of states X_C, X_P, X_D such that:

Neg For every trace $\rho \in \Gamma_F$, there exists i and j with $i \leq j$ such that $\rho[i] \in X_C$, $\rho[j] \in X_P$, and there is no k with $i < k < j$ such that $\rho[k] \in X_D$.
Pos For every trace $\rho \in \Gamma_T$, if for some i and j, $i \leq j$, $\rho[i] \in X_C$, $\rho[j] \in X_P$, then there exists k such that $i < k < j$ and $\rho[k] \in X_D$.

Theorem 1. *The prohibition synthesis problem is NP-complete.*

Proof. The prohibition synthesis problem is clearly in NP (a non-deterministic Turing machine can guess the three sets and check in polynomial time that they satisfy the conditions). To prove that it is NP-hard, we reduce 3SAT (satisfiability of a set of clauses with 3 literals) to prohibition synthesis.

---

[1] Clearly, alternative definitions of norms are also possible. For example, since trucks do not cease being trucks while driving along the street, we can also state the prohibition as $(p \wedge q, P(r), \neg p)$, or we can prohibit a truck driving fast on p: $(\top, P(p \wedge q \wedge r), \bot)$.

3SAT is an NP-complete problem. An instance of 3SAT is a set of clauses, where each clause is a disjunction of at most 3 literals, for example, $\{(x_1 \vee x_2 \vee \neg x_3), (\neg x_1 \vee \neg x_2 \vee x_4)\}$. The question is whether the set of clauses is satisfiable, that is, whether there is an assignment of truth values 0 and 1 to the propositional variables that makes all the clauses true; in other words, is there an assignment such that each clause contains at least one true literal. In the example above, assigning 0 to x_3 and 1 to x_4, and, for example, 0 to x_1 and to x_2, makes both clauses true.

To start the reduction from 3SAT to prohibition synthesis, suppose an instance of 3SAT is given; that is, we have a set of clauses $C_1, \ldots, C_n$ over variables $x_1, \ldots, x_m$. We generate an instance of the prohibition synthesis problem such that it has a solution if, and only if, $C_1, \ldots, C_n$ are satisfiable (each clause contains at least one true literal). We construct the corresponding instance of the prohibition synthesis problem as follows. The set of states in the prohibition synthesis problem consists of two states s and t (s and t are a technical device; intuitively they serve as the detachment condition and the violation of the prohibition), and for each variable x_i, we need two states u_i and v_i. When we 'translate' a clause into a trace, we insert u_i into the trace if x_i occurs positively in the clause, and v_i if it occurs negatively. Intuitively, u_i in X_D will be a proxy for 'x_i should be assigned 1', and v_i in X_D will be a proxy for 'x_i should be assigned 0'. We give the rest of the construction below. Comments in square brackets explain the intuition for each step in the construction.

The set of negative traces Γ_F contains:

- a two state trace (s, t) [together with $s, t \notin X_C \cap X_P$ below, this forces $s \in X_C$ and $t \in X_P$];
- for every variable x_i in the input, a trace (s, v_i, t, s, u_i, t) [this ensures that either v_i or u_i are not in X_D].

The set of positive traces Γ_T contains: ·

- a single state trace (s) [so s cannot be in $X_C \cap X_P$];
- (t) [so t cannot be in $X_C \cap X_P$];
- for every variable x_i in the input: (s, v_i, u_i, t) [this means that either v_i or u_i are in X_D]; (v_i); (u_i); (v_i, t); (u_i, t); (s, v_i); (s, u_i);
- for every pair of variables x_i, x_j in the input: (v_i, u_j); (u_j, v_i) [this together with preceding traces ensures that v_i and u_i are not in X_C or X_P];
- for each clause C in the input over variables x_j, x_k, x_l: (s, z_j, z_k, z_l, t) where z_i is u_i if x_i occurs in C positively, and v_i if it occurs negatively.

It is easy to see that the reduction from the 3SAT instance to the prohibition synthesis instance is polynomial in the number m of variables (quadratic) and in the number n of clauses (linear).

We claim that there exists an assignment f of truth values $0, 1$ to $x_1, \ldots, x_m$ such that all the clauses $C_1, \ldots, C_n$ are true if, and only if, there is a solution to the prohibition synthesis problem above, where $X_C = \{s\}$, $X_P = \{t\}$, and for every i, $u_i \in X_D$ iff $f(x_i) = 1$ and $v_i \in X_D$ iff $f(x_i) = 0$.

'only if' direction. Assume that an assignment f that makes $C_1, \ldots, C_n$ true exists. Let $X_C = \{s\}$ and $X_P = \{t\}$. For every i, place u_i in X_D if $f(x_i) = 1$ and $v_i \in X_d$ if

$f(x_i) = 0$. This produces a solution to the prohibition synthesis problem because: s, t satisfies **Neg**; for every i, either u_i or v_i are not in X_D, so s, v_i, t, s, u_i, t satisfies **Neg**. Positive traces satisfy **Pos**: either s followed by t does not occur on a trace, or u_i, v_i occur between s and t and one of them is in X_D, or (from the clause encoding) one of the literals in the clause is true, so for positive x_i it means that u_i is in X_D and **Pos** is satisfied, or for negative $\neg x_i$ it means that v_i is in X_D and again **Pos** is satisfied.

'if' direction: Assume there is a solution to the prohibition synthesis problem. It is clear (see the comments in square brackets above) that it has to be of the form $X_C = \{s\}$, $X_P = \{t\}$ and X_D containing some u_is and v_is. In particular, since (s, v_i, u_i, t) is a positive trace, for every i either u_i or v_i must not be in X_D. Set $f(x_i)$ to be 1 if u_i in X_D and 0 otherwise. Then each clause $C = \{\sim x_j, \sim x_k, \sim x_l\}$ (where $\sim x_j$ denotes x_j if it occurs positively or $\neg x_j$ if it occurs negatively) is satisfied by f since for every clause there will be one literal which is true. This is because (s, z_j, z_k, z_l, t) is a positive trace, and either for some positive literal x_i, u_i is in X_D, or for some negative literal $\neg x_i$, v_i is in X_D, so u_i is not in X_D, so $f(\neg x_i) = 1$.

3.2 Obligation Synthesis

We now consider the *obligation synthesis problem*.

Definition 5. *The* obligation synthesis problem *is the following decision problem:*

Instance *A finite set of propositions L, a finite set Γ of finite traces partitioned into Γ_T and Γ_F, where each trace is given as a sequence of state descriptions.*
Question *Are there three propositional formulas ϕ_C, ϕ_O, and ϕ_D over L such that*
　Neg *every trace in Γ_F violates $(\phi_C, O(\phi_O), \phi_D)$*
　Pos *no trace in Γ_T violates $(\phi_C, O(\phi_O), \phi_D)$*

Analogously to the prohibition synthesis problem, the obligation synthesis problem can be equivalently restated in terms of states: are there three sets of states X_C, X_O and X_D such that:

Neg For every trace $\rho \in \Gamma_F$, there exist i and j with $i \leq j$ such that $\rho[i] \in X_C$, $\rho[j] \in X_D$, and there is no k with $i \leq k \leq j$ such that $\rho[k] \in X_O$
Pos For every trace $\rho \in \Gamma_T$, if for some i and j, $i \leq j$, $\rho[i] \in X_C$, $\rho[j] \in X_D$, then there exists k such that $i \leq k \leq j$ and $\rho[k] \in X_O$.

Theorem 2. *The obligation synthesis problem is NP-complete.*

Proof. The obligation synthesis problem is clearly in NP. To prove that it is NP-hard, we again use a reduction from the 3SAT problem.

As before, consider a set of clauses $C_1, \ldots, C_n$ over variables $x_1, \ldots, x_m$, which is an instance of 3SAT. We generate an instance of the obligation synthesis problem such that it has a solution iff $C_1, \ldots, C_n$ are satisfiable. The idea of the reduction is similar to that for prohibitions. We use two auxiliary states s and t, intuitively to serve as the detachment condition and the deadline, and make sure that neither of them is also the obligation, but now instead of inserting a deadline between s and t in positive traces, we insert an obligation. We want to make some subset of $\{v_i : i \in [1, \ldots m]\} \cup \{u_i :$

$i \in [1, ...m]\}$ to be the obligation (X_O), so that exactly one of v_i, u_i for each i is in X_O. Then $u_i \in X_O$ can encode that x_i is true, and $v_i \in X_O$ that x_i is false, and we can make the encoding work by creating a positive trace corresponding to each clause so that at least one of the literals in the clause should be true.

The set of negative traces contains:

- a 2 state trace (s, t) [this forces either $s \in X_C \cap \overline{X_D} \cap \overline{X_O}$, $t \in X_D \cap \overline{X_C} \cap \overline{X_O}$, or $s \in X_C \cap X_D \cap \overline{X_O}$, or $t \in X_C \cap X_D \cap \overline{X_O}$. To rule out the latter two possibilities, we require below that s and t on their own are positive traces.]
- for every variable x_i in the input, a trace (s, v_i, t, s, u_i, t) [this ensures that either v_i or u_i are not in X_O, because there is one $(s, .., t)$ sub-trace that does not contain a state from X_O].

The set of positive traces contains:

- a one state trace (s) [so s cannot be in $X_C \cap X_D \cap \overline{X_O}$]
- a one state trace (t) [so t cannot be in $X_C \cap X_D \cap \overline{X_O}$]
- for every variable x_i in the input, a trace (s, v_i, u_i, t) [this ensures that either v_i or u_i are in X_O]
- for each clause C in the input over variables x_j, x_k, x_l, a trace (s, z_j, z_k, z_l, t) where z_i is u_i if x_i occurs in C positively, and v_i if it occurs negatively.

The reduction is linear in the number of variables and clauses.

We claim that there exists an assignment f of $0, 1$ to $x_1, \ldots, x_m$ satisfying $C_1, \ldots, C_n$ if, and only if, there is a solution to the obligation synthesis problem above where $s \in X_C$, $t \in X_D$, and for every i, $u_i \in X_O$ iff $f(x_i) = 1$ and $v_i \in X_O$ iff $f(x_i) = 0$. The proof of this claim is analogous to that of Theorem 1.

Assume that an assignment f satisfying $C_1, \ldots, C_n$ exists. Let $X_C = \{s\}$ and $X_D = \{t\}$. For every i, place u_i in X_O iff $f(x_i) = 1$ and $v_i \in X_O$ iff $f(x_i) = 0$. It is easy to check that this is a solution to the obligation synthesis problem.

Assume there is a solution to the obligation synthesis problem. It is clear (see the comments in brackets above) that any solution should satisfy $s \in X_C \cap \overline{X_D} \cap \overline{X_O}$ and $t \in X_D \cap \overline{X_C} \cap \overline{X_O}$. Since (s, v_i, t, s, u_i, t) is a negative trace for every i, this means that it contains an unsatisfied conditional obligation. This means that for every i, either v_i or u_i is not in X_O. Since (s, v_i, u_i, t) is a positive trace, then in any solution, for every i, either u_i or v_i has to be in X_O. Hence we can use the membership in X_O to produce a boolean valuation of variables x_i (1 if $u_i \in X_O$, and 0 if $v_i \in X_O$). Since for every clause $C = \{\sim x_j, \sim x_k, \sim x_l\}$, the trace (s, z_j, z_k, z_l, t) (where z_i is v_i if $\sim x_i = \neg x_i$, and u_i if $\sim x_i = x_i$) is a positive trace, at least one of z_i is in X_O. This means that the valuation based on the membership in X_O satisfies all the clauses (since at least one literal in each clause will evaluate to 1).

4 Complexity of Synthesising a Set of Norms

In this section, we consider the problem of synthesising a set of norms. To motivate the problem, we first give an example where classifying positive and negative traces correctly requires more than one norm.

Example 2. Let the language L be $\{p, q_1, q_2, r_1, r_2\}$ where, for the sake of intuition, p denotes a particular kind of customer who needs to be greeted in a particular way (r_1) before they pass the greeter (q_1) and $\neg p$ is all other customers who need to be greeted in a different way (r_2), before q_2.

$$\Gamma_T = \{\, \rho_1 = (s_1 = p \wedge \neg q_1 \wedge \neg q_2 \wedge \neg r_1 \wedge \neg r_2, \ s_2 = p \wedge \neg q_1 \wedge \neg q_2 \wedge r_1 \wedge \neg r_2,$$
$$s_3 = \neg p \wedge q_1 \wedge \neg q_2 \wedge \neg r_1 \wedge \neg r_2, \ s_4 = \neg p \wedge \neg q_1 \wedge \neg q_2 \wedge \neg r_1 \wedge r_2) \,\}$$
$$\Gamma_F = \{\, \rho_2 = (s_1 = p \wedge \neg q_1 \wedge \neg q_2 \wedge \neg r_1 \wedge \neg r_2),$$
$$\rho_3 = (s_3 = \neg p \wedge q_1 \wedge \neg q_2 \wedge \neg r_1 \wedge \neg r_2) \,\}$$

This example can only be solved by two norms, because a trace consisting only of state s_1 is a violation (ρ_2), but s_1 alone cannot be prohibited because the trace $\rho_1 = (s_1, s_2, s_3, s_4)$ is in Γ_T. So, the trace (s_1) must be ruled out by an obligation: after s_1, there should be s_2 or s_3 or s_4. From trace ρ_4 in Γ_F, (s_3) is a violation, so s_3 must either be prohibited, or it must be ruled out by an obligation, that is, after s_3, s_4 should happen. If s_3 is prohibited, then $\rho_1 = (s_1, s_2, s_3, s_4)$ would be a violation, but it isn't. So after s_3, s_4 should happen. Therefore two obligations are required, for example, $(p, O(r_1), q_1)$ and $(\neg p, O(r_2), q_2)$.

Similarly, two or more prohibitions may be required if different things are prohibited in different contexts.

If there is a set of norms separating Γ_T and Γ_F, then its size is trivially bounded by the number of all different non-equivalent norms given the language L. Since L is finite, there are $2 \times 3 \times 2^{2^{|L|}}$ possible conditional norms (there are $2^{|L|}$ state descriptions, $2^{2^{|L|}}$ possible formulas in disjunctive normal form that can be parts of the norm, 3 positions on which they can occur, and 2 types of conditional norms). There are $O(2^{2^{2^{|L|}}})$ sets of non-equivalent norms. However, it is possible to produce a much better bound on the maximal size of the set of norms correctly classifying Γ_T and Γ_F than a triple exponential in $|L|$.

Theorem 3. *If it is possible to correctly classify Γ_T and Γ_F by a set N of norms, then this can be done by a set of norms of size at most $|\Gamma_F|$.*

Proof. First, observe that we do not need more than one norm to exclude each trace in Γ_F. So we need to have at most $|\Gamma_F|$ norms. Second, if a set N of norms is not violated on any of Γ_T traces, then no norm from $N' \subseteq N$ is violated on a Γ_T trace.

Definition 6. *The* multiple conditional norm synthesis problem *is the following decision problem:*

Instance *A finite set of propositions L; an integer m; a finite set of finite traces Γ partitioned into Γ_T and Γ_F, each trace given as a sequence of state descriptions over L.*
Question *is there a set N of conditional prohibitions and obligations over L with $|N| \leq m$ such that*
    Neg *every trace in Γ_F violates one of the norms in N*

Pos *no trace in Γ_T violates any of the norms in N.*

Theorem 4. *The problem of synthesising a set of conditional prohibitions or conditional obligations is NP-complete.*

Proof. For membership in NP, observe that it is possible to guess a set $m \le |\Gamma_F|$ norms and check in polynomial time that they correctly classify the traces.

Hardness follows from the NP-hardness parts of Theorems 1 and 2.

5 Complexity of Minimal Revision

In this section, we consider the problems of (minimally) revising conditional prohibitions and obligations. These problems are relevant when there is an existing norm that does not achieve the system objective, and we wish a minimal modification of the existing norm that does achieve the objective.

Assume we are given a set of traces and a conditional norm $(\phi_C, Z(\phi_Z), \phi_D)$, (where $Z \in \{P, O\}$) and need to change it in a minimal way so that it classifies the traces correctly. The editing distance between conditional norms can be defined in various ways, e.g., for formulas ϕ_C, ϕ_Z, ϕ_D in disjunctive normal form, this could be the sum of the numbers of added and removed disjuncts for all three formulas. Note that the set of non-equivalent propositional formulas built from the set L is finite, and so is the number of possible different conditional prohibitions or obligations. Regardless of how the distance between different conditional norms is defined, for a fixed set of propositional variables L there is a maximal editing distance $max(L)$ between any two norms using formulas over L.

5.1 Complexity of Minimal Prohibition Revision

Given some distance measure $dist$ defined for any two conditional prohibitions α_1 and α_2 over L, the decision problem for minimal prohibition revision can be stated as:

Definition 7. *The (decision form) of the* minimal prohibition revision problem *is as follows:*

Instance *A finite set of propositions L; a number m; a finite set Γ of finite traces partitioned into Γ_T and Γ_F; a conditional prohibition $(\phi_C, P(\phi_P), \phi_D)$ over L.*
Question *Are there three propositional formulas ϕ'_C, ϕ'_P, and ϕ'_D over L such that*
  Dist $dist((\phi_C, P(\phi_P), \phi_D), (\phi'_C, P(\phi'_P), \phi'_D)) \le m$
  Neg *every trace in Γ_F violates $(\phi'_C, P(\phi'_P), \phi'_D)$*
  Pos *no trace in Γ_T violates $(\phi'_C, P(\phi'_P), \phi'_D)$*

Theorem 5. *Let $dist(\alpha_1, \alpha_2)$ be computable in time polynomial in the size of α_1 and α_2, and the range of $dist$ over norms built over propositions from L be bounded by $max(L)$. Then the minimal prohibition revision problem is NP-complete.*

Proof. The membership in NP follows from the fact that a solution can be guessed and checked in polynomial time.

NP-hardness is by reduction from the prohibition synthesis problem. Note that if a solution to the prohibition synthesis problem exists, it will be at most at distance $max(L)$ from the input norm. So to solve the prohibition synthesis problem, we can ask for a solution to the minimal prohibition revision problem with $m = max(L)$.

5.2   Complexity of Minimal Obligation Revision

Given some distance measure $dist$ defined for any two conditional obligations α_1 and α_2 over L, the decision problem for minimal obligation revision can be stated as:

Definition 8. *The (decision form) of the* minimal obligation revision problem *is as follows:*

Instance *A finite set of propositions L; a number m; a finite set Γ of finite traces partitioned into Γ_T and Γ_F; a conditional obligation $(\phi_C, O(\phi_O), \phi_D)$ over L.*
Question *Are there three propositional formulas ϕ'_C, ϕ'_O, and ϕ'_D over L such that*
  Dist $dist((\phi_C, O(\phi_O), \phi_D), (\phi'_C, O(\phi'_O), \phi'_D)) \leq m$
  Neg *every trace in Γ_F violates $(\phi'_C, O(\phi'_O), \phi'_D)$*
  Pos *no trace in Γ_T violates $(\phi'_C, O(\phi'_O), \phi'_D)$*

Theorem 6. *Let $dist(\alpha_1, \alpha_2)$ be computable in time polynomial in the size of α_1 and α_2, and the range of $dist$ over norms built over propositions from L be bounded by $max(L)$. Then the minimal obligation revision problem is NP-complete.*

Proof. The membership in NP follows from the fact that a solution can be guessed and checked in polynomial time. Analogously to the minimal prohibition revision problem, NP-hardness is by reduction from the obligation synthesis problem; if a solution to the obligation synthesis problem exists, it will be at most at distance $max(L)$ from the input norm. So to solve the obligation synthesis problem, we can ask for a solution to the minimal obligation revision problem with $m = max(L)$.

6   Related Work

There has been a considerable amount of work on the automated synthesis of norms. In this section, we briefly review some of the main approaches, focussing on work that is most closely related to our approach.

We first review 'offline' approaches, in which norms are synthesised at design time. Shoham and Tennenholtz [34] (see also [16]), consider the problem of synthesising a *social law* that constrains the behaviour of the agents in a MAS so as to ensure that agents in a *focal* state are always able to reach another focal state no matter what the other agents in the system do. They show that synthesising a useful social law is NP-complete. Van der Hoek *et al.* [18] recast the problem of synthesising a social law as an ATL model checking problem. The authors show that the problem of whether there exists a social law satisfying an objective expressed as an arbitrary ATL formula (feasibility) is NP-complete, while for objectives expressed as propositional formulae, feasibility (and synthesis) is decidable in polynomial time. Bulling and Dastani [10] consider norm synthesis for LTL objectives. In their approach, agents are assumed to have LTL-defined preferences with numerical values, and the aim of the synthesis is to produce a norm that enforces the objective for some Nash equilibrium. The problems they consider are weak and strong implementation, and norm-based mechanism design. A norm weakly implements a normative behaviour function if there exists a Nash equilibrium that satisfies the LTL formula. A norm strongly implements a normative behaviour function iff all

Nash equilibria satisfy the formula. Weak implementation is Σ_2^P-complete in the size of the CGS, preferences, objective and norm. The strong implementation problem can be solved by a deterministic polynomial-time oracle Turing machine that can make two non-adaptive queries to an oracle in Σ_2^P and is both Σ_2^P-hard and Π_2^P-hard. Weak implementation existence is Σ_2^P-complete. Strong implementation existence is Σ_3^P-complete. In [19], the synthesis of dynamic prohibitions (that is, prohibitions corresponding to Mealy machines) for CTL objectives is shown to be EXPTIME-complete. In [32], the synthesis of dynamic norms for LTL objectives and Nash equilibria is shown to be 2EXPTIME-complete when considering the existence of a Nash equilibrium satisfying the objective, and in 3EXPTIME for enforcing all Nash equilibria to satisfy the objective. Other work on norm synthesis using logical specifications of objectives includes [2, 36]. Alechina et al. [4] introduce the concept of norm approximation in the context of imperfect monitors. A conditional norm is synthesized to approximate an 'ideal' norm in order to maximize the number of violations that an imperfect monitor can detect. We assume, however, perfectly monitorable norms, and we aim at synthesizing norms that are better aligned with the MAS objectives by using execution data. In contrast to the approach we present here, these approaches assume a complete model the agents' behaviour is available, e.g., in the form of a transition system or a Kripke structure.

Morales et al. present LION [28], an algorithm for the synthesis of liberal normative systems, i.e., norms that place as few constraints as possible on the actions of agents. To guide the synthesis process, LION makes use of a normative network: a graph structure that characterises the generalisation relationship between different norms, which is used to synthesise more general, that is, more liberal, norms when possible. The norms synthesised by LION are so-called action-based norms, which prohibit agents to perform actions in certain states [5]. In our work, we focus on the problem of revising conditional norms with deadlines, which are behaviour-based, or path-based, norms, prohibiting (or obliging) agents from exhibiting certain behaviours. While both our work and LION synthesise norms to avoid undesirable system states, in our work we focus on the problem of synthesising norms from data collected during the execution of the system (i.e., traces of agent behaviour), while in [28], the synthesis considers properties of the normative system (e.g., liberality) which are independent of the behaviour of the agents in the MAS. We consider the liberality of norms an interesting possible extension of our work that could be integrated as a criterion when selecting a new norm among possible revisions. Christelis et al. [12] present an EXPTIME algorithm based on AI planning for synthesising state-based prohibitions that set preconditions to the actions the agents can perform in a regimentation setting. In our work, we do not assume that norms can be regimented.

Another strand of work focuses on the 'online' synthesis of norms, where norms emerge from the interactions of agents in a decentralised way, e.g., [3, 33]. Unlike our approach, such approaches typically assume that the agents are cooperative, and/or that some minimal standards of behaviour can be assumed. However, cooperation between agents cannot be always assumed, particularly in open MAS.

Closer to our work are online approaches that use agents' behaviour to guide centralised norm synthesis. For example, Morales et al. [27] present algorithms for the online synthesis of compact action-based norms when the behaviour of agents leads to undesired system states. In contrast, we consider conditional norms with deadlines that regulate patterns of behaviour. In other work, Morales *et al.* have used game theoretic concepts to guide norm synthesis [29,30]. Their control loop includes game recognition, payoff learning, and norm replication. Their approach to norm synthesis makes use of evolutionary processes to determine, off-line and via simulation, effective and evolutionary stable norms, which are then enforced at run-time. However, while the resulting norms are evolutionary stable, their approach requires sufficient knowledge about the agents, their goals and the environment in which they operate, to permit simulation of their interactions. In our work, instead, we focus on a setting where the only labeled traces of agent behaviors are available. Miralles *et al.* [26] present a framework for the adaptation of MAS regulations at runtime. They consider norms expressed via norm patterns (i.e., IF-THEN rules associated with constraints on the operators and on the values that the norm components can take). The authors describe an adaptation mechanism based on Case Based Reasoning. Adaptation is performed at runtime individually by a number of assistant agents and then, via a voting mechanism, a final adaptation is approved. The decision on how to adapt norms is taken based on similar previously seen cases. On similar lines, Dell'Anna *et al.* [14] propose a framework for the runtime selection of alternative norms based on runtime data and for the revision of the sanctions of norms based on the knowledge of agents preferences. Unlike these approaches, we do not assume knowledge of the agents' internals, e.g., their preferences [14] or their reasoning and communication capabilities [26]. Corapi *et al.* [13] and Athakravi *et al.* [7] discuss the application of Inductive Logic Programming (ILP) [15] to norm synthesis and norm revision. In their work, the desired properties of the system are described through use cases (event traces associated to a desired outcome state), and ILP is used to revise the current norms so to satisfy the use-cases. In their approach, norms and desired outcome are strictly coupled: the desired outcomes of execution traces are expressed in the same language of the norms and, therefore, are directly enforceable. In our approach we consider MAS objectives that cannot be directly enforced, and we use norms as a means to achieve such objectives (e.g., a speed limit norm is a means to achieve vehicles' safety, but it is not possible to directly enforce safety on vehicles: "no accidents should occur" is not directly enforceable on drivers). In our work, the only knowledge of the MAS objectives available to the revision mechanism, is a given boolean labeling of the execution traces. The causal relation between norms and MAS objectives is not given. Because we do not assume that the underlying causal structure of the domain is known to our revision mechanism, we are unable to generate provably correct norm revisions as in ILP-based approaches like those of Corapi *et al.* [13] and related ones (e.g., [21,31]). ILP-based approaches and our approach can therefore be seen as representing different trade-offs between the amount of background knowledge assumed about the possible causes of norm violations, and the guarantees that can be given regarding a particular (candidate) revision. Mahmoud *et al.* [25] propose an algorithm for mining regulative norms that identifies recommendations, obligations, and prohibitions by analyzing events that trigger rewards and penalties. They focus on agents joining an open MAS who have to learn the unstated norms; we, instead, study how to alter existing norms from the point of view of a centralized authority.

Finally, our work is influenced by research on norm change, including logics for norm change [8, 22], the study of the legal effects of norm change, analyzed and formalized by [17], and the contextualization of norms [20], which studies how to refine norms to make them suitable for specific contexts. In our framework, this corresponds to modifying the detachment condition and the deadline of the norms.

7 Conclusions

We considered the problem of synthesising and minimally revising norms to achieve a system objective from labelled traces of agent behaviour in a multi-agent system (MAS). We considered a setting where the internals of the agents in the MAS are unknown and where norms are expressed in a different language from that of the system objective that they intend to bring about. In such setting, explicit knowledge about the relationship between the enforced norms, the agents' behavior and the MAS objective is not given, and the norm synthesis and revision rely on traces of agent behaviour labeled as positive or negative, depending on whether each satisfies or not the system objective. We showed that the problems of norm synthesis and minimal revision are NP-complete. In future work, we plan to investigate the synthesis of approximate norms (i.e., norms that do not classify all traces perfectly), and more tractable heuristic approaches to norm synthesis and revision where, for instance, only a bounded number of candidate revisions of a norm are synthesized based on the available data and the semantics of conditional norms, and the most accurate norm (i.e., the norm with highest accuracy w.r.t. the labeled traces) is selected.

References

1. van der Aalst, W.M.P.: Process Mining - Data Science in Action, 2nd edn. Springer, Heidelberg (2016). https://doi.org/10.1007/978-3-662-49851-4
2. Ågotnes, T., van der Hoek, W., Rodríguez-Aguilar, J.A., Sierra, C., Wooldridge, M.J.: On the logic of normative systems. In: Veloso, M.M. (ed.) Proceedings of the 20th International Joint Conference on Artificial Intelligence (IJCAI 2007), pp. 1175–1180 (2007)
3. Airiau, S., Sen, S., Villatoro, D.: Emergence of conventions through social learning. Auton. Agents Multi-Agent Syst. **28**(5), 779–804 (2014)
4. Alechina, N., Dastani, M., Logan, B.: Norm approximation for imperfect monitors. In: International conference on Autonomous Agents and Multi-Agent Systems, AAMAS 2014, pp. 117–124 (2014)
5. Alechina, N., Logan, B., Dastani, M.: Modeling norm specification and verification in multiagent systems. FLAP **5**(2), 457–490 (2018). https://www.collegepublications.co.uk/downloads/ifcolog00022.pdf
6. Artikis, A., Pitt, J.: A formal model of open agent societies. In: Proceedings of the Fifth International Conference on Autonomous Agents, AGENTS 2001, pp. 192–193 (2001)
7. Athakravi, D., Corapi, D., Russo, A., Vos, M.D., Padget, J.A., Satoh, K.: Handling change in normative specifications. In: International Conference on Autonomous Agents and Multi-agent Systems, AAMAS 2012, pp. 1369–1370 (2012)
8. Aucher, G., Grossi, D., Herzig, A., Lorini, E.: Dynamic context logic. In: Proceedings of LORI, pp. 15–26 (2009)

9. Boella, G., van der Torre, L.W.N.: Regulative and constitutive norms in normative multiagent systems. In: Principles of Knowledge Representation and Reasoning: Proceedings of the Ninth International Conference (KR2004), Whistler, Canada, 2–5 June 2004, pp. 255–266 (2004)

10. Bulling, N., Dastani, M.: Norm-based mechanism design. Artif. Intell. **239**, 97–142 (2016)

11. Chopra, A., van der Torre, L., Verhagen, H., Villata, S. (eds.): Handbook of Multiagent Systems. College Publications, London (2018)

12. Christelis, G., Rovatsos, M.: Automated norm synthesis in an agent-based planning environment. In: Proceedings of The 8th International Conference on Autonomous Agents and Multiagent Systems-Volume 1, pp. 161–168. International Foundation for Autonomous Agents and Multiagent Systems (2009)

13. Corapi, D., Russo, A., Vos, M.D., Padget, J.A., Satoh, K.: Normative design using inductive learning. Theory Pract. Log. Program. **11**(4–5), 783–799 (2011)

14. Dell'Anna, D., Dastani, M., Dalpiaz, F.: Runtime revision of sanctions in normative multi-agent systems. Auton. Agents Multi-Agent Syst. **34**(2), 1–54 (2020). https://doi.org/10.1007/s10458-020-09465-8

15. Dzeroski, S., Lavrac, N.: Inductive logic programming: techniques and applications (1994)

16. Fitoussi, D., Tennenholtz, M.: Choosing social laws for multi-agent systems: minimality and simplicity. Artif. Intell. **119**(1), 61–101 (2000)

17. Governatori, G., Rotolo, A.: Changing legal systems: legal abrogations and annulments in defeasible logic. Log. J. IGPL **18**(1), 157–194 (2010). https://doi.org/10.1093/jigpal/jzp075

18. van der Hoek, W., Roberts, M., Wooldridge, M.J.: Social laws in alternating time: effectiveness, feasibility, and synthesis. Synthese **156**(1), 1–19 (2007)

19. Huang, X., Ruan, J., Chen, Q., Su, K.: Normative multiagent systems: the dynamic generalization. In: Kambhampati, S. (ed.) Proceedings of the 25th International Joint Conference on Artificial Intelligence (IJCAI 2016), pp. 1123–1129 (2016)

20. Jiang, J., Aldewereld, H., Dignum, V., Tan, Y.: Norm contextualization. In: Coordination, Organizations, Institutions, and Norms in Agent Systems VIII - 14th International Workshop, COIN 2012, Held Co-located with AAMAS 2012, Valencia, Spain, 5 June 2012, Revised Selected Papers, pp. 141–157 (2012)

21. Katzouris, N., Artikis, A., Paliouras, G.: Incremental learning of event definitions with inductive logic programming. Mach. Learn. **100**(2), 555–585 (2015)

22. Knobbout, M., Dastani, M., Meyer, J.C.: A dynamic logic of norm change. In: Proceedings of ECAI, pp. 886–894 (2016)

23. Lorenz, R., Senoner, J., Sihn, W., Netland, T.: Using process mining to improve productivity in make-to-stock manufacturing. Int. J. Prod. Res., 1–12 (2021)

24. Loreti, D., Chesani, F., Ciampolini, A., Mello, P.: Generating synthetic positive and negative business process traces through abduction. Knowl. Inf. Syst. **62**(2), 813–839 (2020)

25. Mahmoud, M.A., Ahmad, M.S., Yusoff, M.Z.M., Mostafa, S.A.: A regulative norms mining algorithm for complex adaptive system. In: Ghazali, R., Deris, M.M., Nawi, N.M., Abawajy, J.H. (eds.) SCDM 2018. AISC, vol. 700, pp. 213–224. Springer, Cham (2018). https://doi.org/10.1007/978-3-319-72550-5_21

26. Miralles, J.C., López-Sánchez, M., Salamó, M., Avila, P., Rodríguez-Aguilar, J.A.: Robust regulation adaptation in multi-agent systems. TAAS **8**(3), 13:1–13:27 (2013)

27. Morales, J., Lopez-Sanchez, M., Rodriguez-Aguilar, J.A., Vasconcelos, W., Wooldridge, M.: Online automated synthesis of compact normative systems. ACM Trans. Auton. Adapt. Syst. (TAAS) **10**(1), 1–33 (2015)

28. Morales, J., López-Sánchez, M., Rodríguez-Aguilar, J.A., Wooldridge, M., Vasconcelos, W.: Synthesising liberal normative systems. In: Proceedings of the 2015 International Conference on Autonomous Agents and Multiagent Systems, pp. 433–441. International Foundation for Autonomous Agents and Multiagent Systems (2015)

29. Morales, J., Wooldridge, M., Rodríguez-Aguilar, J.A., López-Sánchez, M.: Evolution-ary synthesis of stable normative systems. In: Proceedings of the 16th Conference on Autonomous Agents and MultiAgent Systems, AAMAS 2017, São Paulo, Brazil, 8–12 May 2017, pp. 1646–1648 (2017)
30. Morales, J., Wooldridge, M., Rodríguez-Aguilar, J.A., López-Sánchez, M.: Off-line synthe-sis of evolutionarily stable normative systems. Auton. Agents Multi-Agent Syst. **32**(5), 635–671 (2018). https://doi.org/10.1007/s10458-018-9390-3
31. Muggleton, S.H., Lin, D., Pahlavi, N., Tamaddoni-Nezhad, A.: Meta-interpretive learning: application to grammatical inference. Mach. Learn. **94**(1), 25–49 (2014)
32. Perelli, G.: Enforcing equilibria in multi-agent systems. In: Agmon, N., Taylor, M.E., Elkind, E., Veloso, M. (eds.) Proceedings of the 18th International Conference on Autonomous Agents and Multiagent Systems (AAMAS 2019), pp. 188–196 (2019)
33. Savarimuthu, B.T.R., Cranefield, S.: Norm creation, spreading and emergence: a survey of simulation models of norms in multi-agent systems. Multiagent Grid Syst. **7**(1), 21–54 (2011)
34. Shoham, Y., Tennenholtz, M.: On social laws for artificial agent societies: off-line design. Artif. Intell. **73**(1–2), 231–252 (1995)
35. Tinnemeier, N., Dastani, M., Meyer, J.J., van der Torre, L.: Programming normative arti-facts with declarative obligations and prohibitions. In: Proceedings of the IEEE/WIC/ACM International Conference on Intelligent Agent Technology (IAT 2009), pp. 69–78 (2009)
36. Wooldridge, M., van der Hoek, W.: On obligations and normative ability: towards a logical analysis of the social contract. J. Appl. Logic **3**(3), 396–420 (2005)

Embracing AWKWARD! Real-Time Adjustment of Reactive Plans Using Social Norms

Leila Methnani[1]([⊠])[ID], Andreas Antoniades[2][ID], and Andreas Theodorou[1][ID]

[1] Department of Computing Science, Umeå University, Umeå, Sweden
{leila.methnani,andreas.theodorou}@umu.se
[2] Guildford, Surrey, UK

Abstract. This paper presents the AWKWARD architecture for the development of hybrid agents in Multi-Agent Systems. AWKWARD agents can have their plans re-configured in real time to align with social role requirements under changing environmental and social circumstances. The proposed hybrid architecture makes use of Behaviour Oriented Design (BOD) to develop agents with reactive planning and of the well-established OperA framework to provide organisational, social, and interaction definitions in order to validate and adjust agents' behaviours. Together, OperA and BOD can achieve real-time adjustment of agent plans for evolving social roles, while providing the additional benefit of transparency into the interactions that drive this behavioural change in individual agents. We present this architecture to motivate the bridging between traditional symbolic- and behaviour-based AI communities, where such combined solutions can help MAS researchers in their pursuit of building stronger, more robust intelligent agent teams. We use DOTA2—a game where success is heavily dependent on social interactions—as a medium to demonstrate a sample implementation of our proposed hybrid architecture.

Keywords: Reactive planning · Normative agents · Hybrid systems · Multi-agent systems · Games AI

1 Introduction

In a Multi-Agent System (MAS) the ability for individual agents to adjust their behaviour when interacting with each other and their environment is critical to the system's success [18]. Yet, agents in MAS need to dynamically re-orient their priorities away from their individual—often selfish—goals and towards the system's collective goals and vice versa as their environment changes.

One technique used to develop agents in highly dynamic environments is Behaviour-Based Artificial Intelligence (BBAI) [11]. Instead of trying to model the environment, BBAI strictly focuses on the actions that an agent can take

---

A. Antoniades—Independent scholar.

N. Ajmeri et al. (Eds.): COINE 2022, LNAI 13549, pp. 54–72, 2022.
https://doi.org/10.1007/978-3-031-20845-4_4

and limiting search within a predefined plan for responsive and robust goal-oriented behaviour [15, 22]. While this approach does indeed increase the search speed, it reduces the flexibility of the system as it is able to react only to *what its developers have specified*. Moreover, BBAI on its own is insufficient when applied to MAS. It does not account for social interactions between agents or any team work explicitly, and thus fails any consideration of real-world challenges where accounting for social behaviours is required.

In this paper, we combine BBAI with formal approaches to get the 'best of both worlds' by developing a hybrid architecture: Agents With KnoWledge About Real-time Duties (AWKWARD). We integrated the OperA framework [19] with Behaviour-Oriented Design (BOD) [15] for their individual and combined strengths in order to produce socially-aware BBAI agents. With OperA, we model the interactions between agents, which contributes towards both governing social behaviour as well as increasing transparency of emerging system behaviour. Transparency could help developers debug the system more effectively and help naive users understand the model [35]. With BOD, we can build reactive planning agents that are suited to interact within uncertain and dynamic environments. We have implemented a 'toy example', presented in this paper, for the popular video game DOTA2. Video games have traditionally been used to test AI solutions due to their highly dynamic virtual worlds, which DOTA2 offers as a test bed. Note, we do not consider the specifics of the DOTA2 implementation as our contribution; our focus and contribution is the AWKWARD architecture.

The paper is structured as follows: in Sect. 2, we discuss Behaviour Oriented Design and OperA as the backbone of our architecture, outlining the relevant characteristics of each. In Sect. 3, we introduce the AWKWARD architecture, followed by a sample implementation of the architecture in Sect. 4 and results presented in Sect. 5. In the penultimate Sect. 6, we look at related work done in normative agents, comparing and contrasting those architectures with our own. Finally in Sect. 7, we summarise our contributions and identify future work.

2 Background

2.1 Behaviour Oriented Design

BOD is a BBAI approach that uses hierarchical representations of an agent's priorities [15]. These representations express both the priority of the agent in terms of the goals it needs to achieve, and the contexts in which sets of actions may be applicable [12]. Another important feature is the usage of the parallel-rooted hierarchy, which allows for the quasi-parallel pursuit of behaviours and a hierarchical structure to aid the design of the agent's behaviour. On each plan cycle, the planner alternates between checking for what is currently the highest-level priority that should be active and then progressing work on that priority. Wortham et al. [36] detail the building blocks of a reactive plan in BOD, which are summarised as follows:

1. **Drive Collection (DC):** The root node of the plan's hierarchy: contains a set of Drives. The DC is responsible for giving attention to the highest priority Drive as at any given cycle only Drive can be active.
2. **Drive:** Allows for the design and pursuit of a specific behaviour. Each Drive has its own release condition of one or more Senses. Even when it is not the focus of the planner attention, each Drive maintains its execution state allowing the quasi-parallel execution of multiple drives.
3. **Competence:** A self-contained basic reactive plan representing the priorities within the particular plan. Each Competence contains at least one non-concurrent Competence Element (CE). Each of these elements is associated with both a priority relative to the other elements and a context which can perceive and report when that element can execute. The highest-priority action that can be executed will do so when the Competence receives attention.
4. **Action Pattern:** Fixed sequences of actions and perceptions used to reduce the design complexity, by determining the execution order in advance.
5. **Action:** A possible 'doing' of the agent, such the use of an actuator to interact with the environment; i.e. the means of altering the world and self.
6. **Sense:** A reading of the world or internal status from a sensor of the agent, such as measuring distance between specified units in the world; i.e. the means of reporting environmental and agent status.

BOD aims to enforce the good-coding practice 'Don't Repeat Yourself' by splitting the behaviour into two core modules: the *planner* and the *behaviour library* [14]. The former reads and 'runs' the plan at set intervals. The latter contains the blocks of code used by the two primitive plan elements, Actions and Senses. The rest of the plan elements are textually listed in dedicated files, written in Lisp-like format [15], read by the planner. A plan file contains descriptions of both the plan elements and of the connections between the elements.

2.2   OperA

OperA is an agent organisation framework for the design and development of MAS consisting of three intermingling models [19]:

1. **Organisational Model (OM):** Describes objectives and the concerns of the organisation from a social perspective. The development of an OM is approached from a top down perspective, that is, with overarching goals and a means to reach them.
2. **Social Model:** Outlines the agent's role enactment in the form of social contracts. These social contracts describe what capabilities and responsibilities each role demands.
3. **Interaction Model:** Defines interaction agreements between role-enacting agents in the form of interaction contracts. These contracts serve as verification for the fulfilment of interaction agreements between relevant actors specified by organisational objectives as defined in the OM.

OperA requires that all interactions are expressed as *scene* scripts. A scene is a formal specification defining which *roles* within the organisation partake in the interaction, what *landmarks* from the environment indicate the scene's start, and what resulting signals describe its termination. More importantly, the specification contains a set of *rules* describing the social norms that the participating agents are expected to follow for the scene's full duration. OperA norms use the deontic expressions of obligation, prohibition and permission as a means of describing an agent's social behaviour and further validating whether it satisfies or violates organisational expectations.

The OperA framework provides a formal specification that depends on organisational structures and global objectives of the organisation as a whole [19]. Moreover, OperA offers an interaction model between agents without requiring knowledge of the internal architecture of the individual agent itself; this quality in particular is our primary motivation for selecting OperA as a normative MAS framework. Further motivation is offered in Sect. 6 where we compare our selection with other related methodologies.

3 The AWKWARD Architecture

The AWKWARD architecture, depicted in Fig. 1, is a hybrid-systems architecture designed for agents operating in multi-agent systems. It consists of three modules, each with a distinct purpose: 1) the reactive planner; 2) the OperA module; and 3) the behaviour library. Our solution, inspired by the dual-process theory presented by [26], employs a 'fast' system 1 and a 'slow' system 2 working in tandem for efficient decision making while taking into consideration its wider environmental and social context.

3.1 The AWKWARD Planner

The 'fast system' consists of the reactive planner. The planner allows the agent to act upon its intuitions: plans with multiple drives are triggered based on its environmental and internal changes. Each change may enable short-term or long-term goals for the agent to achieve. Reactive planning has the advantage of faster action-selection and the ability to manage dynamic and unpredictable environments [11,15]. Most specifically, we use the BOD paradigm due to its proven use in virtual environments, e.g. games [9,21,34] and simulations [13]. BOD, unlike other BBAI approaches, allows the execution of multiple behaviours in pseudo-parallel and has a strong emphasis on modularity and reusability.

BOD plans form a hierarchical tree structure that is traversed from the root to the leaves in order of priority. This order determines the agent's behaviour given the world circumstance it finds itself in. The hierarchy is predetermined by the plan developer and indicated in the plan. In AWKWARD, plans are written as JSON files. At its initiation, the *Plan Parser* component parses the plan to memory, accessed through the *Plan Manager* component, storing the relationships between the plan elements and the hierarchical order of those plan

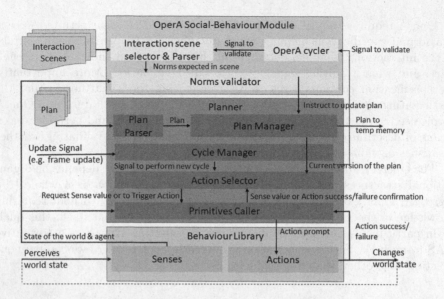

Fig. 1. Conceptual diagram of the AWKWARD architecture. The diagram is colour coded; in yellow, representing our System 1, are the parts of the OperA module, in blue are the components of system 2, i.e. the reactive planner; and in green the code components and files shared during execution by multiple agents. (Color figure online)

elements. Each agent's DCs can be constructed from the same drive elements, but will differ only in the order of execution, resulting in different expressed behaviours per agent. By initiating all roles with the same plan (i.e. same drive collection hierarchy) and enforcing social norms on agents who violate interaction agreements by explicitly re-prioritising drives, we can shape role- and interaction-dependent plans as needed by the current environment state.

At set intervals, referred to as *ticks*, the planner's *Cycle Manager* prompts the *Action Selector* component to re-evaluate the agents' perceived conditions to check if a new plan element needs to be executed or the currently running one should continue doing so. This continuous re-evaluation of the current plan elements, called the *plan cycle*, requires access from the planner to the behaviour library. That is, during each cycle, the planner retrieves the sensory inputs in the form of Sense plan elements, and may trigger actuators in the form of Action plan elements. The plan cycle is set on a fixed frequency based on an external update signal; for example, in our toy implementation, the plan cycle is set on every frame update inline with previous implementations of BOD in games [21].

On every tick, the Action Selector component retrieves the plan from memory and checks the Drive Collections (DCs) in a hierarchical order. If the conditions of a DC are satisfied, as determined by its corresponding Sense elements, it is executed. The planner then traverses through the drive elements of the DC, checking if they are eligible to be executed or not. These comparisons are done by checking by comparing current sensory reading against a set of preconditions, expressed as sense elements, to determine if the behaviour should be pursued or not by using simple boolean logic. If a drive fires, the planner stops its search at the current tick. This approach of local search enables agents to produce complex behaviours with minimal computational resources as there is no need to explore every possible behaviour at each time [22]. If the drive fired is a different one from the previous cycle, then the existing one 'pauses.' In other words, at the DC level, different drives can be in different states of execution enabling a quasi-parallel pursuit of multiple behaviours. Instead, the agent focuses—like our system 1 does—on whatever the highest priority behaviour that should be triggered is, e.g. staying alive, instead of unnecessarily checking if lower priority behaviours could also be triggered [15,36].

3.2 The OperA Module

In AWKWARD, the 'slow' system is the OperA module. It validates the social behaviour of the agent and provides direction to the reactive planner upon the completion—either with a success or failure—of a drive's execution. As discussed in Sect. 2, OperA is instantiated with a collection of Interaction Scenes, i.e. formal specification defining which roles within the organisation partake in the defined interaction. Using the senses found in the behaviour library module, the Cycle Manager component prompts the OperA module to check whether a scene has been initiated or terminated.

While a scene is running, the OperA module verifies that the agent's behaviour fulfils all social obligations that the agent has towards the other agents participating in the same scene. If the agent does not fulfil its obligations, then the OperA module instructs the planner to rearrange the priority of the drives in the currently running Drive Collection. This rearrangement is done by pushing upwards in the hierarchy any drive that corresponds to the desirable social behaviour. The OperA module is informed through formal specifications about which drive should correspond to which social behaviour. It identifies them within the current in-memory version of the plan by using a string equality operation. When the adjustment of drives is done, the new plan is stored in the system's memory, overwriting the old version. The OperA module checks if the re-prioritisation has produced behaviour that falls within the social and organisational norms the agent needs to comply with. If not, the OperA module continues to adjust the plan's drives further until the expected social behaviour is achieved. For this social norm validation, OperA uses the same senses as the planner component does to check which plan elements should be executed.

In its past implementations, a single instance of OperA operated at a global level [2,3], i.e. it was responsible for agents and interactions in the model. In AWKWARD, each agent contains its own local instance of OperA; i.e. each AWKWARD agent only checks its own behaviour in its current interaction scene. An advantage of this approach is that it allows us, at least in larger environments, to keep track of the multiple localised interaction scenes that the agent can be in simultaneously.

The use of a localised instance of OperA takes inspiration from Dennett's description of social constructs, where local efforts are made by agents to "steer their part of the whole contraption while [remaining] blissfully ignorant of the complexities on which the whole system depends" [17]. That is to say, each agent does not need to have any conceivable notion of the global system's intricacies, but rather a partial comprehension which may suffice for competence. In practical terms, as demonstrated in our toy example that is further discussed in Sect. 4, by having local copies of OperA carried with each agent also means that an AWKWARD agent is not constrained to interacting with other AWKWARD agents only. Rather, the agent can consider and interact with any agent architecture, as well as humans. Moreover, an AWKWARD agent does not require perfect knowledge of all agents in the same environment—which is impossible to maintain in certain scenarios, e.g. competitive games—to continuously adjust and moderate its behaviour within a defined socio-organisational role.

3.3 Behaviour Library

While each agent has its own individual plan structure, a single instance of the behaviour library can be shared across all agents. It is the collection of all possible primitives (i.e. Senses and Actions) as discussed in Sect. 2.1. It is accessed through global function calls in the primitives' tick functions. The behaviour library must therefore maintain a direct pointer to the agent that makes any particular function call in order to return values appropriate to the agent that requested them. By having a single behaviour library for all agents, we not only enable code reusability, but also reduce memory footprint of the agents and support the hosting of a remote behaviour library that runs complex actions and senses [14].

As discussed above, the behaviour library is accessible by both the planner and the OperA modules as they each provide control over the agent's means of environmental perception, internal status, and any actuators available. This decision to reuse the same Senses enables code reusability but also constrains OperA's knowledge to that of the agent, which it uses for the action-selection process. Arguably, this is also a more realistic implementation of Kahneman's dual-system theory [26]: our system 1 acts reactively and system 2 acts deliberately, but the embodiment with its sensors and actuators, i.e. behaviour library, is shared by both systems.

4 Implementation in DOTA2

We developed a 'toy example' in DOTA2, a popular game characterised by its extremely steep learning curve and complex emerging behaviour through the interactions of the different actors between themselves and their environment. We selected this game due to its complexity, inherent need for a MAS approach, recognition in the AI research community, and access to a public API for AI researchers[1]. Moreover, DOTA2 has been used in the past by the AI community; OpenAI [7] developed agents that were able to outperform 99% of the DOTA2 player base. Our interest, unlike OpenAI, extends beyond the scope of the individual agent and creating human-beating agents. Instead, we used this highly dynamic environment to demonstrate how AWKWARD can be implemented and have BBAI agents working together in a team by using OperA to model and validate their social interactions.

4.1   DOTA2

In the game, two opposing teams of five players (i.e. agents) navigate through terrain, striving to destroy a structure in their enemy's base known as the Ancient, while also defending their own. There are five roles—or positions—to fill per team. Each team agent is a *hero* that is assigned a position complementary to their given skill-set. For instance, a hero with healing capabilities can fulfil the responsibilities of a *Position 5* role, which includes supporting a hero in the *Position 1* role. In the early game, the Position 1 role is one of the weakest members. As the match progresses, Position 1 typically becomes the strongest on the team. However, to reach that state, a social norm exercised in most games involves giving Position 1 priority, at least in certain scenes, to perform the self-advancing activity known as *farming*. However, given specific circumstances, supporting roles may break that norm to farm in favour of advancing themselves. Hence, it is important to alternate strategies between pursuing behaviours for the benefit of others on the team and for your own personal performance. The resulting team of agents demonstrate emergent behaviour in the arena as they interact. This emergent behaviour can be difficult to perfectly model or even understand from the observer's perspective.

4.2   The Reactive Planner Module and Behaviour Library

As we discussed in the previous section, AWKWARD consists of a planner module and a behaviour library. In order for each agent to behave in compliance with its assigned role, its dedicated plan must consist of a distinctly ordered collection of drives (i.e. DCs). In our DOTA2 implementation, the plan is described in a JSON string that is parsed by the planner. We synchronised the planner update frequency with the game's internal execution update; i.e. the planner ticks the DC to check its drives on every frame update. In our toy example, we implemented a sample DC with multiple drives.

One of our implemented drives is the DE-FarmLane, represented in Formalism 1. The drive prompts the behaviour of seeking out enemy units called *creeps* in the hero's assigned lane in the environment and striking them when they are low on health in order to achieve what is referred to as a *last hit*. Last hits result in a kill and a gold bounty for the hero to collect. Gold is the currency used to purchase items in-game providing heroes with added attributes and abilities in

---

[1] Available at: https://developer.valvesoftware.com/wiki/Dota_Bot_Scripting.

battle. For example, a *healing salve* can be purchased and consumed to aid in health regeneration.

The option for health regeneration is captured by Formalism 2. This drive is executed in response to the agent's internal state: a measure of low health, as defined by the agent designer. It is important to note that two drives such as the external state of *farm time* in DE-FarmLane and internal state of *low health* in DE-Heal, could be true at the same time. In our current implementation, which behaviour is expressed is determined by plan structure; namely the order of executing drives. For example, if DE-Heal is prioritised over DE-FarmLane, then it will execute for as long as the world satisfies its *low health* condition, or until a drive of higher priority is able to run. For instance, if the agent has low health while simultaneously taking damage the plan designer might prioritise a behaviour that more urgently involves retreating.

$$\text{farm time} \Rightarrow \left| \left\langle \begin{array}{l} \text{laning phase ended?} \Rightarrow \textit{goal} \\ \text{creep can be last hit?} \Rightarrow \text{lastHitCreep} \\ \text{creep wave far?} \Rightarrow \text{goToCreepWave} \\ \Rightarrow \text{goToAssignedLane} \end{array} \right\rangle \quad (1)$$

$$\text{low health} \Rightarrow \left| \left\langle \begin{array}{l} \text{full health?} \Rightarrow \textit{goal} \\ \text{healing ability?} \Rightarrow \text{use healing ability} \\ \text{healing item?} \Rightarrow \text{use healing item} \\ \text{enough gold?} \Rightarrow \text{buy healing item} \\ \Rightarrow \text{retreat} \end{array} \right\rangle \quad (2)$$

The drive element DE-Retreat, represented in Formalism 3, prompts the behaviour of seeking refuge in the occurrence of declining health. This drive, as it is currently implemented, only fires when the hero is below 30% health and directs the hero towards their home base where their *fountain* resides and provides protection while regenerating health.

$$\text{under attack} \Rightarrow \left| \left\langle \begin{array}{l} \text{full health?} \Rightarrow \textit{goal} \\ \text{low health AND taking damage?} \Rightarrow \text{retreat} \end{array} \right\rangle \quad (3)$$

Drives may fire Competences or Action Patterns. The competences consist of an ordered list of competence elements that fire other competences or action patterns. The action patterns consist of a sequence of one or more actions—a primitive element found in the behaviour library along with senses. For instance, Formalism 1 depicts DE-FarmLane and lists lastHitCreep as a competence element that fires the action pattern shown in Formalism 4. The action patterns consist of selectTarget followed by rightClickAttack, which are defined in the behaviour library.

$$\langle selectTarget \rightarrow rightClickAttack \rangle \quad (4)$$

An agent's individual behavioural desire is shaped by how its plan element are arranged and executed. Consider again the drive element DE-FarmLane, which encourages a hero to individually collect as much bounty from last hitting lane creeps as possible. All heroes have this drive in their plans, and while it is a common desire for all members of the organisation to maximise their individual farm, it would not benefit the collective team if all members were to continuously act selfishly. For instance, in the early game a hero with the role of Position 1 is often vulnerable and weak with little of the gold needed to mature their abilities and grow their arsenal. It is therefore the duty of the Position 5 role to sacrifice farm for the sake of their allied member who requires it more at this early stage. Social interactions become particularly interesting and important for us to capture here. This is also where the OperA framework shines, as it enables the definition of social role assignments and interaction agreements for the advancement of the whole team unit.

4.3   The OperA Module Implementation

We use social interactions to alter the order in which a reactive agent's drives are fired. Accomplishing this real-time adjustment should demonstrate successful expression of social behaviour. That is, altering selfish priorities for the collective good of the organisation the individual hero is a member of. The OperA module requires a record of the relevant members and their associated roles within the society. Currently, each hero's role assignment also determines their lane assignment in the environment, which further characterises their "right".

For example, Table 1 outlines the role of *Position 1*, indicating that their ultimate objective is to ensure their team's victory, which can only be done by collecting enough items to become powerful. Their sub-objectives are therefore to farm as much as possible, buying items with earned gold from farm. They have the right to do so in their assigned zone: the *safe lane*—named as such due to its proximity to safety zones. An example norm that applies to a Position 1 hero is the obligation to farm enemy creeps when they are close by. In contrast, Table 2 shows the role table for Position 5, who is not permitted to farm while Position 1 is nearby. This sacrifice is to ensure Position 1 gains enough gold to quickly advance their role and carry the team in the later phases of the game.

Table 1. Position 1 role defined using the OperA framework

Role id	Position 1
objectives	Carry team to victory
sub-objectives	Farm and buy items
rights	High priority in safe lane
rules	IF enemy creep around THEN OBLIGED to farm

In the OperA module, relevant norms are constructed by parsing JSON strings with their descriptions. Each norm has a name identifier, an associated

Table 2. Position 5 role defined using the OperA framework

Role id	Position 5
objectives	Support team to victory
sub-objectives	Heal allies and take fights
rights	Low priority in safe lane
rules	IF Position 1 nearby THEN NOT PERMITTED to farm

Table 3. Interaction Scene for Priority Lane Farming

Scene	Priority lane farming
roles	Carry and support
landmarks	Partner and creeps nearby
results	Partner not nearby

rules	IF highest priority around THEN
	    OBLIGED to farm
	ELSE
	    NOT PERMITTED to farm

behaviour, and a deontic operator. The behaviour corresponds to the suitable drive element of the agent's planner. The deontic operators we focus on for this implementation are NOT PERMITTED and OBLIGED. The PERMITTED operator is a softer norm that induces no change to the plan in the current implementation. A norm also has a reference to an assigned agent's plan. It is validated by checking the agent's active drive against the expected (norm) behaviour, and whether it is permissible or required within a given circumstance. If a norm is violated, sanctions should be applied. In our implementation, a norm can alter the plan in response to a violation. Recall that our planner implementation allows for the removal and insertion of drive elements at runtime.

While norms can—and should—be associated with the individual agent, what is most interesting for our purposes is the use of norms to characterise interaction scenes between agents. An OperA interaction scene has a unique name identifier, a list of roles involved in the scene, a list of landmarks that indicate the start of a scene, a list of results that indicate the end of a scene, and the rules that indicate the norms that constrain the agents' behaviours such that they remain within the social expectations of the team (Table 3). In our implementation of scene objects, the landmarks and results correspond to sense primitives that were re-used from the reactive plan elements, as do the rule conditions that determine the appropriate norm to apply in the scene.

Consider again the agent's DE-FarmLane (Formalism 1). This drive is fired when the senses isFarmingTime and isSafeToFarm return true. We have defined farming time as the early game (approximately the first 10 min.) and safety corresponds to the fight activity and whether any enemy heroes are threatening the agent's farm ability. For the purposes of this demonstration, we assume it is always safe to farm and the sense will return true. The competence elements that the farming drive consists of checks conditions in a prioritised order: if the agent is not at the creep wave, they must move there. (Unlike action patterns which always execute in the same order, competences will skip this element if the condition returns false). If the agent is already at the creep wave, then the next condition check is whether any enemy creep around can be last hit. A creep can be last hit when their health is lower than the hero's attack damage and is located within attack range. If this condition is true, the agent will select the appropriate target and attempt to land the last hit. Notice that the drive is entirely self-directed and lacks any social consideration. That is, each agent, while expressing farming behaviour, will pay no mind to whether they have the highest priority around or not. An agent pair farming in the same lane is not optimal behaviour from a social perspective. The agents must abide by social norms for this given circumstance, and OperA can facilitate this interaction using scene scripts. The result is preservation of interaction agreements and altered plans that better suit each agent's role requirements.

While this farm priority check is a simple example that can just as easily be incorporated into each agent's plan, we argue that it will become limiting and wasteful over the course of the game. We observed that when social awareness was incorporated into an individual agent's plan, the structure not only became longer to read and more complicated to understand, but also resulted in increased idle time while an agent was attempting to express farming behaviour. When an agent of higher priority is farming, the agent should not continue to attempt to farm, but should instead fire a different drive for productivity. This coordination is best handled by an organisational/social-aware structure, like OperA. We argue that the individual agent itself should not have too many intricate details about interactions, especially considering the long-time horizons of a game like DOTA2 where social behaviour itself is expected to shift along with the various game phases. In fact, OperA scene scripts very nicely accommodate this game attribute. If behaviour can be altered by OperA, then the reactive planners become simpler to construct. The complexity is captured and described by the OperA interaction models.

5 Results

In this paper, we are exclusively concerned with developing a system that can alter agent plans in response to social interactions, regardless of whether other entities in the society have a similar architecture or not. Hence, we designed the evaluation of our sample implementation to reflect that. For the scope of this project, we focus only on the first 10 minutes of the game; within this time in particular, farming priority is important in terms of behaviour adjustment due to expected social norms.

The interaction under evaluation is described by the Priority Farm scene as defined by an interaction scene object. The particular behaviour that is expected is for the Position 5 agent—the AWKWARD bot—to give up its own farm for the benefit of the ally of higher priority in the same lane. In this case, the relevant ally is the Position 1 agent—the default bot.

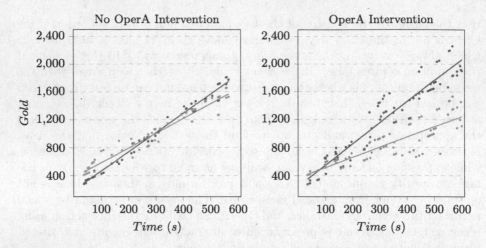

Fig. 2. (Left) Similar rate of gold acquisition between Position 5 (orange) and Position 1 (blue) DOTA2 agents when OperA makes no alterations to Position 5's plan during the Priority Farm interaction scenes. (Right) Diverging rate of gold acquisition between Position 5 and Position 1 DOTA2 agents as a result of AWKWARD rearranging the plan for the agent in the Position 5 role. Trend lines represent average over $N = 5$ trials. (Color figure online)

To demonstrate how these changes in the plan impacts the performance of agents, we used gold acquisition as a quantitative metric. This is the standard metric used for players' performance evaluation in DOTA2 tournaments. The agent's value of gold is measured over the course of the first 10 min. of the game. The right subplot in Fig. 2 shows the divergence in gold acquisition over time between the AWKWARD bot of position 5 and the default DOTA2 bot of position 1 over five trials. This divergence can be explained by the AWKWARD bot's social behaviour change; OperA banning farm will result in the role sacrificing its own gain and promoting its ally's acquisition of gold instead. The AWKWARD bot's social adjustment is to deny itself from farming when the priority ally (Position 1) is around.

In this scenario, we mark the moments in time where plan changes are expected to occur due to social interactions, but OperA is not inducing the change in order to see the difference in each bot's gain. While both roles still acquire gold, Position 1 has acquired less than expected, and both agents approximately match each other's gain.

In contrast, the left subplot in Fig. 2 illustrates a different trend when the AWKWARD bot does *not* change its plan within the social context. These plots show the two roles on par with one another in terms of gold acquisition over time. When the AWKWARD bot does not alter its plan and continues to attempt to farm, even while the ally of higher priority (Position 1) is also farming in the same lane. The difference in gold acquisition between scenarios can be seen over numerous trials (the dotted lines shows the average linear trend over 5 trials).

The data varies in time and gold value due to added randomness across game instances, but the overall trends remain similar.

6   Related Work

The AWKWARD architecture combines the normative framework OperA with the Behaviour-Based AI architecture BOD. In this section, we review and compare our architecture to relevant approaches found in the literature. As a complete survey of the literature is beyond the scope of this article, we focus on the most relevant approaches that we considered during the conceptualisation of the AWKWARD architecture.

6.1   Behaviour-Based AI

Various approaches of Behaviour-Based AI have been proposed for achieving real-time performance in embodied—physical or virtual—agents including the Subsumption Architecture [10], Pengi [1], and ANA [29]. These bottom-up reactive planning approaches use condition-action pairs without—or with minimal—internal state; i.e. a simple functional mapping between perceived environmental stimuli and their appropriate responses. Such reactive approaches have proven highly effective for a variety of problems [30]. However, in comparison to BOD, these approaches expect little regularity in the arbitration of behaviour; i.e. all possible behaviours must be considered at all times. Moreover, they cannot store information dynamically, thus putting the onus on the developer to predict possible stimuli and develop the appropriate behaviours. BOD overcomes these issues by further decomposing behaviours into "things that need to be checked regularly, things that only need to be checked in a particular context, and things that one can get by not checking at all" [15].

While BOD also originated as a robotics cognitive architecture with its POSH implementation [15]—and most recently Instinct [36]—it has made its way to virtual environments such as games, e.g. pyPOSH in Unreal Tournament [9], POSH-Sharp in StarCraft [21], and UNPOSH in Unity [34]. However, in these implementations of BOD, there was no mechanism to verify that the agents adhere to their social roles. Instead, unlike our AWKWARD implementation, the plan developer had to ensure that any social norms were accounted for during the plan's development, limiting the possible interactions between agents and team-level performance of the agents.

6.2   Normative Agents and Self-organisation

The AWKWARD architecture is related to previous work done in the development of *normative agents*. Early work in the literature for normative agents proposes architectures that extend Belief, Desire, Intention (BDI) models with norms [16,27,28]. These agents deliberate around the generation and selection of both goals and plans. For instance, [8] describe their (Beliefs, Obligations,

Intentions, and Desires) BOID agent architecture that appends obligations as a mental attitude in addition to its beliefs, desires and intentions. However, as [20] argue, BDI agents focus towards their own goals instead of social interactions—both with other artificial and human agents—making such approaches unsuitable for multi-agent systems where cooperation between agents is necessary.

Another related approach is N-Jason, a norm-aware BDI agent interpreter equipped with the programming language for agent norm compliance at run-time [28]. It extends Jason/AgentSpeak(L) with addition of normative concepts such as obligations, permissions, prohibitions, deadlines, priorities, and duration. Similar to N-Jason, N-2APL is also a BDI agent architecture that supports norm-aware deliberation [4]. N-2APL allows agents to adopt normative behaviour in the form of deontic obligations and prohibitions with specified deadlines. OperA being a framework for formal specifications of social interactions instead of a complete architecture, enables us to define explicitly the social interactions in the form of scene specifications while also keeping the reactive planner component independent; i.e. operational without the OperA module.

Relevant work also includes existing methodologies for the development of normative agents in multi-agent organisations such as Moise [23] and its extension Moise+ which adds an inheritance on the roles and structural verification features [24,25]. Moise+ is based on notions of *roles*, *groups*, and *missions*, enabling explicit specification of MAS organisations that agents can reason about and organisational platforms can enforce [25]. Moise+ offers an implicit description of an interaction protocol through deontic links that specify agent permissions and obligations within their assigned missions. An agent belongs to groups where they are offered a set of permitted roles and missions. Thus, upon changing roles and missions, groups are also subject to change, allowing for task-oriented coalitions to be defined. While interactions in Moise+ are task-driven, OperA leads by social expectation in the form of explicit contracts; a main motivation for its adoption in the work presented here.

All of these approach capture and represent social norms in order to enable agents to self organise. However, they rely on integrating the social norm enforcement directly into the decision making system. In our architecture, we allow for both reactivity and social deliberation as the situation demands. This ensures that our agents can act efficiently in their environment on their own, i.e. act as complete complex agents, while also organising themselves based on their social roles—and corresponding responsibilities—when they are a part of a larger organisation. Moreover, our decision to use a distributed version of OperA ensures that our AWKWARD agents can interact with other AWKWARD agents, non-AWKWARD agents, and even humans.

Finally, AWKWARD considers that all agents have the capacity to act self-ishly and altruistically to varying degrees determined by their roles and social interactions. In contrast to above approaches, we use a reactive planning architecture for the individual agent motivated by its ability to handle uncertainty and dynamic environments. We assign obligations via external expectations that may be subject to change. This approach of global coordination also differs from other work proposed for developing normative reactive planning agents, such as the NoA architecture [27]. While NoA adopts norms and deliberates over their activation, our proposed framework concerns itself with dynamically imposing, monitoring and enforcing norms through global coordination, and then distributed enforcement, rather than individual deliberation.

6.3   Hybrid Approaches with Reactive Planning

AWKWARD combines formal reasoning, in the form of the OperA module, with reactive planning. A related approach is the logic-based subsumption architecture, where the different control layers that make up a subsumption system have been axiomatised using first-order logic [5,6]. The benefit of this approach is the introduction of non-monotonic reasoning into reactive planning; i.e. developers can understand and easily add control layers to the subsumption planner at run time [6]. Similarly, the Layered Argumentation System combines—at hardware level—fuzzy reasoning and non-monotonic reasoning for run-time generation of reactive plans [32,33]. These combinations of reactive and formal reasoning approaches bridge together communities—one of our goals—but their focus has been to improve the overall performance of the agent by combining the two paradigms instead of enabling cooperation between multiple agents.

With the latter goal in mind, ABC^2 architecture combines classical planning with reactive approaches [31]. ABC^2, similar to AWKWARD, emphasises cooperation between agents. In ABC^2 each agent has to define and broadcast their own 'skills'; i.e. it requires active communication and coordination instead of promoting self-coordination as AWKWARD's OperA implementation does. AWKWARD keeps the reactive and formal parts of the system completely separate from each other; i.e. our reactive planner—sans social consideration—can operate without the OperA module.

AWKWARD uses both formal reasoning and reactive planning as complementary approaches to each other. However, unlike past approaches, this combination is done on an architectural level. By keeping the reactive planner separate from the normative system, our reactive planner can operate without the normative reasoning module—even if the agent is not behaving within the limits of its socio-organisational role.

7   Conclusions and Future Work

In this paper, we presented the AWKWARD architecture for hybrid systems: agents that combine normative reasoning, in the form of OperA, and behaviour-based AI methods, in the form of BOD, at an architectural level. Combining the advantages of BOD and OperA, AWKWARD achieves real-time adjustment of agent plans for evolving social roles as it verifies—and adjust plans to ensure—adherence to any socio-organisational role prescribed to the agent. We provided a toy example, implemented in the game DOTA2, where we demonstrated how

AWKWARD enables continual manipulation of agent's behaviour over changing environmental and social circumstances.

With the planner and OperA module implemented in DOTA2, we have demonstrated how OperA can influence the behaviour of reactive planners under defined social circumstances. However, manually designing and building reactive plans can be inefficient and time consuming for system developers, especially as plans scale. As a next step, we intend to investigate methods of optimising plan structure automatically. To do this, Reinforcement Learning techniques can be employed to guide the discovery of an optimal ordering and OpenAI Gym acts as a favourable toolkit for this task. Additionally, we are interested in extending the scope to cover variable autonomy, where varying levels of decision-making control can be passed between a human player—who either directly controls a hero in the game or oversees a team of bots—and artificial agents.

Acknowledgements. Theodorou was supported by the Wallenberg AI, Autonomous Systems and Software Program (WASP) funded by the Knut and Alice Wallenberg Foundation. We would like to thank Dignum V. for her input on OperA. All code is available at: https://github.com/lulock/dota.

References

1. Agre, P., Chapman, D.: Pengi: an implementation of a theory of activity. In: Proceedings of the Sixth National Conference on Artificial Intelligence (1987)
2. Aldewereld, H., Dignum, V.: OperettA: organization-oriented development environment. In: Dastani, M., El Fallah Seghrouchni, A., Hübner, J., Leite, J. (eds.) LADS 2010. LNCS (LNAI), vol. 6822, pp. 1–18. Springer, Heidelberg (2011). https://doi.org/10.1007/978-3-642-22723-3_1
3. Aldewereld, H., Dignum, V., Jonker, C.M., van Riemsdijk, M.B.: Agreeing on role adoption in open organisations. KI-Künstliche Intelligenz **26**(1), 37–45 (2012)
4. Alechina, N., Dastani, M., Logan, B.: Programming norm-aware agents. In: Proceedings of the 11th International Conference on Autonomous Agents and Multiagent Systems, vol. 2, pp. 1057–1064 (2012)
5. Amir, E., Maynard-Reid, P.: Logic-based subsumption architecture. In: Artificial Intelligence (2004)
6. Amir, E., Maynard-Zhang, P.: LiSA: a robot driven by logical subsumption (2001)
7. Berner, C., et al.: DOTA2 with large scale deep reinforcement learning. arXiv preprint:1912.06680 (2019)
8. Broersen, J., Dastani, M., Hulstijn, J., van der Torre, L.: Goal generation in the BOID architecture. Cogn. Sci. Q. **2**, 428–447 (2002)
9. Brom, C., Gemrot, J., Michal, B., Ondrej, B., Partington, S.J., Bryson, J.J.: Posh tools for game agent development by students and non-programmers. In: IEEE 9th Computer Games Conference (CGames 2006) (2006)
10. Brooks, R.: A robust layered control system for a mobile robot. IEEE J. Robot. Autom. **2**(1), 14–23 (1986)
11. Brooks, R.A.: Intelligence without representation. Artif. Intell. **47**, 139–159 (1991)
12. Bryson, J.J.: Action selection and individuation in agent based modelling. In: Sallach, D.L., Macal, C. (eds.) Proceedings of Agent 2003: Challenges in Social Simulation, pp. 317–330. Argonne National Laboratory, Argonne (2003)

13. Bryson, J.J., Ando, Y., Lehmann, H.: Agent-based modelling as scientific method: a case study analysing primate social behaviour. Philos. Trans. Roy. Soc. B Biol. Sci. **362**, 1685–1699 (2007)
14. Bryson, J.J., Theodorou, A.: How society can maintain human-centric artificial intelligence. In: Toivonen-Noro, M., Saari, E., Melkas, H., Hasu, M. (eds.) Human-Centered Digitalization and Services. Springer, Singapore (2019). https://doi.org/10.1007/978-981-13-7725-9_16
15. Bryson, J.J.: Intelligence by design: principles of modularity and coordination for engineering complex adaptive agents. Ph.D. thesis, MIT (2001)
16. Castelfranchi, C., Dignum, F., Jonker, C.M., Treur, J.: Deliberative normative agents: Principles and architecture. In: International Workshop on Agent Theories, Architectures, and Languages (1999)
17. Dennett, D.C.: The age of post-intelligent design. In: The Age of Artificial Intelligence: An Exploration (2020)
18. Dignum, F.: Agents for Games and Simulations II: Trends in Techniques, Concepts and Design. Springer, Heidelberg (2011). https://doi.org/10.1007/978-3-642-18181-8
19. Dignum, V.: A model for organizational interaction: based on agents, founded in logic. Ph.D. thesis, SIKS (2004)
20. Dignum, V., Dignum, F.: Agents are dead. Long live agents! In: 19th International Conference on Autonomous Agents and Multi-Agent Systems (AAMAS) (2020)
21. Gaudl, S., Davies, S., Bryson, J.J.: Behaviour oriented design for real-time-strategy games: an approach on iterative development for StarCraft AI. In: Foundations of Digital Games (FDG) (2013)
22. Guzel, M.S., Bicker, R.: A behaviour-based architecture for mapless navigation using vision. Int. J. Adv. Robot. Syst. **9**, 18 (2012)
23. Hannoun, M., Boissier, O., Sichman, J.S., Sayettat, C.: MOISE: an organizational model for multi-agent systems. In: Monard, M.C., Sichman, J.S. (eds.) IBERAMIA/SBIA 2000. LNCS (LNAI), vol. 1952, pp. 156–165. Springer, Heidelberg (2000). https://doi.org/10.1007/3-540-44399-1_17
24. Hübner, J.F., Sichman, J.S.a., Boissier, O.: A model for the structural, functional, and deontic specification of organizations in multiagent systems. In: Proceedings of the 16th Brazilian Symposium on Artificial Intelligence: Advances in Artificial Intelligence (2002)
25. Hübner, J.F., Sichman, J.S., Boissier, O.: Developing organised multiagent systems using the MOISE+ model: programming issues at the system and agent levels. Int. J. Agent Oriented Softw. Found. Eng. **1**, 370–395 (2007)
26. Kahneman, D., Frederick, S.: A model of heuristic judgment. In: The Cambridge Handbook of Thinking and Reasoning (2005)
27. Kollingbaum, M.J., Norman, T.J.: Norm adoption and consistency in the NoA agent architecture. In: Dastani, M.M., Dix, J., El Fallah-Seghrouchni, A. (eds.) ProMAS 2003. LNCS (LNAI), vol. 3067, pp. 169–186. Springer, Heidelberg (2004). https://doi.org/10.1007/978-3-540-25936-7_9
28. Lee, J., Padget, J., Logan, B., Dybalova, D., Alechina, N.: N-Jason: Run-time norm compliance in AgentSpeak. In: International Workshop on Engineering Multi-Agent Systems (2014)
29. Maes, P.: Situated agents can have goals. Robot. Auton. Syst. **6**, 49–70 (1990)
30. Mataric, M.J.: Behaviour-based control: examples from navigation, learning, and group behaviour. J. Exp. Theor. Artif. Intell. **9**, 323–336 (1997)

31. Matellán, V., Borrajo, D.: ABC(2) an agenda based multi-agent model for robots control and cooperation. J. Intell. Robot. Syst. **32**, 93–114 (2001). https://doi.org/10.1023/A:1012009429991
32. Song, I., Governatori, G.: Designing agent chips. In: 5th International Joint Conference on Autonomous Agents and Multiagent Systems (AAMAS 2006) (2006)
33. Song, I., Governatori, G., Diederich, J.: Automatic synthesis of reactive agents. In: 11th International Conference on Control, Automation, Robotics and Vision (ICARCV) (2011)
34. Theodorou, A., Bandt-law, B., Bryson, J.J.: The sustainability game: AI technology as an intervention for public understanding of cooperative investment. In: IEEE Conference on Games (2019)
35. Theodorou, A., Wortham, R.H., Bryson, J.J.: Designing and implementing transparency for real time inspection of autonomous robots. Connect. Sci. **29**, 230–241 (2017)
36. Wortham, R.H., Gaudl, S.E., Bryson, J.J.: Instinct : a biologically inspired reactive planner for embedded environments. In: ICAPS 2016 PlanRob Workshop (2016)

Self-learning Governance of Black-Box Multi-Agent Systems

Michael Oesterle[1]([✉]) [iD], Christian Bartelt[1] [iD], Stefan Lüdtke[1] [iD],
and Heiner Stuckenschmidt[2] [iD]

[1] Institute for Enterprise Systems (InES), University of Mannheim,
Mannheim, Germany
{oesterle,bartelt,luedtke}@es.uni-mannheim.de
[2] University of Mannheim, Mannheim, Germany
heiner@informatik.uni-mannheim.de

Abstract. Agents in Multi-Agent Systems (MAS) are not always built
and controlled by the system designer, e.g., on electronic trading platforms. In this case, there is often a system objective which can differ
from the agents' own goals (e.g., price stability). While much effort has
been put into modeling and optimizing agent behavior, we are concerned
in this paper with the platform perspective. Our model extends Stochastic Games (SG) with dynamic restriction of action spaces to a new self-
learning governance approach for black-box MAS. This governance learns
an optimal *restriction policy* via Reinforcement Learning.

As an alternative to the two straight-forward approaches—fully centralized control and fully independent learners—, this novel method
combines a sufficient degree of autonomy for the agents with selective
restriction of their action spaces. We demonstrate that the governance,
though not explicitly instructed to leave any freedom of decision to the
agents, learns that combining the agents' and its own capabilities is
better than controlling *all* actions. As shown experimentally, the self-
learning approach outperforms (w.r.t. the system objective) both "full
control" where actions are always dictated without any agent autonomy,
and "ungoverned MAS" where the agents simply pursue their individual
goals.

Keywords: Multi-Agent System · Governance · Self-learning system ·
Reinforcement Learning · Electronic institution

1 Introduction

1.1 Motivation

Multi-Agent Systems (MAS) are widely used as a general model for the interaction of autonomous agents, and have been applied to a vast range of real-world
settings, for example Algorithmic Trading [1], Traffic Management [33], and
Multi Player Video Games [25] (see [42] for a recent survey of MAS applications).

© The Author(s), under exclusive license to Springer Nature Switzerland AG 2022
N. Ajmeri et al. (Eds.): COINE 2022, LNAI 13549, pp. 73–91, 2022.
https://doi.org/10.1007/978-3-031-20845-4_5

Example 1. Consider a stock market where high-frequency trading algorithms typically generate the vast majority of orders. Obviously, agents in this setting act autonomously and in a self-interested manner in order to maximize their profit. As is known, this behavior leads to problems like high volatility and extreme stock price behavior [26]. It is therefore crucial for regulators to provide both stability (i.e., ensure that extreme price movement flash crashes will not happen) and opportunity (i.e., ensure that investors can still use intricate, proprietary strategies to make profit).

In this example—as in many other applications areas—the agents cannot (or should not) be fully controlled, but must have a sufficient degree of freedom regarding their actions. At the same time, some level of control needs to be imposed on the agents such that a system objective can be achieved.

The scope of this paper is therefore a subclass of MAS with three more assumptions, inspired by the concept of *Electronic Institutions* (EI) [4] as described in Sect. 2:

(a) The agents are truly autonomous entities whose goals and strategies cannot be known ("black boxes"), but only observed through their actions,
(b) in addition to the agents' individual goals, there is a *system objective* which does not necessarily coincide with any of the former goals, and
(c) agent actions can be restricted by a *governance* which has the power to enforce such restrictions.

We propose a novel approach to governing an MAS which combines the restriction concept of EI with dynamic rule-setting, provided by a Reinforcement Learning (RL) component (the *governance*). This governance observes the public information of the MAS, i.e., actions and transitions, and learns optimal restrictions, which depend on the system state and the respective agent's observation.

A common method for governing agents in an EI is the use of *norms* with a focus on rewards and sanctions as the means of influencing agent behavior, while the action space itself is not affected. This makes two essential assumptions about the agents: First, "the effectiveness of these norms depends heavily on the importance of the affected social reality for the individual" [6], and second, the normative awareness needs to be comparable for all participating agents (*interpersonal utility comparison*). For unknown agents, we argue that these assumptions cannot be expected to hold true, which is why we base our governance on (mandatory) restrictions of the agents' action sets. The dynamic nature of the rule-setting process (*rule synthesis*) is due to the fact that agents themselves can act strategically and are therefore able to exploit any static rule set.

Of course, the governance's "power to restrict" requires some sort of physical control over the MAS. This requirement is satisfied in a wide range of applications, for example by any digital platform where agents are software components, and actions are chosen by exchanging messages. Therefore, we assume the adherence to restriction to be given in this work.

1.2 Illustration of the Governance Approach

The simultaneous execution and learning of a *Governed Multi-Agent System* (GMAS) is shown in Fig. 1 (see the formal model in Sect. 3 for the definition and explanation of the variables, and Algorithm 1 for the actual run-time loop). The governance is used, i.e., its restriction policy is queried, at every execution step of the MAS to determine the set of allowed and forbidden actions, whereas the learning happens in between those execution steps.

In each learning step, the governance optimizes its restriction policy in order to maximize the system objective, given the observation of the last step. At the same time, the agents can update their own action policies, but this is not part of the GMAS (black-box agents).

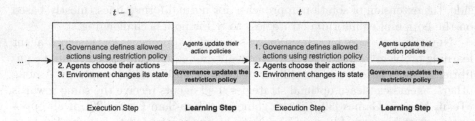

Fig. 1. Sequence of execution and learning steps in a Governed Multi-Agent System

1.3 Contribution

We show in this paper how a self-learning governance with the ability to restrict action spaces can add value to an MAS. This is demonstrated by comparing its performance to two natural alternatives (see also [37]):

- *Ungoverned MAS* (UMAS), in which the agents alone decide on their actions, such that coordination or cooperation (if any) evolves on its own, and
- *Fully Controlled MAS* (FMAS), where the governance prescribes all agent actions, leaving no room for autonomous decisions.

The main contributions of this work are: We give a formal definition of a Governed Multi-Agent System (Sect. 3), we conceptualize an RL governance for this model, analyzing the assumptions made in the model and describing the governance's learning behavior (Sect. 4), and we present experiments (Sect. 5) to demonstrate that this method can significantly outperform both alternatives: UMAS and FMAS.

2 Related Work

Most MAS literature focuses on the agents' perspective, attempting to improve their learning behavior [32,35]. The underlying model, the *Stochastic Game*

(SG), is both an extension of a *Markov Decision Process* (MDP) to multiple agents, and an extension of a *Normal-Form Game* to multiple states. Hence, methods from both Stochastic Processes and Game Theory have been adapted to this setting. Both in Game Theory and in Machine Learning, it is very common to assume discrete time steps and therefore a synchronized interaction between agents. We will make use of this assumption for the interaction between environment, agents and governance (see Sect. 3).

For a single-agent (stationary) MDP, the most common approach—Reinforce-ment Learning—includes a variety of algorithms which have been proven to converge to an optimal strategy [38]. What makes it hard to transfer these algorithms to multi-agent settings is the fact that the rewards and transitions in an SG depend on the joint action of all agents, making the system non-stationary from the perspective of each agent. Coming from the game-theoretic side, the extension of solution approaches for normal-form games (mostly based on the notion of equilibrium strategies) to SG is no less challenging.

Nevertheless, there have been many successful approaches to the multi-agent learning problem by introducing new concepts for equilibria (e.g. correlated equilibria [19] and cyclic equilibria [43]) or by making additional assumptions: Among others, agents can learn optimal strategies if all agents receive the same rewards (Team Markov Games [39]), if the game is a Zero-Sum Game [23], if all opponents are stationary [13], or if the "rate of non-stationarity" is bounded by a *variation budget* [12]. The general problem of finding an optimal strategy in a model-free, general-sum SG, however, is still an open challenge [42].

As a consequence, researchers have introduced additional support for the learning agents. This support can be either restricted to the interaction between the agents, or it can involve another entity besides the agents.

For the first type, agents are usually allowed to exchange additional information in order to find optimal strategies [11,21] (see also the recent MARL surveys of Zhang et al. [42] and Gronauer and Diepold [20]).

The second type relies on non-agent components to solve the learning problem: In its most general notion, the concept of *Environment-Mediated Multi-Agent Systems* (EMMAS) states: "When designing a system that is based only on local interactions in the environment and the emergent properties resulting from these interactions, it is a difficult research problem on the one hand to obtain the required global behavior of the system and on the other hand to avoid undesired global properties", and therefore suggests to "off-load some of the agent complexity into the processes of the dynamic agent environment" [40].

Electronic Institutions (EI) [16,30] provide an *institution* as the entity which regulates agent interactions, among many other features. The framework contains an "implementation of the control functionality of the institution infrastructure [which] takes care of the institutional enforcement", which can refer to both *norms*—which can be violated—and enforced *rules*. While these two terms are not always used consistently, we use here the convention that rules are "norms that can be effectively controlled and thus enforced, such that violation is impossible" [27].

The EI framework itself does not only describe rule-setting capabilities, but also Agents, Roles, a Performative Structure, and Normative Rules, among others [16]. The same holds for alternative models for social coordination, e.g., ANTE [24], or INGENIAS [18] ([3] includes details of all these frameworks). However, we use only one feature of EI: The ability to restrict the space of available actions for the participating agents. This has been described as an important part of an EI by Esteva et al.: "An electronic institution defines a set of rules that structure agent interactions, establishing what agents are permitted and forbidden to do" [15]. Aldewereld et al. emphasize that "organisational objectives are not necessarily shared by any of the individual participants, but can only be achieved through their combined action" [3], and that "one cannot make any assumptions about the inner workings of participants. [...] Rather, external aspects of the participants (actions, interactions, etc.) have to be leveraged to create the required coordination structures" [3].

Norms are a very common approach for achieving system goals in MAS. The distinction between norms and rules ("[Norms] are a concept of social reality [...] Therefore, it is possible to violate them" [6]) has been made many times in the literature; they have been called "social conventions" and "explicit prescriptions" [14], "legalistic view of norms" and "interactionist view of norms" [9], "norms" and "regimented norms" [6], or "norms" and "hard constraints" [17,27].

Normative Multi-Agent Systems (NorMAS) [8,14] embrace the idea that agent communities can self-regulate their interactions without a controlling force. Therefore, the field focuses on (violable) norms, their creation or emergence, observation, revision, adherence or violation, and sanctioning mechanisms. However, this requires the two assumptions mentioned in Sect. 1.1: Norm-awareness and inter-agent utility comparability. In our opinion, these requirements do not hold for black-box agents with individual goals ("How to deal with a lack of normative awareness and if it is being considered, how to check the lack of normative awareness if an agent's knowledge base is not accessible?" [6]). In consequence, our focus lies on the other type of institutional enforcement: Rules for allowed and forbidden actions.

The original implementation of EI (and its development environment EIDE [31]) envisaged a clear distinction between rule/norm creation at design-time and agent interaction at run-time (i.e., all rules/norms are given independently of the agents and do not change during execution). A logical next step was the Autonomic Electronic Institutions (AEI) approach [5,10]: Acknowledging the fact that static norms are not always sufficient for dealing with self-adapting agents, it moved norm creation from the design time to the run-time and allowed for dynamic changes. EI was therefore extended to include an evolutionary norm adaptation mechanism (e.g., a genetic algorithm). As we will see later, this is somewhat similar to our governance (defining and updating institutional rules at run-time).

Like multi-agent learning in general, normative capabilities in MAS can either be part of the agents [34], or part of an additional entity [2] (or both). While early work defined static norms at design-time [7,37], the field has since evolved towards run-time norm creation, synthesis and adaptation [28], applying methods like Automated Theorem Proving [29] or Deep Learning [2] to NorMAS.

This development towards dynamic norm creation and adaptation has, to our knowledge, not yet been examined for rules (i.e., hard constraints). In this paper, we fill the gap by demonstrating that dynamic rules do have the potential to enhance the capabilities of an MAS. Moreover, the RL approach employed here for the governance component is shown to be well-suited for on-line learning of a restriction policy in an environment where the agents and their behavior can only be observed from outside.

3   Model

3.1   Notation

Vectorized Variables. Let $\mathcal{S}$ be a set, and I be an index set. A single variable $s \in \mathcal{S}$ is written in regular face, whereas a vector $\boldsymbol{s} = (s_i)_{i \in I} \in \mathcal{S}^I$ is written in bold face. The index set is usually omitted when the context is clear. Variables that change over time always have the current time step as a superscript, as in $s^{(t)}$ or $\pi_i^{(t)}$.

Categorical Distribution. Given a finite set $\mathcal{S}$, $\Delta(\mathcal{S})$ denotes the set of all discrete probability distributions over $\mathcal{S}$, i.e., the set of all functions $p : \mathcal{S} \to [0, 1]$ with $\sum_{s \in \mathcal{S}} p(s) = 1$.

Image and Support. Let $f : A \to B$ be a function. Then $\mathrm{im}(f) := \{f(x) : x \in A\}$ is the *image* of f. If $B = \mathbb{R}$, $\mathrm{supp}(f) := \{x \in A : f(x) \neq 0\}$ is the *support* of f.

3.2   Multi-Agent System

Consider a *Partially Observable Stochastic Game* (POSG) over discrete time steps $t \in \mathbb{N}_0$, i.e., a 7-tuple $(I, \mathcal{S}, \mathcal{O}, \boldsymbol{\sigma}, \mathcal{A}, \boldsymbol{r}, \delta)$ with agent set $I = \{1, ..., n\}$, state set $\mathcal{S}$, observation set $\mathcal{O}$, observation functions $\sigma_i : \mathcal{S} \to \mathcal{O} \, \forall i \in I$, fundamental action set $\mathcal{A}$ with $k := |\mathcal{A}| \in \mathbb{N}$, agent reward functions $r_i : \mathcal{S} \times \mathcal{A}^I \to \mathbb{R} \, \forall i \in I$ and a probabilistic transition function $\delta : \mathcal{S} \times \mathcal{A}^I \to \Delta(\mathcal{S})$.

Each agent has an (unknown) stochastic action policy $\pi_i : \mathcal{O} \times 2^{\mathcal{A}} \to \Delta(\mathcal{A})$ which defines its behavior. These policies take as input not only the agent's current observation, but also a set $A \subseteq \mathcal{A}$ of allowed actions. Referring to the assumption of non-violable rules (see Sect. 1.1), we take as a given that forbidden actions are never chosen, hence $\mathrm{supp} \, \pi_i(s, A) \subseteq A \, \forall i \in I, s \in \mathcal{S}$.

An action policy is called *static* if it is constant in t; otherwise it is called *dynamic*. Note that a static policy π can still be non-deterministic, since the concrete action is sampled from the categorical distribution $\pi(o, A) \in \Delta(A)$.

3.3   Governance

The governance component returns a set $A \subseteq \mathcal{A}$ of allowed actions when given an input pair consisting of the overall environmental state and an agent's observation. This function is called the *governance policy* $\pi_G : \mathcal{S} \times \mathcal{O} \to 2^{\mathcal{A}}$. Note that the set of allowed actions can never be empty, i.e., $\varnothing \notin \mathrm{im}(\pi_G)$.

In contrast to a standard MAS, where the environment provides all the input for the agents' action policies, there is now an intermediary step in which the governance computes the set of allowed actions for each agent, which is then passed to the agent's policy in addition to its observation.

The system objective is given as a reward function $r_G : \mathcal{S} \times \mathcal{A}^I \to [0, 1]$, allowing the governance to directly measure the success of its restrictions after each environment step. The normalized range of r_G is chosen for ease of comparability.

Definition 1. *A* Governed Multi-Agent System *(GMAS) is the 9-tuple*

$$(I, \mathcal{S}, \mathcal{O}, \boldsymbol{\sigma}, \mathcal{A}, \boldsymbol{r}, \delta, \pi_G, r_G).$$

The governance is a *centralized controller* insofar as it observes the entire MAS and defines restrictions in a centralized way. However, the fundamental difference to the usual notion of "centralized control" is that the governance leaves a substantial amount of autonomy to the agents. This is not enforced by its design, but emerges naturally: The synergy between the governance's and the agents' capabilities gives a performance advantage over full control, causing the governance to allow multiple actions at most times (see Sect. 5).

3.4   Sequence of Actions in a GMAS

Figure 2 shows the exchange of data in one execution step (see Fig. 1) of a GMAS: The environment provides the agents with their respective rewards and observations, while passing to the governance the environment state, the governance reward and agent observations ❶. The governance then calculates the sets of allowed actions for each agent, and passes them to the respective agent ❷. Finally, the agents choose their actions and communicate them

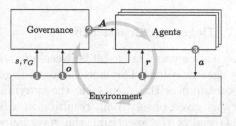

$s \in \mathcal{S}$: Environmental state $A \subseteq \mathcal{A}^I$: Allowed actions
$r_G \in \mathbb{R}$: Governance reward $r \in \mathbb{R}^I$: Agent rewards
$o \in \mathcal{O}^I$: Agent observations $a \in \mathcal{A}^I$: Agent actions

Fig. 2. Execution step of a GMAS

back to the environment ❸ which executes the transition. For simplicity and clarity of presentation, all n queries to the governance have been wrapped up into one arrow.

In pseudocode (see Algorithm 1), the run-time loop is very similar to the standard execution of an RL environment (e.g., in OpenAI Gym), with an additional governance step.

Algorithm 1: Run-time loop of a governed MAS

Data: GMAS $G = \left(I, \mathcal{S}, \mathcal{O}, \boldsymbol{\sigma}, \mathcal{A}, \boldsymbol{r}, \delta, \pi_G^{(0)}, r_G\right)$

Choose initial environmental state $s^{(0)} \in \mathcal{S}$;

for $t \in \{0, ..., T\}$ **do**
    // Execution step
    for $i \in I$ **do**
        $o_i^{(t)} \leftarrow \sigma_i(s^{(t)})$ // Compute agent observation from state
        $A_i^{(t)} \leftarrow \pi_G(s^{(t)}, o_i^{(t)})$ // Get allowed actions from governance
        $a_i^{(t)} \leftarrow \pi_i(o_i^{(t)}, A_i^{(t)})$ // Get chosen action from agent
    end
    $r^{(t)} \leftarrow r(s^{(t)}, a^{(t)})$ // Get rewards
    $s^{(t+1)} \leftarrow \delta(s^{(t)}, a^{(t)})$ // Execute transition

    // Learning step
    $\pi_G^{(t+1)} \leftarrow \text{train}(\pi_G^{(t)})$ // Train governance
    for $i \in I$ **do**
        $\pi_i^{(t+1)} \leftarrow \text{train}(\pi_i^{(t)})$ // Train agent
    end
end

3.5 Degree of Restriction

There is a natural trade-off between achieving the system objective and preserving agent freedom: The more actions the governance forbids, the higher its level of control over the agents—in the extreme case, only a single action is allowed for any given observation, resulting in a fully-deterministic trajectory. On the other end of the spectrum, the governance always allows all actions, reducing the GMAS to an ordinary MAS.

It is therefore reasonable to measure the *degree of restriction,* i.e., the percentage of forbidden actions, and to assess this metric in relation to the governance's performance:

Definition 2. *For an individual agent $i \in I$ and time step $t \in \mathbb{N}_0$, the degree of restriction is defined as*

$$\rho_i^{(t)} := 1 - \frac{\left|\pi_G\left(s^{(t)}, o_i\left(s^{(t)}\right)\right)\right|}{|\mathcal{A}|} \in [0, 1].$$

The overall degree of restriction $\rho^{(t)} := \frac{1}{n} \sum_{i \in I} \rho_i^{(t)}$ is simply the mean over all agents. The higher the degree of restriction, the lower the autonomy of the agents.

It should be noted that real-world agents oftentimes cannot choose every action at every step. Instead, only a subset of actions is feasible, depending on the environmental state (*parametric action spaces*). In this case, the degree of restriction should be defined as the ratio between forbidden actions and feasible actions.

4   Model Analysis

4.1   Fairness

Agents who make the same observation $o \in \mathcal{O}$ at a time step t are always allowed to perform the same actions $\pi_G\left(s^{(t)}, o\right)$. This is in line with a common-sense definition of fairness: The governance treats all agents the same way. To achieve this, learning (i.e., a change of the governance policy) cannot take place within a time step, but only after all agents have been given their action sets.

4.2   Learning

The GMAS model does not specify any particular learning algorithm, but only requires a governance policy π_G to be available for querying at all times. The restriction policy can be any function $\mathcal{S} \times \mathcal{O} \to 2^{\mathcal{A}}$, but, of course, the governance's goal is to find a restriction policy which maximizes the reward r_G, given the agents' behavior. Since the governance interacts with the ungoverned MAS in a cycle of information, reward and action, RL seems to be the natural way to optimize this policy.

From this perspective, the governance itself is a Reinforcement Learning agent which acts on the entire MAS as its environment: The governance interacts with the MAS environment and the agents, but only sees how its own actions (i.e., defining sets of allowed actions) influence its reward and the environmental state. Therefore, it can be treated as a reinforcement learner with action policy π_G and reward r_G. Its environment has the transition function $\delta' : \mathcal{S} \times \left(2^{\mathcal{A}}\right)^I \to \Delta(\mathcal{S})$ with $\delta'(s, A) := \delta\left(s, \pi(\sigma(s), A)\right)$, which is a composition of observation functions σ, agent policies π and MAS transition function δ.

δ' is not explicitly known to the governance, such that a model-free algorithm must be used. Moreover, since the governance policy is the action policy of the governance, standard model-free RL algorithms like A3C, DQN or PPO can be directly applied. The governance is structurally equivalent to a multi-label classifier: Its policy outputs a subset of the (finite) fundamental action set. Thus, specialized network architectures for this type of classifier could also be applied in order to build a more effective governance policy.

Since agents can (and probably will) change their behavior according to the current restriction policy, a GMAS is inherently dynamic and therefore an *online* learning problem: Both sides (agents and governance) react to the other side's actions and strategies by continuously adapting their own action policies. The initial restriction policy can be a random function, or it can be set to simply allow all actions, i.e., $\pi_G^{(0)}(s, o) := \mathcal{A} \; \forall s \in \mathcal{S}, o \in \mathcal{O}$. At run-time, the governance needs to learn continuously in order to keep up with changing agent behavior.

Therefore, there is no distinction between traning and evaluation as in classical RL, but the governance learning process continues throughout the lifecycle of the GMAS.

4.3 Stationarity

It is known [12] that, for a stationary MDP, near-optimal regret bounds can be achieved via RL. The situation is more complicated in the non-stationary case, depending on whether non-stationarity occurs in discrete steps (piece-wise stationarity) or continuously (among other criteria).

The transition function δ is assumed to be stochastic, but stationary. Therefore, the defining factor for the stationarity of a GMAS, seen from the governance's view, is the set of agent policies π: δ' is stationary if and only if all agent policies are static.

While using static pre-trained models is very common for NLP, Computer Vision and Speech Recognition [41], this is unusual for agent models, since on-line learning lies at the heart of useful behavior in an unknown world. Nevertheless, safety-critical agent-based systems like fully autonomous cars will likely require some sort of certification ensuring that they behave (exactly or approximately) in a certain way, which means that their policy should not, even when learning how to deal with unforeseen situations, be allowed to deviate too far from the approved policy.

Hence, we cannot generally assume that a GMAS is stationary, but in some domains there can be (quasi-)stationary agents, which means that the governance is likely to perform better than in a setting where the agents adapt their strategies arbitrarily fast.

5   Experimental Evidence

The goal of the experiments is to investigate the effect of the governance. For this purpose, we define a game in which the agents need to agree on an action, and then compare three types of systems: Ungoverned MAS (UMAS) which does not have a governance component at all, Fully Controlled MAS (FMAS), and Governed MAS (GMAS).

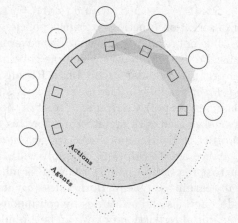

Fig. 3. The dining diplomats' problem

5.1   The Dining Diplomats' Problem

Consider an MAS with agent set $I = \{1, ..., n\}$ and action set $\mathcal{A} = \{1, ..., k\}$ for all agents. The agents are positioned in a circle such that each agent can only see their immediate neighbors (see Fig. 3). At each step, the agents play a card corresponding to one of their available actions. The environmental state represents the currently played cards, i.e., $S = A^n$ and $O = A^3$.

The agents' goal is to learn to coordinate their actions in order to play the same cards. In the style of the famous *dining philosophers' problem*, we call this problem the *dining diplomats' problem*, requiring the participating agents to come to an agreement under imperfect information.

5.2 Reward Functions

Consider two reward functions—a *state-based* reward and an *observation-based* reward:

$$r_s : S \rightarrow \mathbb{R}, \ r_s(s) = \begin{cases} 1 & \text{if } s_1 = \cdots = s_n \\ 0 & \text{else} \end{cases}$$

$$r_o : O \rightarrow \mathbb{R}, \ r_o(o) = \begin{cases} 1 & \text{if } o_1 = o_2 = o_3 \\ 0 & \text{else} \end{cases}$$

The state-based reward function only differentiates between "no coordination" and "full coordination", while the observation-based reward also shows local coordination between three agents (i.e., the observation space of one agent). The three system types use these reward functions as follows:

	Agents	Governance
UMAS	r_o	–
FMAS	r_s	r_s
GMAS	r_o	r_s

In the FMAS type, agents and governance have the same information about achieving their goals, so the governance cannot use the agents as an additional source of intelligence. In GMAS, however, the agents have access to more detailed information through r_o. Hence, the two pivotal dimensions are (a) access to low-level/high-level information and (b) dense and sparse rewards.

5.3 Configurations

We compare the three types for four different problem sizes: Tiny ($n = 5, k = 3$), small ($n = 10, k = 5$), medium ($n = 15, k = 7$) and large ($n = 20, k = 10$). This allows us to see clearly at which complexity the non-GMAS types fail to achieve coordination, and therefore highlights the value added by the synergy.

The size $|S| = k^n$ of the state space grow polynomially in the number of actions, but exponentially in the number of agents: In the tiny configuration, there are $3^5 = 243$ states, while this number is $5^{10} \approx 10^7$ for the small configuration, $7^{15} \approx 4 \cdot 10^{12}$ for the medium configuration, and 10^{20} for the large configuration.

5.4   Frameworks and Algorithms

For our experiments, we used the *RLlib* library [22] for multi-agent learning, which is based on the *Ray* distributed computing framework. Both agents and governance use a standard configuration of the Proximal Policy Optimization (PPO) algorithm [36].

The interaction between agents, governance, and environment requires a sequential MAS execution: The governance needs to act (i.e., produce a set of allowed actions) before an agent can choose from this set. All agent actions, in turn, cause the environment to proceed to the next state. Therefore, the governance is queried n times for each environmental step, while the agents each only act once during the same period.

All experiments were run in ten independent samples for $5 \cdot 10^6$ steps each (empirically determined to ensure sufficient convergence of the action policies).

5.5   Reproducibility

The source code to perform the experiments and generate the graphs is publicly available as a Jupyter notebook, allowing for simple reproduction of the results. The exact results shown in Fig. 4 are stored as Tensorboard log files in the same public repository.

5.6   Results

The results of the experiments can be found in Fig. 4. The governance reward r_G, as the main performance indicator, is shown on the left side, while the graphs on the right depict the corresponding degree of restriction ρ (see Definition 2).

Since the reward at every step is either 0 or 1, the governance reward $r_G^{(t)}$ is the average reward over time, i.e., the percentage of steps where full coordination of all agent actions has been achieved.

In each graph, the mean of the ten samples (thick line) and the individual samples (thin lines) are plotted. The numbers vary strongly between samples, i.e., the mean should be seen as a general trend, but not as the "average run".

Since the governance policy is initialized randomly, all governed types start with $\rho^{(0)} \approx \frac{1}{2}$. The progression of ρ depends on whether the governance is able to learn a "fully controlling" way to create a high reward. If it succeeds, ρ goes up to $\frac{k-1}{k}$ and stays there. Otherwise, the governance must utilize the agents' freedom, and therefore allows more than one action. Notably, the degrees of restriction turn out to be roughly equal in the FMAS and GMAS types.

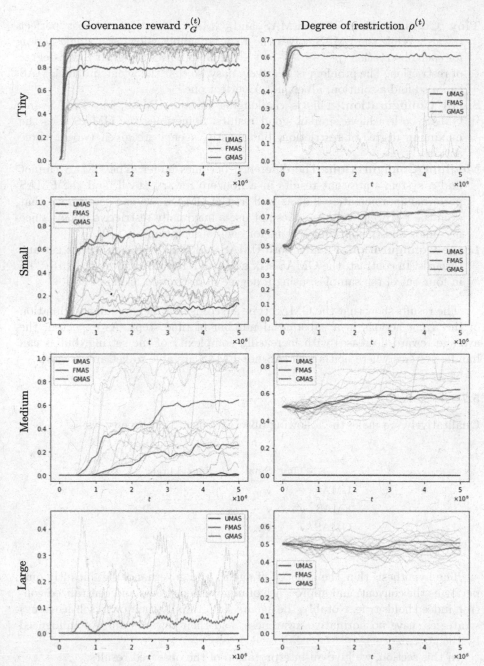

Fig. 4. Experimental results. Thick lines show the mean of $r_G^{(t)}$ and $\rho^{(t)}$ over ten independent samples, while thin lines are the results of the individual samples.

Tiny Configuration. Both FMAS and GMAS achieve an almost perfect reward. While the FMAS solves the task by simply allowing a single action for each observation ($\rho^{(t)} \rightarrow \frac{k-1}{k} = \frac{2}{3}$), the GMAS uses a slightly lower degree of restriction. The problem is relatively easy, so that the agents in the UMAS can also find a solution, albeit not a perfect one.

Small Configuration. This is challenging for the UMAS, but FMAS and GMAS both achieve similar, good results. Sometimes the GMAS uses the maximum degree of restriction, but mostly, agents are given two or three actions.

Medium Configuration. The difference becomes larger: The UMAS cannot find a system state that results in a nonzero reward at all, and the FMAS performs approximately half as well as the GMAS. We can see from ρ that even the FMAS governance does not use a maximally restrictive policy, since it cannot find the optimal actions for each observation.

Large Configuration. Finally, both UMAS and FMAS are not able to get any rewards. In contrast, the GMAS still achieves a reward of more than 15–20% in four out of ten samples, using a degree of restriction around 50%.

The results show that the GMAS type succeeds in achieving full coordination of the agent actions in a substantial number of time steps. As expected, the average reward decreases with increasing complexity of the setting, but it can handle systems where neither UMAS nor FMAS are able to get any rewards.

5.7   Discussion

Qualitatively, we make the following observations of the three types:

	Tiny	Small	Medium	Large
UMAS	✓	✓		
FMAS	✓	✓	✓	
GMAS	✓	✓	✓	✓

The hypothesis that the synergy of agents and governance significantly outperforms the conventional approaches of ungoverned agents and centralized control, indeed holds true. Notably, the agents simply apply their own (self-learning) strategies, have no normative awareness, and their rewards are not influenced by the governance.

In this section, we give an interpretation of the observed results:

System Objective and Degree of Restriction. The governance in the GMAS type has the power of fully controlling the MAS—it could simply allow only one action for any state and observation. Therefore, the crucial observation in the experiments is that the degree of restriction does *not* converge to $\frac{k-1}{k}$.

Instead, the right side of Fig. 4 clearly shows that the governance leaves a substantial amount of freedom to the agents, and that this freedom causes the governance reward to be much higher than using full control (i.e., the FMAS type).

The balance between governance control and agent freedom is constantly changing, depending on how well the system objective (as measured by the governance reward function) is achieved. It is a crucial feature of our approach that the optimal balance is determined via RL and not defined in advance.

Micro-level and Macro-level Knowledge. There are different types of knowledge in the GMAS: The governance can see the entire environmental state and knows which states are most desirable, but does not know effective actions to get there, since its reward function only indicates whether the system objective has been fully achieved. The agents, on the other hand, lack a view of the big picture, but have a better grasp of how to act on a lower level, since their reward function tells them when they are locally coordinated.

In the UMAS, the overall state is not available to the agents at all, not even through the governance. This prevents the agents from finding a globally coordinated solution, even though they can coordinate locally. In the FMAS, the governance sees the big picture, but cannot figure out the necessary actions for the agents to move in the right direction.

The combination of these two levels allows the GMAS to reach global coordination—without ever being instructed how to combine agent and governance knowledge. This setting was chosen since it represents a common pattern in MAS: Individual agents are situated at a specific location in the environment and only able to perceive their surroundings, i.e., a small part of the environment. On the other hand, this small part is where their actions have the biggest impact. The system designer or operator, in contrast, sees the environment as a whole, but does not have the micro-level knowledge about optimal or even useful agent actions. Therefore, the goal is clear, but the way to get there is unknown.

Incentives for Autonomy and Restriction. The governance can freely choose the restrictions without being penalized for high degrees of restriction. Consequently, there is no real incentive for the governance to allow multiple actions: The chosen degree of restriction directly reflects the highest expected reward. In the small scenarios, we observe that allowing only one action per observation is a feasible strategy which leads to high rewards. As the scenarios get more complex, however, the governance policy is not maximally restrictive anymore: The governance learns that the autonomous decisions of the agents are more helpful than centralized control. Still, by selectively forbidding actions, the governance can support the agents' action policies.

Penalties for Restrictions A reasonable goal for the governance is to use the least amount of restrictions to achieve its objective, and therefore strive to

Body

reduce the degree of restriction whenever this does not counteract the system objective. To this end, we experimented with giving the governance a penalty in proportion to the current degree of restriction by redefining its reward function as $r'_G := r_G - \alpha \cdot \rho$ with a constant weighting parameter α. This resulted in a much lower reward (even when ignoring the penalty), making the governance drop nearly all restrictions early in the training, before it then defined new, more effective restrictions. However, the penalty often prevented the governance from sufficiently exploring the possible restrictions, so there were many samples where there was never any reward, even in small scenarios.

6   Conclusion and Future Work

In this paper, we have motivated the need for governed MAS, a synergy-based approach for black-box MAS with an additional system objective. We have demonstrated that full control as well as ungoverned learning agents fail to achieve their goals even in simple scenarios; a challenge solved considerably better by GMAS.

The model and experiments give rise to several questions for future work:

– In the experiments presented here, the objectives of agents and governance were strongly correlated. How can the approach be applied to an arbitrary combination of goals, and how do conflicts in the objective functions influence learning?
– What does an extension of the restriction policy to continuous action spaces look like?
– How do action space restrictions compare (empirically and theoretically) to other forms of governance, e.g., norms or inter-agent communication?
– Is the approach viable for asynchronous MAS (e.g., cyber-physical systems)?

Acknowledgements. This work is supported by the German Federal Ministry for Economic Affairs and Energy (BMWi).

References

1. Abdunabi, T., Basir, O.: Holonic intelligent multi-agent algorithmic trading system (HIMAATS). Int. J. Comput. Appl. **21**, 54–61 (2014)
2. Aires, J.P., Meneguzzi, F.: Norm conflict identification using deep learning. In: AAMAS Workshops (2017)
3. Aldewereld, H., Boissier, O., Dignum, V., Noriega, P., Padget, J. (eds.): Social Coordination Frameworks for Social Technical Systems. Springer, Cham (2016). https://doi.org/10.1007/978-3-319-33570-4
4. Arcos, J.L., Esteva, M., Noriega, P., Rodríguez-Aguilar, J.A., Sierra, C.: Environment engineering for multiagent systems. In: Engineering Applications of Artificial Intelligence (2004)
5. Arcos, J.L., Rodríguez-Aguilar, J.A., Rosell, B.: Engineering autonomous electronic institutions. In: Weyns, D., Brueckner, S.A., Demazeau, Y. (eds.) EEMMAS 2007. LNCS (LNAI), vol. 5049, pp. 76–87. Springer, Heidelberg (2008). https://doi.org/10.1007/978-3-540-85029-8_6

6. Balke, T., et al.: Norms in MAS: definitions and related concepts, p. 31. Schloss Dagstuhl-Leibniz-Zentrum fuer Informatik (2013)
7. Barbuceanu, M.: Coordinating agents by role based social constraints and conversation plans. In: AAAI/IAAI (1997)
8. Boella, G., van der Torre, L., Verhagen, H.: Introduction to normative multiagent systems. Comput. Math. Organ. Theory 12(2), 71–79 (2006). https://doi.org/10.1007/s10588-006-9537-7
9. Boella, G., van der Torre, L., Verhagen, H.: Introduction to the special issue on normative multiagent systems. Auton. Agents Multi-Agent Syst. 17(1), 1–10 (2008). https://doi.org/10.1007/s10458-008-9047-8
10. Bou, E., López-Sánchez, M., Rodríguez-Aguilar, J.A.: Towards self-configuration in autonomic electronic institutions. In: Noriega, P., et al. (eds.) COIN 2006. LNCS (LNAI), vol. 4386, pp. 229–244. Springer, Heidelberg (2007). https://doi.org/10.1007/978-3-540-74459-7_15
11. Cacciamani, F., Celli, A., Ciccone, M., Gatti, N.: Multi-agent coordination in adversarial environments through signal mediated strategies. In: Proceedings of the 20th International Conference on Autonomous Agents and MultiAgent Systems. International Foundation for Autonomous Agents and Multiagent Systems, Richland (2021)
12. Cheung, W.C., Simchi-Levi, D., Zhu, R.: Reinforcement learning for non-stationary markov decision processes: the blessing of (more) optimism. In: Proceedings of the 37th International Conference on Machine Learning, ICML 2020, Virtual Event, 13–18 July 2020 (2020)
13. Conitzer, V., Sandholm, T.: AWESOME: a general multiagent learning algorithm that converges in self-play and learns a best response against stationary opponents. Mach. Learn. 67, 23–43 (2003). https://doi.org/10.1007/s10994-006-0143-1
14. Conte, R., Falcone, R., Sartor, G.: Introduction: agents and norms: how to fill the gap? Artif. Intell. Law 7(1), 1–15 (1999). https://doi.org/10.1023/A:1008397328506
15. Esteva, M., et al.: Electronic institutions development environment. In: AAMAS Demo Proceedings, vol. 3. International Foundation for Autonomous Agents and Multiagent Systems (2008)
16. Esteva, M., Rodríguez-Aguilar, J.-A., Sierra, C., Garcia, P., Arcos, J.L.: On the formal specification of electronic institutions. In: Dignum, F., Sierra, C. (eds.) Agent Mediated Electronic Commerce. LNCS (LNAI), vol. 1991, pp. 126–147. Springer, Heidelberg (2001). https://doi.org/10.1007/3-540-44682-6_8
17. Frantz, C., Pigozzi, G.: Modelling norm dynamics in multi-agent systems. J. Appl. Logic 5, 491–564 (2018)
18. Gomez-Sanz, J.J.: Ingenias. In: Aldewereld, H., Boissier, O., Dignum, V., Noriega, P., Padget, J. (eds.) Social Coordination Frameworks for Social Technical Systems. Springer, Cham (2016). https://doi.org/10.1007/978-3-319-33570-4_5
19. Greenwald, A., Hall, K.: Correlated-Q learning. In: Proceedings of the Twentieth International Conference on International Conference on Machine Learning, ICML2003. AAAI Press (2003)
20. Gronauer, S., Diepold, K.: Multi-agent deep reinforcement learning: a survey. Artif. Intell. Rev. 55, 895–943 (2021). https://doi.org/10.1007/s10462-021-09996-w
21. Hwang, K., Jiang, W., Chen, Y.: Model learning and knowledge sharing for a multiagent system with Dyna-Q learning. IEEE Trans. Cybern. 45(5), 978–990 (2015)
22. Liang, E., et al.: RLlib: abstractions for distributed reinforcement learning. In: ICML (2018)

23. Littman, M.L.: Markov games as a framework for multi-agent reinforcement learning. In: Proceedings of the Eleventh International Conference on International Conference on Machine Learning, ICML 1994. Morgan Kaufmann Publishers Inc., San Francisco (1994)

24. Lopes Cardoso, H., Urbano, J., Rocha, A., Castro, A.J.M., Oliveira, E.: ANTE: a framework integrating negotiation, norms and trust. In: ldewereld, H., Boissier, O., Dignum, V., Noriega, P., Padget, J. (eds.) Social Coordination Frameworks for Social Technical Systems, vol. 30. Springer, Cham (2016). https://doi.org/10.1007/978-3-319-33570-4_3

25. Marín-Lora, C., Chover, M., Sotoca, J.M., García, L.A.: A game engine to make games as multi-agent systems. Adv. Eng. Softw. **140**, 02732 (2020)

26. McGroarty, F., Booth, A., Gerding, E., Chinthalapati, V.L.R.: High frequency trading strategies, market fragility and price spikes: an agent based model perspective. Ann. Oper. Res. **282**(1), 217–244 (2019). https://doi.org/10.1007/s10479-018-3019-4

27. Mellema, R., Jensen, M., Dignum, F.: Social rules for agent systems. In: Aler Tubella, A., Cranefield, S., Frantz, C., Meneguzzi, F., Vasconcelos, W. (eds.) COIN/COINE 2017/2020. LNCS (LNAI), vol. 12298, pp. 175–180. Springer, Cham (2021). https://doi.org/10.1007/978-3-030-72376-7_10

28. Morales, J.: On-line norm synthesis for open Multi-Agent systems. Ph.D. thesis, Universitat de Barcelona (2016)

29. Neufeld, E., Bartocci, E., Ciabattoni, A., Governatori, G.: A normative supervisor for reinforcement learning agents. In: Platzer, A., Sutcliffe, G. (eds.) CADE 2021. LNCS (LNAI), vol. 12699, pp. 565–576. Springer, Cham (2021). https://doi.org/10.1007/978-3-030-79876-5_32

30. Noriega, P.: Agent-mediated auctions: the fishmarket metaphor. Ph.D. thesis, Universitat Autonoma de Barcelona (1997)

31. Noriega, P., de Jonge, D.: Electronic institutions: the EI/EIDE framework. In: Aldewereld, H., Boissier, O., Dignum, V., Noriega, P., Padget, J. (eds.) Social Coordination Frameworks for Social Technical Systems. LGTS, vol. 30, pp. 47–76. Springer, Cham (2016). https://doi.org/10.1007/978-3-319-33570-4_4

32. Nowé, A., Vrancx, P., De Hauwere, Y.M.: Game theory and multi-agent reinforcement learning. In: Wiering, M., van Otterlo, M. (eds.) Reinforcement Learning: State-of-the-Art. Springer, Heidelberg (2012). https://doi.org/10.1007/978-3-642-27645-3_14

33. Padakandla, S., K. J., P., Bhatnagar, S.: Reinforcement learning algorithm for nonstationary environments. Appl. Intell. **50**(11), 3590–3606 (2020). https://doi.org/10.1007/s10489-020-01758-5

34. Riad, M., Golpayegani, F.: Run-time norms synthesis in multi-objective multi-agent systems. In: Theodorou, A., Nieves, J.C., De Vos, M. (eds.) COINE 2021. LNCS, vol. 13239, pp. 78–93. Springer, Cham (2021). https://doi.org/10.1007/978-3-031-16617-4_6

35. Rizk, Y., Awad, M., Tunstel, E.: Decision making in multi-agent systems: a survey. IEEE Trans. Cogn. Dev. Syst. **10**, 514–529 (2018)

36. Schulman, J., Wolski, F., Dhariwal, P., Radford, A., Klimov, O.: Proximal policy optimization algorithms (2017)

37. Shoham, Y., Tennenholtz, M.: On social laws for artificial agent societies: off-line design. Artif. Intell. **73**(1), 231–252 (1995)

38. Sutton, R.S., Barto, A.G.: Reinforcement Learning: An Introduction. A Bradford Book, Cambridge (2018)

39. Wang, X., Sandholm, T.: Reinforcement learning to play an optimal nash equilibrium in team Markov games. In: NIPS (2002)
40. Weyns, D., Brückner, S., Demazeau, Y.: Engineering Environment-Mediated Multi-Agent Systems. Springer, Heidelberg (2007). https://doi.org/10.1007/978-3-540-85029-8
41. Zaib, M., Sheng, Q.Z., Zhang, W.E.: A short survey of pre-trained language models for conversational AI-A NewAge in NLP (2021)
42. Zhang, K., Yang, Z., Başar, T.: Multi-agent reinforcement learning: a selective overview of theories and algorithms. In: Vamvoudakis, K.G., Wan, Y., Lewis, F.L., Cansever, D. (eds.) Handbook of Reinforcement Learning and Control. SSDC, vol. 325, pp. 321–384. Springer, Cham (2021). https://doi.org/10.1007/978-3-030-60990-0_12
43. Zinkevich, M., Greenwald, A., Littman, M.L.: Cyclic equilibria in Markov games. In: Proceedings of the 18th International Conference on Neural Information Processing Systems, NIPS 2005. MIT Press, Cambridge (2005)

Computational Theory of Mind
for Human-Agent Coordination

Emre Erdogan[1]([⊠]) [iD], Frank Dignum[1,2] [iD], Rineke Verbrugge[3] [iD],
and Pınar Yolum[1] [iD]

[1] Utrecht University, Utrecht, The Netherlands
{e.erdogan1,p.yolum}@uu.nl
[2] Umeå University, Umeå, Sweden
dignum@cs.umu.se
[3] University of Groningen, Groningen, The Netherlands
l.c.verbrugge@rug.nl

Abstract. In everyday life, people often depend on their theory of mind, i.e., their ability to reason about unobservable mental content of others to understand, explain, and predict their behaviour. Many agent-based models have been designed to develop computational theory of mind and analyze its effectiveness in various tasks and settings. However, most existing models are not generic (e.g., only applied in a given setting), not feasible (e.g., require too much information to be processed), or not human-inspired (e.g., do not capture the behavioral heuristics of humans). This hinders their applicability in many settings. Accordingly, we propose a new computational theory of mind, which captures the human decision heuristics of reasoning by abstracting individual beliefs about others. We specifically study *computational affinity* and show how it can be used in tandem with theory of mind reasoning when designing agent models for human-agent negotiation. We perform two-agent simulations to analyze the role of affinity in getting to agreements when there is a bound on the time to be spent for negotiating. Our results suggest that modeling affinity can ease the negotiation process by decreasing the number of rounds needed for an agreement as well as yield a higher benefit for agents with theory of mind reasoning.

Keywords: Social cognition · Communication · Affinity ·
Abstraction · Heuristics · Negotiation · Human-inspired computational
model

1 Introduction

Theory of Mind (ToM) is the ability of reasoning about the mental content of other people, such as their beliefs and desires, making it possible to understand and predict their behaviour [9,25,27]. Being an important part of social cognition, the capability of ToM develops early in life and bestows on humans a plethora of social skills such as negotiating, teaching, and tricking. Recursively employing ToM provides a direct path to reason about how others use ToM,

N. Ajmeri et al. (Eds.): COINE 2022, LNAI 13549, pp. 92–108, 2022.
https://doi.org/10.1007/978-3-031-20845-4_6

which is widely known as "higher-order ToM" (e.g., "I believe that Alice does not know that Bob is planning a baby shower for her"), and is particularly helpful for adapting to the complex dynamics of social life.

Agent-based computational models have previously been used to analyze the effectiveness of ToM in competitive [11,13] and cooperative [14] games and mixed-motive situations [15,16,21] in which the models are based on recursive reasoning and behaviourally limited by the complexity and rules of the games. Baker *et al.* [5] model ToM within a Bayesian framework using partially observable Markov decision processes and test its performance in a simple spatial setting. Osten *et al.* [26] propose a multiagent ToM model that extends the model described in [11] and evaluates its performance in a multiplayer stochastic game. Winfield [35] shows how robots can use a ToM model in improving their safety, making decisions based on simple ethical rules, and imitating other robots' goals. In most of the studies around computational ToM models, the results are generally promising and demonstrate that the use of ToM leads to better outcomes for the studied tasks. Still, the existing models have not been widely adopted as a computational tool in many real-life settings. We argue that for a ToM model to be applicable, it needs to adhere to the following criteria:

Generic: Most of the existing models (see [11–15,26,32]) are built for a specific game-theoretic setting in mind. The models thus are based on the rules of the game as well as interpreted semantics of the strategies. This creates a limitation because it is not straightforward to use these models outside of these settings. We argue that real-life social interaction is generally more complex and for a more comprehensive model of ToM, agents should take into account a variety of both context-dependent and context-independent information such as traits, as well as social frames of reference such as roles, norms, and values [6,30]. Ideally, a computational ToM model should be *generic*; i.e., independent of the particular setting to which it is applied so that it can be used in a variety of settings.

Feasible: In general terms, ToM is about beliefs and knowledge an agent has or can derive about the mental attitudes of other agents. Without a proper control, the number of elements in an agent's belief and knowledge set can increase rapidly over time. This has two immediate disadvantages. First, it will not be clear to the agent which beliefs about the other agents would be useful to consider in a given context, leading to complex decision processes. Second, the volume of information will make it more difficult for the agent to make fast and accurate inferences about others. On the other hand, the agent can benefit from a control mechanism which can sort out the relevant and important information according to the context that the agent operates in. Thus, for a more efficient computational model, it is necessary to ensure that the agent can abstract from existing information to yield *feasible* computation of ToM.

Human-Inspired: In various social contexts, humans are known to rely on social skills that are based on more automatic and fast-working heuristics and require less conscious effort, such as repetition (i.e., repeating behaviours that yield desirable results), imitation (i.e., mimic others) [20], and stereotypes [17]. These agile mechanisms can be especially helpful for humans in social interactions where the time spent on reasoning and/or the cognitive resources allocated are vital concerns. For an agent to better explain the behaviour of humans that it interacts with, its ToM should be *human-inspired*, such that it should be able to capture and interpret the heuristics that humans use in every day dealings.

An important area where ToM could be of particular use is hybrid intelligence [1], where an agent can coordinate with a human towards a particular goal, where the agent would have varying capabilities that could complement those of the human to yield the goal. As an example, consider a wearable physical activity monitor agent à la Fitbit that works with a human to ensure that the human establishes a healthy life. Typical interactions with such devices take the form of information passing, such as that the device periodically informs the human what more she has to do (e.g., "take another 200 steps"), milestones she has achieved (e.g., "you received a Tiger badge"); or it requests information (e.g., "enter the foods consumed today"). Take the first type of interaction. This necessitates the human to take an action that is not easy to do and thus requires nudging from the agent. Ideally, if the agent could have a ToM for the human, it could create strategies as to how to proceed with such requests. The long-term goal of our research is thus to design and develop a generic, feasible, and human-inspired ToM that could be applicable in such settings to improve human-agent coordination and thus to facilitate hybrid intelligence.

As an initial step towards this goal, we develop an abstraction framework for ToM over which we construct an abstraction heuristic. The underlying idea is to employ an agent's belief and knowledge set to produce a more abstract, complex *interaction state* that can be readily used by the agent. To investigate the principle of abstraction we use the concrete concept of *affinity* that summarizes how we relate to someone based on many things we know about that person and our history of interactions. Computational affinity captures how humans use affinity in their interactions and can be used in tandem with ToM reasoning when designing agent models. To demonstrate its usage and power in human-agent interaction, we employ it in two-agent negotiation. Our results show that capturing affinity improves agent-agent coordination and agents who perform ToM reasoning obtain outcomes that are better than agents who do not.

The rest of this paper is organized as follows. Section 2 describes abstraction heuristics and computational affinity. Section 3 explains our framework and how we integrate ToM with affinity in negotiation. Section 4 evaluates our proposed model over two-agent simulations. Section 5 discusses our results, addresses related research in the literature, and points to future research directions.

2 Abstraction Heuristics and Affinity

Humans are known to use behavioural simplification mechanisms in their decision-making processes (e.g., stereotypes, biases) [34]. Inspired by this idea, we envision an abstraction-guided ToM agent paradigm that simplifies its beliefs and knowledge into compact representations that can serve for heuristics. Computationally, what we call an "abstraction mechanism" is an agent apparatus that does the following (Fig. 1):

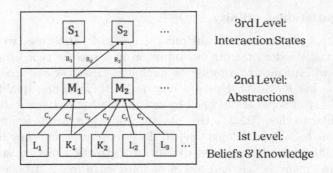

Fig. 1. Abstraction procedure: Individual beliefs (L_i) and knowledge (K_j) are used to create abstractions M_k that are then used in interactions S_n.

1. It takes a set of beliefs and knowledge as input.
2. Using a shared prominent characteristic of such input, it produces an intermediate output in the form of a simple yet more abstract belief or piece of knowledge, or simply an *abstraction*, which shares the same characteristic.
3. Applying rules that govern the role of the intermediate output, it produces interaction states for the agent to operate in.

We claim that such an abstraction procedure embedded in a ToM agent should produce interaction states that can be used in a variety of settings, are simple enough to easily mesh with the agent's decision-making processes, and capture and interpret the related human behaviour. Figure 1 shows our layered approach to such an abstraction mechanism. The first layer holds the set of beliefs and knowledge about others that could come from different sources, such as observations or explicitly stated information from others. While the agent can keep this set, it does not operate at that level but instead creates abstractions in the second level. The first level influences the second level; thus, if the agent observes more information at the first level, the abstractions in the second level might change. The abstractions in the second level influence how the agents operate in the third level. One can think of the third level as pertaining to the application in question. Figure 1 also shows that beliefs and knowledge can have multiple characteristics C_k, C_l, etc. which guide the production of the corresponding abstractions M_k, M_l etc.; multiple abstractions can be used to produce an interaction state S_n with respect to the corresponding rule R_n.

Note that abstractions are not designed to prevent agents from using their beliefs and knowledge directly. Instead, abstractions act as additions that require low maintenance and that are used whenever possible to avoid having to use too much information. Here, we do not intend to provide a full-fledged abstraction model that addresses and gives possible solutions to all kinds of challenges a ToM agent may face during its lifetime. We will discuss some important points that can help us further develop our abstraction mechanism in Sect. 5

2.1 Computational Affinity

We propose that in principle, this abstraction approach can be used with complex human notions. We demonstrate our intuition in a specific type of abstraction mechanism, which captures *affinity*: "a feeling of closeness and understanding that someone has for another person because of their similar qualities, ideas, or interests" [24]. People are inclined to get along with and gravitate to others that are similar to them [22,33]. One practical outcome of this feeling is generating generous behaviour: People tend to do favors for others they like [2]. We claim that affinity can be captured within an abstraction mechanism in which one can merge many beliefs and pieces of knowledge (e.g., "I believe that he leads a healthy life *like me.*") into a more abstract belief that shares the same characteristic ("I believe that he is *very similar to me.*") and then to an interaction state ("I feel a strong affinity towards him because I believe that he is very similar to me.") which can be more effectively used within a rule set when making decisions ("I feel a strong affinity towards him. I can do small favors to people that I feel strong affinity towards. Thus, I will do a small favor for him.").

Observing a similarity is essential for affinity [7]. In our computational framework, we limit similarity to interacting agents having the same opinions on a subject and use opinions as comparable tokens that are Boolean in nature (e.g., healthy living is important: yes/no). Moreover, we limit observation to communication, meaning that opinions are private and unobservable unless the agent shares them with another agent. Following this intuition, we provide three different definitions of computational affinity that pertain to how it is brought about. Note that the aim is not to come up with the most precise definition but with reasonable, alternative definitions that an agent might adopt.

All definitions are based on the agents exchanging opinions. Thus, we consider each agent A to have a set of fixed opinions on various subjects.

Definition 1. *For an agent A to have a **type-1 affinity** towards another agent B, at least one of the opinions B tells A must match with that of A.*

The most important aspect of this form of affinity is that it is static, meaning that after A establishes affinity towards B, even if B later tells its opinion on another subject that does not match with that of A, A does not lose its affinity. However, in real life, affinity is not always static; thus, we define another type of affinity to capture its dynamic nature:

Definition 2. *For an agent A to have a **type-2 affinity** towards another agent B, the most recent opinion B tells A must match with that of A.*

Still, affinity does not have to depend only on the latest matching opinion. For example, agents can do multiple comparisons before establishing affinity. Thus, we give another, more concrete way to define affinity computationally:

Definition 3. *For an agent A to have a **type-3 affinity** towards another agent B, the majority of opinions B tells A must match with those of A (i.e., the number of matching opinions is bigger than zero and not smaller than the number of non-matching opinions).*

Note that the abstraction mechanism that the agents employ is relatively simple: Comparing just one pair of opinions is enough to produce (or change) the abstract belief of similarity which agents further employ to decide whether to establish affinity or not. Even with this simple mechanism, we observe that computational affinity as an abstract entity that has a life-cycle: it is born, lives, and dies (and can be brought from the dead again). It can be active or passive, subject to the situation the agent is in. Plus, it holds basic information about the relationship between agents. Depending on the communication history of the agents, it can be reciprocal or not since both agents should tell each other their opinions for both of them to have affinity towards the other. Other features that we have not incorporated here can include the duration (e.g., how long it affects the agent's decision) and strength (e.g., how strongly it affects the agent's decision). Next we demonstrate how even a simple abstraction mechanism as described can be useful in human-agent interactions.

2.2 Computational Affinity and ToM

In its core, we observe that a person who has affinity towards another person can act in ways that would be helpful to the second person. This can mean different things depending on the context; here we define it in a two-agent setting and as generic as possible. In simplest terms, an agent A that has an affinity towards another agent B can do *a thing* that is more favorable to B than *the thing* A normally does when it does not have affinity towards B. For example, in a negotiation, a seller A with an affinity towards a buyer B can make an offer that is more favorable for B than the offer A makes when it does not have affinity.

In addition, we want our agents to not just establish affinity but also attribute it as a mental state to others, as people do. Essentially, we also design agents that have ToM about other agents and reason whether another agent has an affinity towards a certain agent or not (e.g., "I believe B has an affinity towards me"). The reasoning mechanism shall rely on basic perspective-taking and the condition that both agents share their opinions (remember that affinity is not inherently mutual). Later on, we will explain how such an agent with ToM can also use this affinity attribution mechanism to its benefit.

In this body of work, we call the ToM agents that can have type-x affinity towards others "type-x affinity agents with 1st order ToM" or shortly "A_1^x agents". Similarly, we denote the agents that do not have ToM as "type-x affinity agents with 0th order ToM" or shortly "A_0^x agents".

3 Negotiation with Computational Affinity and ToM

Now, we discuss how our proposed model can be used for human-agent negotiation. We return to our example in Sect. 1 where a wearable physical activity monitor agent is working with a human to increase the number of steps the human takes. As the underlying mechanism, we choose two-agent negotiation, because it is a robust mixed-motive setting that also provides a good context for exploring behavioural capabilities of ToM agents.

To make our setup concrete, we define an **agent** as an autonomous entity which can either be an **activity monitor agent** or a **human agent**, where the former is working to increase the number of steps taken by the human while the human is reluctant to walk. To achieve its goal, each agent can **make an offer** or **accept an offer** made by the other agent. Furthermore, an agent has fixed **opinions** on various subjects (e.g., healthy living is important: yes/no). It can **tell** the other agent its opinions, including those about the negotiation outcomes themselves, and **compare** a told opinion with its own opinion (same subject).

3.1 Negotiation Framework

The subject matter of negotiation is agreeing on the number of steps to be taken. The negotiation protocol can be briefly described as alternating monotonic concession with communication, a variant of the monotonic concession protocol [31]. Basically, it is a rule set for two agents to **negotiate** and **communicate** in alternating rounds. An agent can both negotiate and communicate with the other agent in the same round in which it can either make a new offer or accept the latest offer made by the other agent (negotiation part) and can tell the other agent its opinions (communication part). Furthermore, negotiations should be done in the form of **monotonic concession**: No agent can make an offer that is less preferred by the other agent than an earlier offer that it made. Lastly, a negotiation **ends** when an agent accepts the latest offer made or a fixed number of rounds pass without an agreement (e.g., 10 total rounds).

Negotiating agents' offers and counter-offers are generally governed by their strategies: a prepared plan of action to achieve a goal under conditions of uncertainty. The negotiation literature is rich with sophisticated strategies [4,28]. In order to focus only on the effects of computational affinity and ToM, we opt for a simple strategy for agents such that each agent makes an offer and adjusts the number of steps with a constant, predetermined value until it goes beyond the **reserve value** (or **reserve price**). For example, a human agent starts the offer at 5000 and increases it with 100 every round until it goes beyond 5500.[1] We call this value of 100 the **unit increment/decrement value** of agents and make all agents use this strategy as the baseline strategy when making offers.

3.2 Negotiating with Affinity and ToM

Agent A that has affinity towards another agent B can give an offer that can be more favorable for B than the offer A gives when it does not have affinity towards B, as we have stated earlier. More specifically, we utilize computational affinity as a regulator for unit increment/decrement values that agents use when making offers. As a design decision, we make reserve values not affected by affinity in our framework. Here, we give an example.

---

[1] In this case, for example the activity monitor agent could start with an offer of 5700 and decrease it with 100 until it goes beyond 5300.

Table 1. Four negotiation scenarios Sc_1, Sc_2, Sc_3 and Sc_4 are given (Example 1).

(a) Opinions do not match in Sc_1, but match in Sc_2. Only A tells its opinion.

Sc_1			Sc_2		
R	A	B	**R**	A	B
1	1500		1	1500	
1	O_{yes}		1	O_{yes}	
2		2100	2		2100
3	1600		3	1600	
4		2000	4		1990
5	1700		5	1700	
6		1900	6		1880
7	1800		7	1800	
8		Accepts	8		Accepts

(b) Opinions match and A (resp. B) starts in Sc_3 (resp. Sc_4). Both tell opinions.

Sc_3			Sc_4		
R	A	B	**R**	A	B
1	1500		1		2100
1	O_{yes}		1		O_{yes}
2		2100	2	1500	
2		O_{yes}	2	O_{yes}	
3	1610		3		1990
4		1990	4	1610	
5	1720		5		1880
6		1880	6	1720	
7	1830		7		1770
8		Accepts	8	Accepts	

Example 1. A human agent A of type A_0^1 and an activity monitor agent B of type A_0^1 are negotiating. The reserve values of A and B are set to be 1850 and 1750, respectively. Their respective unit increment/decrement values are both 100 and affinity increases it with 10. Each agent has a Boolean opinion on the same subject O: It can be either O_{yes} or O_{no}. In Tables 1a and 1b, we give four different scenarios (Sc_1, Sc_2, Sc_3, and Sc_4).

Example 1 depicts two crucial points. First, affinity does not always produce a different result (e.g., Sc_1 and Sc_2) and second, either agent can benefit from the result when affinity is reciprocal (e.g., Sc_3 and Sc_4), since the final situation depends on other factors as well (e.g., the reserve values, the starting agent). Additionally, one can see that although reciprocal affinity introduces variance in the agreements (e.g., Sc_3 and Sc_4 in which the accepted offers are 1770 and 1830, respectively), it stays the same on average (e.g., 1800) due to the symmetry in the provided benefits for both agents.

In the previous section, we have noted that an A_1^x agent can use its ToM ability to its benefit when making offers. In particular, when an A_1^x agent concludes that there is a mutual affinity, it can change its unit increment/decrement value so that its offer *adjustments* (not offers themselves) are not as generous as its opponent's adjustments. For example, if an A_1^x activity monitor agent decides that there is a mutual affinity and observes that its opponent's current increment value (i.e., the difference between the latest two offers of the opponent) is 110, it can change its own to a value lower than 110, say 105. With this improvement, it is guaranteed that a reciprocal affinity between an A_1^x and an A_0^y will result in an offer that A_1^x prefers more than A_0^y. Here, we give an illustrating example.

Example 2. A human agent A of type A_1^1 and an activity monitor agent B of type A_0^1 are negotiating. The reserve values of A and B are set to be 1850 and 1750, respectively. Their respective unit increment/decrement values are both 100. Affinity increases it by 10 but mutual affinity increases it only by 5. Each

Table 2. Two negotiation scenarios Sc_5 and Sc_6 are given for A and B. Both tell their opinions in both scenarios (Example 2).

Sc_5: Opinions match, A starts.			Sc_6: Opinions match, B starts.		
R	A	B	**R**	A	B
1	1500, O_{no}		1		2100, O_{no}
2		2100, O_{no}	2	1500, O_{no}	
3	1610		3		1990
4		1990	4	1605	
5	1715		5		1880
6		1880	6	1710	
7	1820		7		1770
8		Accepts	8	Accepts	

agent has a Boolean opinion on the same subject O: It can be either O_{yes} or O_{no}. In Table 2, two different scenarios (Sc_5 and Sc_6) are given.

One can notice in Example 2 that A_1^x is designed to limit its own affinity-induced generousness using ToM. The superiority of A_1^x over A_0^x can be seen in the newly introduced asymmetrical variance in the agreements (e.g., Sc_5 and Sc_6 in which the accepted offers are 1770 and 1820, respectively) and the new average (e.g., $1795 < 1800$), benefiting A_1^x agent A more than A_0^x agent B.

4   Experiments and Results

We are interested in understanding the role of affinity in getting to agreements when there is a bound on the time spent for negotiating. To answer this general question in detail, we have created an experimental setup with four simulation experiments. We configure our negotiation framework (including the reserve values, starting offers, and unit increment and decrement values) so that an agreement can be achieved in a maximum of 12 rounds, even without affinity. In all simulations, activity monitor agents' and human agents' starting offers are set to 2000 and 1000 and reserve values are 1450 and 1550, respectively. Unit increment and decrement values are both set to 100 at the beginning and it is common knowledge that agents do not decrease these values below 100 (agents can increase them in case of affinity). The worst offer an agent can make for itself is with its reserve value. A negotiation begins with two newly created agents, namely, an activity monitor agent and a human agent, where every opinion of agents is created randomly: it can be a "yes" or "no" with the same probability. One of the agents is randomly chosen to start the process and the other agent continues accordingly. In the first two rounds, each agent gives its starting offer.

There are two additional restrictions in the protocol we use. First, an agent tells all of its opinions in the negotiation process. Second, opinions are told in a pre-arranged order (i.e., subject 1, subject 2, subject 3...) where an agent tells only one opinion per round in a conversational flow. This is because we intend to keep the communication as simple as possible and do not want to analyze how different communication patterns affect the life-cycle of affinity. We also want to ensure that affinity can be formed reciprocally in the negotiations.

Every round, an A_0^x agent first checks if the latest offer is acceptable. If yes, it accepts and ends the negotiation. If not, it compares the shared opinion(s) to check whether affinity ensues or not, following the criteria of its affinity definition. If it does not establish affinity, it gives an offer that is 100 higher (resp. lower) than its previous offer, if it is a human (resp. activity monitor) agent. On the other hand, if the agent establishes affinity, it changes 100 to a multiple of 5 between 100 and 150 (including the boundaries) and makes an offer accordingly. Then, it ends its turn by telling one of its opinions according to the sharing order until all are shared. We introduce this randomness into A_0^x agent's offer-making mechanism to make it more dynamic. It is worth to note that this can also indirectly change the agent that gives the final offer.

Every round, an A_1^x agent also checks if the latest offer is acceptable. If yes, it accepts and ends the negotiation. If not, it compares the shared opinion(s) to check whether affinity ensues or not, following the criteria of its affinity definition. Additionally, it also decides whether the other agent has established affinity or not. If the A_1^x agent does not establish affinity or decides that its opponent does not have affinity, it gives an offer that is 100 higher (resp. lower) than its previous offer, if it is a human (resp. activity monitor) agent, like A_0^x agents. Otherwise, it changes 100 to a multiple of 5 between 100 and X (including X) and makes an offer accordingly, where X is equal to the difference between the latest two offers of its opponent (i.e., the opponent's currently observed unit increment/decrement value). It ends its turn by telling one of its opinions according to the sharing order until all are shared. Again, we introduce this opponent-dependent randomness into the offer-making mechanism of an A_1^x agent to make it more dynamic and limit the agent's own affinity-induced generousness.

There are four different experimental variations in which we use only A_m^1 (V1), only A_m^2 (V2), only A_m^3 (V3), and all types of agents (V4), where $m \in \{0, 1\}$ unless told otherwise. Every experimental variation consists of four different opinion settings: In the n-opinion setting, every agent has n opinion(s) on the same n subjects, where $n \in \{1, 2, 3, 4\}$. Per setting, we perform simulations with 10,000 different agent pairs where every agent negotiates once.

4.1 The Effect of Affinity on Agreements

In the first experiment, our aim is to find how affinity affects the number of agreements made when A_0^1, A_0^2, and A_0^3 agents negotiate with each other (V4). An agent is created as an A_0^1, A_0^2, or A_0^3 agent with the same probability. We limit the maximum number of rounds of negotiation to 12. Through the simulation, we also keep track of the final rounds in which agreements are settled.

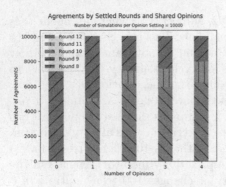
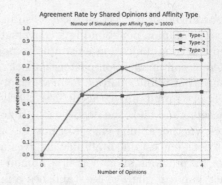

(a) Affinity conceives early agreements.   (b) Agreements and affinity types (all A_0^x).

Fig. 2. Affinity helps coordination.

The stacked bars in Fig. 2a show the number of successful negotiations that are done by A_0^x in the simulation. All different opinion settings are given in the x-axis (i.e., 0-4), while the y-axis shows the total number of achievable agreements; colors and hatches together represent the final round information of the agreements (i.e., 8-12).

When no opinion is shared, all 12 rounds are necessary for reaching an agreement in all simulations. However, even sharing one opinion makes a big difference. We can see in Fig. 2a that nearly half of the agreements are done in 10 rounds in the 1-opinion setting. Other settings also show similar results: The number of agreements that need 12 rounds decreases when the number of shared opinions increases. Hence, we can conclude that when A_0^x agents negotiate, the number of agreements that are settled on earlier than 12 rounds increases with the number of shared opinions. This shows that by modeling affinity explicitly, the agents can reduce the number of interactions needed to agree.

4.2   Affinity Types and Agreement Rates

In the second experiment, our aim is to find how affinity type and number of shared opinions affect the number of agreements made when A_0^x agents negotiate. The experiment consists of the first three variations V1, V2, and V3. We limit the maximum number of rounds of negotiation to 10 to get a better understanding of how different affinity types get to early agreements.

The line plots in Fig. 2b show the percentage of successful negotiations that are achieved by A_0^x in 10 rounds over all negotiations per affinity type.

When no opinion is shared, the number of agreements that can be achieved in 10 rounds is zero. Figure 2b shows that for the experiment's V1 variation with 1-opinion setting, we can see that agents sharing just one opinion makes a significant difference in the number of agreements. When A_0^1 agents negotiate, nearly 0.50 of all simulations end with an agreement. The number increases to 0.68 and 0.75 for 2-opinion and 3-opinion settings. This increase can be explained

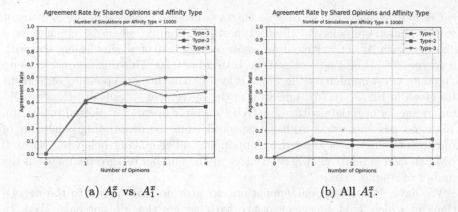

(a) A_0^x vs. A_1^x.   (b) All A_1^x.

Fig. 3. Agreement rates depend on both ToM and affinity type.

by the fact that when the agents exchange more opinions, the probability of finding a negotiating agent pair that has at least one matching opinion increases. In the 4-opinion setting, however, it does not go higher since we set hard limits on the unit increment/decrement values and also due to the overall randomness in the agent creation and offer-making procedures. Thus, it shows that Type-1 affinity affects the agents in such a way that the number of agreements made increases more slowly when the number of rounds is fixed.

When A_0^2 agents negotiate, we see a different pattern. For every opinion setting of the experiment's V2 variation, nearly 0.50 of all simulations end with an agreement. This is mainly because Type-2 affinity is not static like Type-1 affinity and every agent can lose its affinity during the opinion comparison process. Thus, Type-2 affinity affects and changes the average unit increment/decrement value that an agent uses before reaching an agreement, but not as much as Type-1 affinity. On the other hand, A_0^3 agents generate a different pattern that is a mixture of the previous ones. Excluding the 0-opinion setting, the agreement rate in the experiment's V3 variation is on average greater than 0.5 but not as much as the average we see in V1. Hence, we can say that Type-2 and Type-3 affinity types do not create agreements as much as Type-1 affinity.

4.3   Roles of ToM and Affinity in Agreements

In the third (resp. fourth) experiment, our aim is to find how ToM reasoning and affinity together affect the number of agreements made when human agents of type A_0^x (resp. A_1^x) and activity monitor agents of type A_1^y negotiate. Both experiments consist of variations V1, V2, and V3, similar to the second experiment. The maximum number of rounds is set to 10.

The line plots in Fig. 3a (resp. Fig. 3b) show the percentage of successful negotiations that are achieved by A_0^x (resp. A_1^x) human agents and A_1^y activity monitor agents in 10 rounds over all negotiations per affinity type.

Comparing with Fig. 2b, Fig. 3a shows a general decrease in the agreement rates by shared opinions and affinity types. For example, when A_0^x human agents negotiate with A_1^y activity monitor agents, nearly 0.40 of all simulations end with an agreement in the 1-opinion setting, instead of 0.50. This number increases up to 0.60 for the 4-opinion setting which is lower than the corresponding agreement rate given in Fig. 2b (0.76). The drop in the agreement rates is drastic when A_1^x human agents negotiate with A_1^x activity monitor agents, as plotted in Fig. 3b. This is on par with what we have expected from the negotiating behaviour of ToM agents since it is affected by opponents' offer-making behaviour as well: ToM can have a relatively negative effect in the number of agreements when the number of rounds is fixed.

We have done additional simulations to provide more depth to the negotiations in which ToM agents negotiate with agents that do not have ToM. In Fig. 4a, we analyze A_0^x-A_1^y negotiations where all affinity types are used and only one opinion is shared. The x-axis shows the number of agreements done in 10 rounds and the y-axis shows the agreeable offer range (1450−1550). We can see more agreements on the right side of the figure (>1500) than the left side (<1500), implying that A_1^y activity monitor agents end up with offers that are on average better for them (the average offer is approximately equal to 1512). In Fig. 4b, we analyze how an increase in the number of shared opinions changes this asymmetrical benefit. Every line plot shows how number of agreements correlates with the final offers in a specific opinion setting. We can see that the A_0^x human agents in many-opinion settings end up with better offers on average than the A_0^x human agents in few-opinion settings (still not better than their A_1^y monitor agent counterparts). It shows that when more opinions are shared, the superiority of ToM agents over non-ToM agents decreases in negotiations where we explicitly model affinity. This emergent phenomenon reminds us that it is not so easy to develop and maintain affinity with sheer communication (i.e., it also needs a strategy) and it is even harder to benefit from it (i.e., ToM's advantage diminishes).

5   Discussion and Future Work

Within our computational ToM framework, founded on the abstraction mechanism defined in Sect. 2, we propose a human-inspired heuristic called computational affinity for agents to improve coordination in hybrid interactions. We use agents to simulate a human-agent negotiation in the context of activity monitoring. Our findings demonstrate that explicitly modeling affinity can ease the agreement process. We show how sharing more information can also help the activity monitoring agents forge more agreements, albeit depending on the agent's affinity type. Our results indicate that when negotiating with human agents that do not have a ToM, activity monitoring agents that have a ToM end up with agreements that is more favorable to them than to their opponents. Although the communication part of negotiations needs further analysis and strategies on its own [28], the results provide the motivation to develop more

(a) A_1^y benefit more than A_0^x.   (b) ToM's benefit decreases with opinions.

Fig. 4. ToM with affinity benefits agents.

sophisticated ToM agents that can generate affinity and benefit from it, and test them in real-life negotiations to see if and how they can improve human-agent coordination.

Research on computational ToM models suggests that ToM reasoning benefits agents in different ways and even more in the higher orders. De Weerd *et al.* [11] show that agents benefit from higher-order ToM reasoning in competitive game-theoretic settings, although with diminishing returns beyond third-order ToM. Further, they investigate how higher-order ToM can be beneficial for agents in a strictly cooperative game [14] and show that communication can be set up more quickly when agents beyond zero-order ToM play the game. De Weerd *et al.* [15] determine to what extent agents benefit from higher-order ToM reasoning in a mixed-motive situation called the "Colored Trails". The results indicate that there is a considerable benefit in using second-order ToM; however, first-order ToM has a limited effectiveness. Kröhling and Martínez [21] investigate the role of ToM in single-issue negotiations between "context-aware" agents where the negotiation context is modeled by two variables, summarized as necessity and risk. Görür *et al.* [18] propose a ToM agent model for estimating humans' intentions in a shared human-robot task. Brooks and Szafir [8] show how robots can create second-order ToM models by using humans' actions in spatial settings.

Observing and communicating are crucial components of human social behaviour. Our long-term goal is to design socially intelligent agents that can understand how humans "tick" and work with them in synergy. Computationally modeling ToM ability with the abstraction heuristics that we defined in Sect. 2 is a first step toward this goal. Unlike the studies we mention above, we design our human-inspired abstraction procedure to be as generic as possible and generate interaction states which emulate how humans develop and maintain the mental states they experience through their lives. The procedure also provides a useful simplification technique for abstracting information for social agents to yield feasible ToM models of humans they interact with. Affinity, which is essentially based on abstracting observed and communicated similarities, is one particular interaction state we use in this paper. It presents a good starting point, being a human mental state which is also a valuable heuristic in decision-making, and inspires us to computationally formalize other useful interaction states as well.

As a follow-up work, we aim for a more complete model that captures the ways humans abstract their beliefs and knowledge. We will start with a formalization from tip to toe (i.e., beliefs, abstractions, procedure etc.). For that, we need to answer a couple of fundamental questions such as which beliefs to use when abstracting, when to stop the procedure, what to do in case of a belief update, and which interaction states to activate after abstracting. In addition to these issues, a ToM agent should also be able to correctly attribute this abstraction process to others. As we aim to design higher-order ToM agents that can also take into account how their own artificial minds are perceived by others, we plan to benefit from *mind perception theory* [19,23] when investigating the roles of observation and communication in recursive ToM reasoning. Additionally, we consider benefiting from *value-based reasoning* [3,10,29] to develop agents that takes others' values into account when doing ToM reasoning. With a more comprehensive, formalized model, we will further analyze how affinity can be used within other negotiation and communication protocols and strategies as well as get a broader view of its effects in multi-issue negotiations.

Acknowledgements. This research was funded by the Hybrid Intelligence Center, a 10-year programme funded by the Dutch Ministry of Education, Culture and Science through the Netherlands Organisation for Scientific Research, https://hybrid-intelligence-centre.nl, grant number 024.004.022.

References

1. Akata, Z., et al.: A research agenda for hybrid intelligence: augmenting human intellect with collaborative, adaptive, responsible, and explainable artificial intelligence. Computer **53**(08), 18–28 (2020)
2. Aronson, E., Akert, R.M., Wilson, T.D.: Social Psychology, 7th edn. Prentice Hall, Upper Saddle River (2010)
3. Atkinson, K., Bench-Capon, T.: Taking account of the actions of others in value-based reasoning. Artif. Intell. **254**, 1–20 (2018)
4. Baarslag, T., Hendrikx, M.J.C., Hindricks, K.V., Jonker, C.M.: Learning about the opponent in automated bilateral negotiation: a comprehensive survey of opponent modeling techniques. Auton. Agents Multi-Agent Syst. **30**(5), 849–898 (2016)
5. Baker, C.L., Saxe, R.R., Tenenbaum, J.B.: Bayesian theory of mind: modeling joint belief-desire attribution. In: Proceedings of the Thirty-Third Annual Conference of the Cognitive Science Society, vol. 33, no. 33, January 2011
6. Baksh, R.A., Abrahams, S., Auyeung, B., MacPherson, S.E.: The Edinburgh Social Cognition Test (ESCoT): examining the effects of age on a new measure of theory of mind and social norm understanding. PloS ONE **13**(4), e0195818 (2018)
7. Bell, R.A., Daly, J.A.: The affinity-seeking function of communication. Commun. Monogr. **51**(2), 91–115 (1984)
8. Brooks, C., Szafir, D.: Building second-order mental models for human-robot interaction. arXiv preprint arXiv:1909.06508 (2019)

9. Carruthers, P., Smith, P.K.: Theories of Theories of Mind. Cambridge University Press, Cambridge (1996)
10. Cranefield, S., Winikoff, M., Dignum, V., Dignum, F.: No pizza for you: value-based plan selection in BDI agents. In: IJCAI, pp. 178–184 (2017)
11. De Weerd, H., Verbrugge, R., Verheij, B.: How much does it help to know what she knows you know? An agent-based simulation study. Artif. Intell. **199–200**, 67–92 (2013)
12. De Weerd, H., Verbrugge, R., Verheij, B.: Agent-based models for higher-order theory of mind. In: Advances in Social Simulation, Proceedings of the 9th Conference of the European Social Simulation Association, vol. 229, pp. 213–224 (2014)
13. De Weerd, H., Verbrugge, R., Verheij, B.: Theory of mind in the Mod game: an agent-based model of strategic reasoning. In: European Conference on Social Intelligence, pp. 128–136. Springer (2014)
14. De Weerd, H., Verbrugge, R., Verheij, B.: Higher-order theory of mind in the tacit communication game. Biol. Inspir. Cogn. Archit. **11**, 10–21 (2015)
15. De Weerd, H., Verbrugge, R., Verheij, B.: Negotiating with other minds: the role of recursive theory of mind in negotiation with incomplete information. Auton. Agents Multi-Agent Syst. **31**(2), 250–287 (2017)
16. De Weerd, H., Verbrugge, R., Verheij, B.: Higher-order theory of mind is especially useful in unpredictable negotiations. Auton. Agents Multi-Agent Syst. **36**(2), 1–33 (2022)
17. Fiske, S.T.: Stereotyping, prejudice, and discrimination. In: Gilbert, D.T., Fiske, S.T., Lindzey, G. (eds.) Handbook of Social Psychology, vol. 2, 4 edn., pp. 357–411. McGraw-Hill, New York (1998)
18. Görür, O.C., Rosman, B.S., Hoffman, G., Albayrak, Ş.: Toward integrating theory of mind into adaptive decision-making of social robots to understand human intention. In: International Conference on Human-Robot Interaction. Workshop on the Role of Intentions in Human-Robot Interaction (2017)
19. Gray, H.M., Gray, K., Wegner, D.M.: Dimensions of mind perception. Science **315**(5812), 619 (2007)
20. Heyes, C.M.: Imitation, culture and cognition. Anim. Behav. **46**(5), 999–1010 (1993)
21. Kröhling, D., Martínez, E.: On integrating theory of mind in context-aware negotiation agents. In: XX Simposio Argentino de Inteligencia Artificial (ASAI 2019)-JAIIO 48 (Salta), pp. 180–193 (2019)
22. Lazarsfeld, P.F., Merton, R.K.: Friendship as a social process: a substantive and methodological analysis. Freedom Control Mod. Soc. **18**(1), 18–66 (1954)
23. Lee, M., Lucas, G., Gratch, J.: Comparing mind perception in strategic exchanges: human-agent negotiation, dictator and ultimatum games. J. Multimod. User Interfaces **15**(2), 201–214 (2021)
24. Merriam-Webster: Affinity. Merriam-Webster.com dictionary (n.d.). https://www.merriam-webster.com/dictionary/affinity
25. Michlmayr, M.: Simulation theory versus theory theory: theories concerning the ability to read minds. Master's thesis, Leopold-Franzens-Universität Innsbruck (2002)
26. Osten, F.B.V.D., Kirley, M., Miller, T.: The minds of many: opponent modeling in a stochastic game. In: IJCAI, pp. 3845–3851. AAAI Press (2017)
27. Premack, D., Woodruff, G.: Does the chimpanzee have a theory of mind? Behav. Brain Sci. **1**(4), 515–526 (1978)
28. Raiffa, H.: The Art and Science of Negotiation. Harvard University Press, Cambridge (1982)

29. Rangel, A., Camerer, C., Montague, P.R.: A framework for studying the neurobiology of value-based decision making. Nat. Rev. Neurosci. **9**(7), 545–556 (2008)

30. Rosati, A., Knowles, E., Kalish, C., Gopnik, A., Ames, D., Morris, M.: What theory of mind can teach social psychology: traits as intentional terms. In: Malle, B.F., Moses, L.J., Baldwin, D.A. (eds.) Intentions and Intentionality: Foundations of Social Cognition, pp. 287–303. MIT Press, Cambridge (2003)

31. Rosenschein, J.S., Zlotkin, G.: Designing conventions for automated negotiation. AI Mag. **15**(3), 29 (1994)

32. Stevens, C., Taatgen, N.A., Cnossen, F.: Metacognition in the prisoner's dilemma. In: 13th Annual International Conference on Cognitive Modeling, p. 112, April 2015

33. Suls, J., Martin, R., Wheeler, L.: Social comparison: why, with whom, and with what effect? Curr. Direct. Psychol. Sci. **11**(5), 159–163 (2002)

34. Tversky, A., Kahneman, D.: Judgment under uncertainty: heuristics and biases. Science **185**(4157), 1124–1131 (1974)

35. Winfield, A.F.T.: Experiments in artificial theory of mind: from safety to storytelling. Front. Robot. AI **5**, 75 (2018)

Computational Discovery of Transaction-Based Financial Crime via Grammatical Evolution: The Case of Ponzi Schemes

Peter Fratrič[1(⊠)], Giovanni Sileno[1], Tom van Engers[1,2], and Sander Klous[1]

[1] Informatics Institute, University of Amsterdam, Amsterdam, The Netherlands
p.fratric@uva.nl
[2] Leibniz Institute, TNO/University of Amsterdam, Amsterdam, The Netherlands

Abstract. The financial sector continues to experience wide digitalization; the resulting transactional activity creates large amounts of data, in principle enabling public and private actors to better understand the social domain they operate on, possibly facilitating the design of interventions to reduce illegal activity. However, the adversarial nature of frauds and the relatively low amount of observed instances make the problem especially challenging with standard statistical-based methods. To address such fundamental issues to non-compliance detection, this paper presents a proof-of-concept of a methodological framework based on automated discovery of instances of non-compliant behaviour in a simulation environment via grammatical evolution. We illustrate the methodology with an experiment capable of discovering two known types of Ponzi schemes from a modest set of assumptions.

1 Introduction

Financial crime occurs at many levels of society, from credit card fraud, to tax fraud, money laundering, terrorist financing, financial market manipulation, up to the corruption of the highest representatives of individual countries or international political bodies. A unifying aspect of all these instances of non-compliance is that the transaction of assets with the aim of illegal profit is typically conducted in such a way that no suspicion of illicit activity arises. In order to detect non-compliant activity from available evidence, researchers and analysts have applied over the years various computational methods, ranging from rule-based systems, knowledge graphs, machine learning models, to executable models of social systems. Although these applications have shown various levels of success, several issues remain at present, still exploited by non-compliant actors [4,17].

Research Background. Synthetizing non-compliant behaviour into a set of patterns, either explicitly via a set of logical rules, or implicitly by some machine learning method, typically face difficulties as e.g. explainability (for ML-based methods), unavailability of data, high false positive rate, or overlooking the adaptability of non-compliant agents. All these issues make traditional

N. Ajmeri et al. (Eds.): COINE 2022, LNAI 13549, pp. 109–120, 2022.
https://doi.org/10.1007/978-3-031-20845-4_7

approaches both ineffective and inefficient, particularly on the medium-longer term. We will elaborate therefore on three other trends observed in the literature. According to a recent review [3], *network analysis* tools have been slowly finding their way into prominence. These tools capitalize on the ability of networks to represent complex relationships, and at the same time being both interpretable and easy to visualize. Once the transaction graph is formed, the main goal becomes essentially to detect non-compliant individuals, suspicious events, or anomalous structures [1,2]. Several methods of this type have already been proposed in the area of financial fraud detection [23]. Comparatively, approaches based on *modeling and simulation* are covered by a much smaller number of studies [6,18], most of which focus on the possibility of training detection models on simulated data, also to mitigate the issue of high false negatives. Only a few simulation environments were developed in the literature to generate illicit transaction activity. Instead, the issue of adaptivity is addressed mostly in the context of *adversarial machine learning* [12,14,16,25]. However, this approach targets the local fraud space defined by the parametric model determined by the dataset, so it can hardly generalize to illicit behaviour in a global sense, i.e. not included in the data or encoded in the classifier. If we target the design of intelligent agents autonomously learning frauds by interacting with the environment (and so capable of generating new illicit behaviours), the number of studies is even lower, e.g. co-evolutionary methods to discover tax frauds tested in a transaction tax network environment in [15]; reinforcement learning [19] to design an agent learning credit card fraud in an adversarial environment.

Generalizing to any kind of adversarial system where the detection model is tested against a model of an adaptive perpetrator, the research seems to be progressing faster in other areas. For instance, adversarial systems are more extensively studied in the area of artificial intelligence [7], although still on a relatively low scale level. The area of cybersecurity is advancing comparatively faster than the socio-legal domain, probably because the implementation of a model of cyber environment is less of a challenge compared to social systems, which means model-based testing methods can be effectively implemented [24].

Aims and Contribution of the Paper. Fraud schemes target specific vulnerabilities of a socio-legal system and/or psychological weaknesses of its victims, and very often exhibit a modular structure: more complex schemes tend to be modifications of simpler ones. This short paper presents and elaborates on this intuition, focusing on Ponzi schemes (PSs) implemented on distributed ledger, i.e. smart contracts. The reason why we choose specifically smart contract PSs is that the complex legal terminological nuances involved in arbitrary contracts are mitigated with smart contracts because of their mechanistic transaction environment. This, and public availability of data, makes the distributed ledger suitable for the type of investigations. Moreover, due to popularization of this technology, the question of smart contract PS detection is a pressing issue [8,9].

In our study, we pursue a long term goal of developing a *fraud discovery assistant*, where illicit behaviour can be generated depending on presumed observables, socio-psychological modules of the simulation model, or potentially even the implemented countermeasures. At this point of research, we focus on the first (generation) and briefly discuss the second (internal socio-psychological modules) and third (couuntermeasures) aspects. Depending on observables considered, two known types of PSs will be discovered using grammatical evolution. The illicit activity discovered and simulated in the model will be visualized as a series of snapshots of the transaction network.

Case Study: Types of Ponzi Schemes. Various types of smart contract PSs already exist on the Ethereum blockchain [5]. In its *basic* version, each time a new participant enters the scheme, the entry fee is redistributed equally among other participants. A modification that aims to create a community of highly profitable users can be implemented by imposing a preference ordering on the capital redistribution. For example, to exploit risk-appetite and deceivability of society, early-stage investors can be benefited by repaying the premium chrono- logically; therefore, the participants that joined later might not be repaid once the capital is depleted. This type of smart contract PS is known as *waterfall type*. Another type, that is in a way a modification of the previous two types, is the *array* type. In this case, the redistribution mechanism keeps track of which participant was paid last in order to equalize the frequency of payments, but at the same time pays the next participant only if there is enough capital to send a payment exceeding the entry fee of the participant. This means that it prioritizes the size of the user base that is already in profit, therefore it is more likely the scheme will be perceived as a valid investment in the society. Clearly, there can be more sophisticated variations of smart contract PSs, for example including a reward for participants recruiting new users; however, for our current aims, the two previous schemes are sufficient.

2   General Framework

In order to generate and evaluate possible fraud schemes, we propose a frame- work for (re)construction of non-compliant behaviour that requires four opera- tional components. These are: (i) a *search space* defined by an action space (in which a fraud scheme can be constructed); (ii) a *simulation environment* to exe- cute actions of agents including a *non-compliant* (or *fraudulent*) *agent*, in which (iii) a *fitness function* can be calculated to determine how good each scheme is by evaluating its outcome; (iv) a *search algorithm* to explore the search space, that we typically identify with the reasoning mechanism of the non-compliant agent. If all four instruments are well-defined, then it is possible to (re)create the fraudulent behaviour as illustrated on Fig. 1.

Expert knowledge is used to formulate hypotheses about the functioning of the simulation environment and representation of the search space, including relevant observables for the non-compliant agent (search algorithm). The inner loop (continuous lines) searching the space of non-compliant schemes produces a dataset of transaction schemes. The set of hypotheses can be subsequently extended with assumptions that give rise to new instances of non-compliant behaviour (dashed lines).

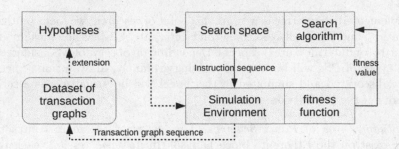

Fig. 1. Overview of methodology to (re)construct non-compliant behaviour

Arguably, a *detection algorithm* is also an important part of the theoretical framework. However, at the current stage of research, we consider it as essentially a different research question subsequent to the generation problem (see the discussion section for insights on future directions). Moreover, note that simulation environment can be also combined with additional goals as assessing algorithmic fairness (see e.g. [11]).

3   Generation of Ponzi Schemes

In general, a simulation model generates a sequence of transactional graph snapshots $G_0, ..., G_T$ as a record of agents interacting in the environment for a finite number of steps T. The fraudulent subgraph sequence $H_0, .., H_t$ for $t < T$ is generated during the simulation process, in association with non-compliant activity. For the sake of this study, the agent-based model will be designed to be minimalistic, which means that only the minimal set of assumptions necessary to approximate PS mechanism will be employed. Since PSs do not in principle depend on transactions that are happening outside the scheme, it is not needed to assume any direct transactional interactions between the agents. While this might intuitively seem an unsound manner to model social systems, it turns out to be an advantage, because it allows us to generate data related to illicit behaviour only by using the assumptions necessary for the illicit behaviour to arise. Obviously, it is true that other forms of interactions happen in the real world during a PS spread, but this extension is needed only for more sophisticated types of schemes (see p. 9).

In practice, no additional economic activity producing value is assumed in the model, which means except for trivial cases every transaction sequence is a PS. This simplifies the modelling as there is no need to define a PS either on a phenomenological or a logical basis. Yet, the adaptation mechanism to find profitable schemes will plausibly work for more complex settings (e.g. societal policies, physical constraints, additional economic actions). Consequently, by relaxing this assumption, more sophisticated schemes can be addressed.

Contract Mechanism. We assume that the initial transaction graph G_0 is an empty graph with $N + 2$ nodes; one node represents the contract, one node

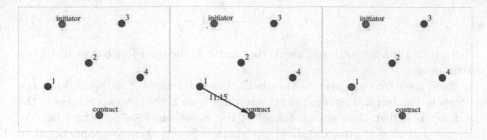

Fig. 2. Initial state is an empty transaction graph G_0 (blue nodes) and subgraph H_0 (red nodes). In G_1 a transfer of 11.15 cash is made between the node 1 and the contract node. In the state G_2 the subgraph H_2 has three nodes. (Color figure online)

represents the initiator of the contract, and N nodes represent the agents that can join the contract. The contract and its members constitute the subgraph sequence $H_0, ..., H_T$ and therefore the initial subgraph H_0 will consist only of two nodes (the contract node and the initiator) and zero edges.

The contract has two attributes: a deposit account and a list of members. In order to join the contract, an agent needs to send an entry fee, that is initialized for each agent randomly from a prespecified distribution. If an agent decides to join the contract, the entry fee is sent to the contract deposit address. The mechanism, specified in the following excerpt, is illustrated on Fig. 2.

```
1  if contract.isTrustworthy(agent.threshold):
2      G.addEdge(agent, contract, agent.entryFee)
3      G.executeTransactions()
```

In the simulation environment, the method `addEdge` adds a directed edge from the node in the first argument to the node in the second argument. The method `executeTransactions` is called on a graph object by an agent to execute transactions defined by the edges. The `threshold` attribute of an agent and the contract method `isTrustworthy` serve to model the agents' attitude, and will be explained in the next section.

Contract Trustworthiness and Agent Trust. During the simulation, the *trustworthiness* of the contract is calculated as a numerical value in the zero-one interval. There is no general agreement what exactly makes a contract trustworthy to people; for the sake of example we consider two plausible basic assumptions, and define a function based on these assumptions[1]. The trustworthiness Tr of a contract is (a) proportional to the relative amount of agents in profit n_+ compared to the number of agents n that have already joined; (b) inversely proportional to the root of the density of agents that joined the contract. Following these two assumptions, we can define the function:

---

[1] The model of trust used in this study is simplistic and serves only for the purpose of demonstration. For overviews on trust models see, e.g. [10,22].

$$Tr(n_+, n) = \frac{1 + n_+}{n} \cdot \left(\frac{n}{N}\right)^{\frac{1}{k}} \tag{1}$$

where $K > 1$ is a societal coefficient, that controls the interplay between the two assumptions.

Each agent has an internal threshold that determines if an agent joins the contract. The method `isTrustworthy` returns `True` if the trustworthiness of the contract is higher than the threshold of the agent, and `False` otherwise. We assume that the internal threshold parameter of each agent is proportional to the entry fee the agent is willing to pay to join the contract, because we deem a plausible assumption that the agents considering to pay more will be equally more skeptical of their investment.

Fitness. Clearly, the profit attained by the PS heavily depends on the Eq. (1), and therefore the scheme initiator needs to decide the optimal redistribution of capital such that the scheme is attractive for the agents in the environment. This means that the initiator needs to balance out short-term profit with long-term sustainability of the scheme. This is a core parameter for this type of non-compliant behaviour. The fitness of a PS is then defined as the amount of capital generated for the initiator, that is, the amount of redistributed capital that ends up in the deposit address of the initiator node.

Search Space Representation. Once the graph G_0 and the subgraph H_0 are initiated, the scheme is defined by its specific capital redistribution structure. This redistribution structure consists of a set of logical rules that evolve the transaction graph, deciding which members should be paid. In our framework, the characteristic form of the PS is expressed as illustrated below:

```
1 if contract.FeeReceived(new_user):
2     H.addNode(new_user)
3     H.addEdge(new_user, contract, new_user.entryFee)
4     G.executeTransactions()
5     try:
6         H.evaluate(instructionSequence)
7         G.executeTransactions()
8     else:
9         exit()
```

The set of instructions `instructionSequence` consists of instruction that modify the payment scheme H_{t-1}. Then the payments defined by the modified graph H_t are carried out by the `executePayments()` method[2]. Note that an entry condition can be considered for potential new users, e.g. a minimal entry fee. For simplicity, we assume no special conditions are in place: anyone can join.

---

[2] It can be argued whether `executePayments` should be called after every instruction, or after graph modifications, e.g. `AddNode` already applied during the evaluation of `instructionSequence`; however, this choice does not affect the model profoundly.

The syntax of the instructions `instructionSequence` will be defined by a context-free grammar, defined in Backus-Naur form below:

```
<instruction> ::= <clause> ; <instruction> | <clause>
<clause>   ::= if (<premise>) <action>
<action>   ::= H.addNode(<node>) | H.addEdge(contract, <node>, <weight>)
 | H.removeEdges(contract, <node>)
```

The actions `addNode`, `addEdge`, and `removeEdges`, add node, edge, and remove edges of the subgraph H_t respectively. The rest of the terminal symbols will be formulated later to illustrate how specific assumptions of observables depend on what kind of scheme is generated. In the trivial case displayed on Fig. 2, the instruction sequence would consist of three instructions: `H.addNode(1)`, `H.addEdge(contract, 1, 11.15)`, and `H.removeEdges(contract, 1)`, where 11.15 is the weight of an edge that corresponds to the amount of currency transferred. As will be defined later, the symbol `<node>` can be replaced by a variable, which means the instruction sequence of the initiator essentially acts as an open formula that is grounded in an event of a new agent joining the PS[3].

Note that not all words generated in the exploration are semantically correct (e.g. adding a node that was already added), which is why the code above requires `try` method to call the `exit()` method if an error is detected on runtime.

4   Experiments and Results

The present work empirically demonstrates how two PS types can be discovered based on the introduction of hypothetically relevant observables, as following the methodology described in Fig. 1. In practice, the context-free grammar presented above is extended with further terminal symbols (standing for the hypothetical relevant predictors), i.e. dedicated *query-methods* (used by agents to perceive some property from the environment), and *premises* (used by agents to condition performance).

In our experiments, the search algorithm used by the agent to discover new instances of illicit schemes from the given set of predictors is *grammatical evolution* [21].[4] For the simulation environment, we will consider $N = 100$ agents and the societal coefficient K of the trustworthiness function will be set to 10. The distribution of the entry fees follows a Beta distribution with both first and second shape parameter equal to two, which means the distribution approximates a Gaussian. The sampled value from the Beta distribution is scaled by a factor of 10 for better readability.

---

[3] This reflects the event-driven architecture integrated into the smart contract programming language Solidity. In general, it captures the cyclic characteristic of fraudulent business models.

[4] In general, grammatical evolution is an evolutionary algorithm where words of a grammar are mapped to integer vectors, and an evolutionary optimization procedure is used to optimize the fitness function. Then integer vectors are mapped back to words.

Waterfall-Type Topology. The basic Waterfall type of PS can be found by including a set of rather trivial terminal symbols into the grammar. In the instruction sequence, it must be indicated who is the initiator of the scheme and who is the new user that wants to join. The `getFee` method returns the entry fee of the agents that already joined. Further on, the possible percentages of either the entry fee or the contract balance to be paid to the contract participants are assumed. A handy piece of information to include is the `NUsers` query-method, that takes as an argument an integer and returns true if the number of market participants is equal to the argument.

```
<premise> ::= TRUE | NUsersEq(<int>)
<node> ::= new_user | initiator
<weight>   ::= <percentage>·getFee(<node>) | <percentage>·contract.balance
<percentage> ::= 0.06 | 0.1 | 0.2 | 0.5 | 1.2 | 2
<int> ::= 1 | 2 | 3 | 4 | 5 | 10 | 50
```

By visually analysing the best 20 generated transaction graph sequences, we have observed that all of them had a star graph structure, that is typical for the waterfall type (Fig. 3). The only deviation from this pattern occurred when the algorithm decided to send capital to the initiator only after a sufficiently high number of contract participants was reached. This means that the evolutionary algorithm discovered that the spread of the PS is greater, and therefore also the amount of capital accumulated, if the capital is redistributed more generously at the beginning.

Array Topology. As already discussed, the waterfall type can be made more efficient if the scheme will have a concept of who was paid last and who should be paid next. Indeed, each time the method `executeTransactions` is called for the waterfall scheme, many of the transactions cannot be executed because the

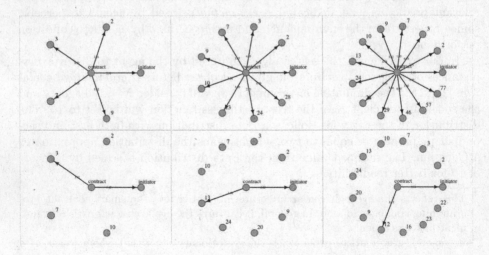

Fig. 3. Snapshots of the transaction graph for the waterfall type (upper row) and the array type (lower row) of Ponzi Schemes (PS).

capital of the contract is depleted. This issue can be resolved by including three more query-methods into the grammar, modifying it as such:

```
<premise> ::= TRUE | NUsersEq(<int>)
   | BalanceFeeHigherAndNotConnected(<node>, <weight>)
<node> ::= new_user | initiator | getNextToPay() | getLastPaid()
```

where getNextToPay and getLastPaid keep track of which agent was paid last and which agent is next in order; BalanceFeeHigherAndNotConnected returns true if the contract node is not connected to the node provided by the first argument and the capital balance of the contract is higher than the second argument. Running the search procedure over the extended search space yields the *array* type of PS. The typical "clock" pattern is depicted on Fig. 3. As in the waterfall case, a number of different transaction patterns were discovered. These mutants differ slightly in the transaction topology, usually adding one or two instructions more into the instruction sequence.

5 Discussion

Convergence. Computation-wise, the evolutionary algorithm for a population of size 100 with other parameters kept default [21] can easily find profitable PSs of Waterfall type in less than 200 iterations. In order to discover the Array-type, the algorithm had to be extended with an adaptive mutation chance parameter to avoid getting trapped in local optima[5] of the Waterfall-type. Moreover, the *maximum depth* parameter, required to ensure termination of the recursive grammar defined above, is increased due to the higher complexity of the scheme.

Extending to Other Types of Ponzi Schemes. Other types of PS can be explored similarly. For instance, to include a PS spread mechanism as those observed in social systems [20], a simple network spread model [13] can be implemented, extending the grammar accordingly. Participants to the scheme has to be rewarded by how many new members they have recruited. Adding to the grammar a query-method that returns the number of new contract participants recruited by an agent would be sufficient in terms of predictors. However, a mechanism that motivates the individual agent to recruit new participants would also need to be present.

Detection supported by generation Without loss of generality, assume we use a certain neural network to decide whether a certain behaviour is compliant or not. This detection model can be trained on labelled data records of a given socio-economic system, and then tested also on labelled data obtained via the simulation environment. The training dataset can be subsequently extended by generated instances of non-compliant behaviour to enhance the performance of the classifier, mitigating the issue of unbalanced datasets as motivated in the introduction. Note that these instances can correspond to previously unobserved

---

[5] See the source code: https://github.com/fratric/Ponzi-Scheme-Discovery.

types of non-compliant behaviour. More interestingly, since the noncompliant agents are assumed to be capable to adapt, the detection model can be also used to incentivize the discovery of new schemes, producing co-evolutionary adversarial dynamics (see e.g. [15]).

Beyond Grammatical Evolution. Grammatical evolution can be challenging to use for more complex applications, both regarding the computational complexity and the representation by a context-free grammar. In systems consisting of several transactional sub-systems, where a variety of transaction operations can occur, the search space represented by a context-free grammar would be too large to be explored using evolutionary operators. In such case, the search algorithm associated with the noncompliant agent (or a group of agents) would require a more sophisticated type of reasoning, e.g. bringing some context into the grammar, such that the noncompliant agent(s) are capable to plan ahead depending on the environment and the actions of other agents, thus allowing modularization of the search space. Moreover, the behaviour of the noncompliant agent ought not to be deterministic, which is also important for generation of rich synthetic data. However, this challenge is similar to planning and cooperation in complex, diverse and stochastic environments which remain still open questions.

6   Conclusions

Our present research deals with exploration of non-compliant behaviours in the context of policy-making. The paper sketched a general computational framework to generate instances of transaction-based financial crime and illustrated its application on a well known case of smart contract Ponzi schemes. It was demonstrated that with only a modest set of assumptions it is possible to generate a sequence of transaction graphs that captures the functional and modular aspects of two well-known types of Ponzi schemes, that differ in their dynamic topology defining the redistribution of capital. We argue that the lines of research revisited in this paper are relatively unexplored and deserve much more attention, as they have the potential to successfully address certain important issues present in the contemporary research on fraud detection. However, more examples of fraud generated in simulation environment needs to be provided before creating a sound basis for deployment into real socio-economical systems.

References

1. Aggarwal, C.C.: An introduction to outlier analysis. In: Outlier Analysis, pp. 1–34. Springer, Cham (2017). https://doi.org/10.1007/978-3-319-47578-3_1
2. Ahmed, M., Naser Mahmood, A., Hu, J.: A survey of network anomaly detection techniques. J. Netw. Comput. Appl. **60**, 19–31 (2016)
3. Al-Hashedi, K.G., Magalingam, P.: Financial fraud detection applying data mining techniques: A comprehensive review from 2009 to 2019. Comput. Sci. Rev. **40**, 100402 (2021)

4. Bao, Y., Hilary, G., Ke, B.: Artificial intelligence and fraud detection. SSRN Electron. J. **7**(2), 223–247 (2020)
5. Bartoletti, M., Carta, S., Cimoli, T., Saia, R.: Dissecting Ponzi schemes on Ethereum: identification, analysis, and impact. Futur. Gener. Comput. Syst. **102**, 259–277 (2020)
6. Brito, J., Campos, P., Leite, R.: An agent-based model for detection in economic networks. In: Bajo, J., et al. (eds.) PAAMS 2018. CCIS, vol. 887, pp. 105–115. Springer, Cham (2018). https://doi.org/10.1007/978-3-319-94779-2_10
7. Caminero, G., Lopez-Martin, M., Carro, B.: Adversarial environment reinforcement learning algorithm for intrusion detection. Comput. Netw. **159**, 96–109 (2019)
8. Chen, W., Zheng, Z., Cui, J., Ngai, E., Zheng, P., Zhou, Y.: Detecting Ponzi Schemes on Ethereum. In: Proceedings of the 2018 World Wide Web Conference on World Wide Web - WWW 2018, New York, New York, USA, pp. 1409–1418. ACM Press (2018)
9. Chen, W., Zheng, Z., Ngai, E.C., Zheng, P., Zhou, Y.: Exploiting blockchain data to detect smart Ponzi schemes on Ethereum. IEEE Access **7**, 37575–37586 (2019)
10. Cho, J.H., Chan, K., Adali, S.: A survey on trust modeling. ACM Comput. Surv. (CSUR) **48**(2), 1–40 (2015)
11. D'Amour, A., Srinivasan, H., Atwood, J., Baljekar, P., Sculley, D., Halpern, Y.: Fairness is not static. In: Proceedings of the 2020 Conference on Fairness, Accountability, and Transparency, New York, NY, USA, pp. 525–534. ACM (2020)
12. Delecourt, S., Guo, L.: Building a robust mobile payment fraud detection system with adversarial examples. In: 2019 IEEE Second International Conference on Artificial Intelligence and Knowledge Engineering (AIKE), pp. 103–106. IEEE (2019)
13. Fu, P., Zhu, A., Ni, H., Zhao, X., Li, X.: Threshold behaviors of social dynamics and financial outcomes of Ponzi scheme diffusion in complex networks. Phys. A **490**, 632–642 (2018)
14. Fursov, I., et al.: Adversarial attacks on deep models for financial transaction records. In: Proceedings of the 27th ACM SIGKDD Conference on Knowledge Discovery & Data Mining, New York, NY, USA, vol. 1, pp. 2868–2878. ACM (2021)
15. Hemberg, E., Rosen, J., Warner, G., Wijesinghe, S., O'Reilly, U.-M.: Detecting tax evasion: a co-evolutionary approach. Artif. Intell. Law **24**(2), 149–182 (2016). https://doi.org/10.1007/s10506-016-9181-6
16. Kumar, N., Vimal, S., Kayathwal, K., Dhama, G.: Evolutionary adversarial attacks on payment systems. In: 2021 20th IEEE International Conference on Machine Learning and Applications (ICMLA), pp. 813–818. IEEE (2021)
17. Kurshan, E., Shen, H., Yu, H.: Financial crime & fraud detection using graph computing: Application considerations & outlook. In: 2020 Second International Conference on Transdisciplinary AI (TransAI), pp. 125–130. IEEE (2020)
18. Lopez-Rojas, E.A., Axelsson, S.: A review of computer simulation for fraud detection research in financial datasets. In: 2016 Future Technologies Conference (FTC), pp. 932–935. No. December, IEEE (2016)
19. Mead, A., Lewris, T., Prasanth, S., Adams, S., Alonzi, P., Beling, P.: Detecting fraud in adversarial environments: a reinforcement learning approach. In: 2018 Systems and Information Engineering Design Symposium (SIEDS), pp. 118–122. IEEE (2018)
20. Nash, R., Bouchard, M., Malm, A.: Investing in people: the role of social networks in the diffusion of a large-scale fraud. Soc. Networks **35**(4), 686–698 (2013)

21. Noorian, F., de Silva, A.M., Leong, P.H.W.: gramEvol: grammatical evolution in R. J. Stat. Softw. **71**(1), 1–26 (2016)
22. Pinyol, I., Sabater-Mir, J.: Computational trust and reputation models for open multi-agent systems: a review. Artif. Intell. Rev. **40**(1), 1–25 (2013)
23. Pourhabibi, T., Ong, K.L., Kam, B.H., Boo, Y.L.: Fraud detection: a systematic literature review of graph-based anomaly detection approaches. Decis. Support Syst. **133**, 113303 (2020)
24. Utting, M., Legeard, B.: Practical Model-Based Testing: A Tools Approach. Elsevier (2010)
25. Zeager, M.F., Sridhar, A., Fogal, N., Adams, S., Brown, D.E., Beling, P.A.: Adversarial learning in credit card fraud detection. In: 2017 Systems and Information Engineering Design Symposium (SIEDS), pp. 112–116. IEEE (2017)

Centralized Norm Enforcement in Mixed-Motive Multiagent Reinforcement Learning

Rafael M. Cheang[1,2]([✉]) [iD], Anarosa A. F. Brandão[1] [iD],
and Jaime S. Sichman[1] [iD]

[1] Laboratório de Técnicas Inteligentes (LTI), Universidade de São Paulo (USP),
São Paulo, Brazil
{rafael_cheang,anarosa.brandao,jaime.sichman}@usp.br
[2] Centro de Ciência de Dados (C2D), Universidade de São Paulo (USP), São Paulo,
Brazil

Abstract. Mixed-motive games comprise a subset of games in which individual and collective incentives are not entirely aligned. These games are relevant because they frequently occur in real-world and artificial societies, and their outcome is often bad for the involved parties. Institutions and norms offer a good solution for governing mixed-motive systems. Still, they are usually incorporated into the system in a distributed fashion, or they are not able to dynamically adjust to the needs of the environment at run-time. We propose a way of reaching socially good outcomes in mixed-motive multiagent reinforcement learning settings by enhancing the environment with a normative system controlled by an external reinforcement learning agent. By adopting this proposal, we show it is possible to reach social welfare in a mixed-motive system of self-interested agents using only traditional reinforcement learning agent architectures.

Keywords: Mixed-motive games · Centralized norm enforcement ·
Multiagent reinforcement learning

1 Introduction

Mixed-motive games, comprise a subset of games in which individual and collective incentives are not entirely aligned. These games describe situations in which the combined effects of every individual's selfishness do not yield a good outcome for the group, a problem also known as the collective action problem [24]. Two basic properties define this type of games [8]: *a)* every individual is incentivized to socially defect and *b)* all individuals are better off if all cooperate than if all defect.

Olson develops the notion of a collective action problem starting from the *raison d'etre* of *organizations* [24]. These, as he describes, are groups that serve to further the interests of their members. The problem emerges when the individuals of such groups also have antagonistic incentives to those common to the collective. Individuals, in this case, are left to choose between harming the organization as whole in favor of their own benefit, or to pass on the opportunity

N. Ajmeri et al. (Eds.): COINE 2022, LNAI 13549, pp. 121–133, 2022.
https://doi.org/10.1007/978-3-031-20845-4_8

for bigger gains in favor of the group. A collective action problem happens when the former is systematically preferred over the latter.

Global warming is a real-world case of the collective action problem. In it, most players—be it an individual, institution, or government—have an incentive to emit as much greenhouse gases as desired—for matters of comfort, financial gains, or popularity—, regardless of how much others are emitting. If collective emissions surpass some threshold to these ends, the system increasingly dips into an undesirable state that is bad for all involved.

It has been noted that real-world communities are capable of circumventing this problem with varying success, conditioned on variables such as group size, the existence of a communication channel, etc. [25,26]. These are tied and serve to strengthen the idea of social norms; a guide of conduct, or the expectation individuals hold of others in certain situations [22].

Social norms and norm enforcement mechanisms can be a useful tool in guiding groups of people out of social dilemmas [17], but they can also be incorporated into multiagent systems (MAS) [5,6]. This institutional machinery provides ways of governing mixed-motive games either via centralized solutions—when a central governing body is tasked with running the institutional apparatus by itself—or decentralized solutions—when the normative system is conducted by the agents in the system.

Decentralized norm-enforcement approaches have been used to deal with degrading system properties in MASs [9,15], such as the collective action problem. However, these decentralized solutions either imply *a)* pro-social behavior from the agents or *b)* some form of direct or indirect retaliatory capacity—e.g. having the choice not to cooperate in future interactions—that is at least similar in intensity to the harm caused by the aggressor. We acknowledge the effectiveness of these solutions in some cases but also recognize they are no *panacea*.

For instance, how can one—agent or group of agents—successfully drive a complex MAS towards social order [5] from within without assuming anything about others' beliefs, intentions, or goals, and given that punishing uncompliant behavior is not desirable or allowed? This problem is akin to many situations in modern society; thus far is impossible to know the beliefs and intentions of every person we might interact with, and not every problem we face is ideally solvable by a "taking matters into own hands" approach.

Consider as an example the problem with burglary. We—as society—don't expect social norms and good moral values to completely solve the problem—although they certainly change the rate to which it happens—and when a burglary does happen, we don't expect the victim to return the favor with a response of similar intensity—like stealing from the aggressor's house.

A similar issue may also occur in MASs. Consider a system of self-driving autonomous vehicles. Every vehicle in it might have an incentive to get to its destination as fast as possible. Suppose that, to this end, a vehicle engages in careless maneuvers and risky overtakes to gain a few extra seconds, harming others—safety and/or performance—close to it in the process. Could we safely assume agents in this system are pro-social to the degree that such a situation would never happen?

This might not always be a good premise. In this example, the system itself is embedded in a competitive environment of firms fiercely fighting for market share. Performance, in the form of getting to the final destination faster, might represent getting a bigger slice of the pie. Does the designer behind the agent have the right incentives to design pro-social agents? Social defection for the sake of financial gains is not unthinkable by any means in the automobile industry[1].

Now, suppose that an uncompliant behavior has been identified by another vehicle close by. Could any form of punishment by the latter be accomplished without compromising the safety of passengers riding in both vehicles? Furthermore, even if we agree on the safety to reciprocate, there are many situations where direct retaliation might be undesirable. For instance, how do we address fairness in these systems? If highly interconnected, even a small violation could be met with a huge wave of public bashing, similar to the problem of internet cancel culture[2].

In case it is not safe to assume other agents will cooperate and it is not desirable that agents directly or indirectly punish each other, we may need to resort to centralized governance of some kind. Jones and Sergot (1994) propose two complementary models of centralized norm enforcement [16]:

1. *Regimentation:* Assumes agents can be controlled by some external entity, therefore non-compliant behavior does not occur.
2. *Regulation:* Assumes agents can violate norms, and violations may be sanctioned when detected.

A drawback of the former is that it constrains agents' autonomy [22]. Furthermore, implementing a regimentation system is not necessarily trivial; edge cases may arise such that violations may still occur [16]. On the other hand, the latter preserves—to some degree—agents' autonomy by allowing their actions to violate norms.

This work proposes a way out of the collective action problem in mixed-motive multiagent reinforcement learning (MARL) environments through centralized regulation. The proposal involves enhancing regular mixed-motive environments with a normative system, controlled by a reinforcement learning (RL) agent playing the role of a regulator; able to set norms and sanctions of the system according to the ADICO grammar of institutions [7]. The primary aim of this proposal is to solve the collective action problem in mixed-motive MARL environments given two assumptions:

1. We have no prior knowledge about the agents' architectures, thus it's impossible to predict their incentives and behaviors.
2. It's not desirable for agents in the system to punish each other.

---

[1] https://www.bbc.com/news/business-34324772.
[2] https://nypost.com/article/what-is-cancel-culture-breaking-down-the-toxic-online-trend/.

We also show that, by employing this method, social control can be achieved using only off-the-shelf, traditional RL agent architectures[3,4].

2   Related Work

Many studies have addressed the collective action problem in mixed-motive MARL environments [9,15,18,20,27]. Still, most of them have tackled this problem from an agent-centric perspective; their solutions involve modifying an RL architecture to the specific needs of multiagent mixed-motive environments. This has been accomplished in different ways, such as allowing agents to have pro-social intrinsic motivation [15,20,27], coupling agents with a reciprocity mechanism [9,18], and deploying agents with a normative reasoning engine [23].

This very same problem—and others—has also been addressed in MASs through the adoption of electronic institutions (EI) [10,11], which specifies among other definitions, a set of rules that determines what the agents in the system ought to do or not under predefined circumstances, similar to the role traditional institutions play [1]. Likewise, the autonomic electronic institution (AEI) is also a framework that can be used to govern MASs and may be better suited to cope with the dynamism of complex systems of self-adapting agents due to its autonomic capabilities (norm-setting at run-time) [1,2].

Our work here presented is similar to the AEI framework in the sense that it also proposes to overcome a system-level problem by dynamically regulating the system's norms at run-time. Still, it differs from such framework by leveraging in a single agent the learning capabilities RL together with the normative concepts spread across a broad literature. Our work also broadly resembles the AI Economist framework proposed by Zhen et al. [33], that allows for the training of RL *social planners*, that learn optimal tax policies in a multiagent environment of adaptable *economic actors* by observing and optimizing for macro-properties of the system (productivity and equality).

In summary, to the best of our knowledge, none of the studies cited above have: *a)* proposed a centralized norm enforcement solution to mixed-motive MARL environments using another RL agent as a central governing authority, and *b)* proposed a solution that uses only traditional RL architectures when peer retaliation is not allowed.

3   Normative Systems and the ADICO Grammar of Institutions

One way of preventing MASs from falling into social disorder [5] is to augment the system with a normative qualifier. Thus, a normative system can be simply

---

[3] By traditional RL agent architectures we mean commonly used in other RL tasks such as A2C [21].

[4] All relevant code and data for this project is available at https://github.com/rafacheang/social_dilemmas_regulation.

defined as one in which norms and normative concepts interfere with its outcomes [22]. In these settings, despite not having an unified definition, a norm can be generally described as a behavioral expectation the majority of individuals in a group hold of others in the same group in certain situations [31].

In normative systems, norms that are not complied with might be subject to being sanctioned. Sanctions can be generally classified into *direct material sanctions*, that have an immediate negative effect on a resource the agent cherish, such as a fine, or *indirect social sanctions*, such as a lowering effect on the agent's reputation, that can influence its future within the system [4]. Nardin [22] also describes a third type of sanction; *psychological sanctions* are those inflicted by an agent to himself as a function of the agent's internal emotional state.

The ADICO grammar of institutions [7] provides a framework under which norms can be conceived and operationalized. The ADICO grammar is defined within five dimensions:

- *A*ttributes: is the set of variables that defines to whom the institutional statement is applied.
- *D*eontic: is a holder from the three modal operations from deontic logic: *may* (permitted), *must* (obliged), and *must not* (forbidden). These are used to distinguish prescriptive from nonprescriptive statements.
- *Aim:* describes a particular action or set of actions to which the deontic operator is assigned.
- *C*onditions: defines the context—when, where, how, etc.—an action is obliged, permitted or forbidden.
- *O*r else: defines the sanctions imposed for not following the norm

Example 1. The norm *All Brazilian citizens, 18 years of age or older, must vote in a presidential candidate every four years, or else he/she will be unable to renew his/her passport* as per defined in the ADICO grammar, can be broken down into: *A:* Brazilian citizens, 18 years of age or older, *D:* must, *I:* vote in a presidential candidate, *C:* every four years, *O:* will be unable to renew his/her passport.

4 Reinforcement Learning (RL)

4.1 Single-Agent Reinforcement Learning

The reinforcement learning task mathematically formalizes the path of an agent interacting with an environment, receiving feedback—positive or negative—for its actions, and learning from them. This formalization is accomplished through the Markov decision process (MDP), defined by the tuple $\langle S, A, R, P, \gamma \rangle$ where S denotes a finite set of environment states; A, a finite set of agent actions; R, a reward function $R : S \times A \times S \rightarrow \mathbb{R}$ that defines the immediate—possibly stochastic—reward an agent gets for taking action $a \in A$ in state $s \in S$, and transitioning to state $s' \in S$ thereafter; P, a transition function $P : S \times A \times S \rightarrow [0, 1]$ that defines the probability of transitioning to state $s' \in S$ after taking action $a \in \mathcal{A}$ in state $s \in \mathcal{S}$; and finally, $\gamma \in [0,1]$, a discount factor of future rewards [29].

In these settings, the agent's goal is to maximize its long-term expected reward G_t, given by the infinite sum $\mathbb{E}[r_{t+1} + \gamma r_{t+2} + \gamma^2 r_{t+3} + \dots + \gamma^n r_{t+n+1}]$. Solving an MDP ideally means finding an optimal *policy* $\pi_* : \mathcal{S} \rightarrow \mathcal{A}$, i.e., a mapping that yields the best action to be taken at each state [29].

4.2   Multi-Agent Reinforcement Learning (MARL)

One critical difference between RL and MARL is that, instead of the environment transitioning to a new state as a function of a single action, it does so as a function of the combined efforts of all agents.

The MDP counterpart in MARL is the Markov Game (MG) [19] also known as Stochastic Game, and it is defined by a tuple $\langle \mathcal{N}, \mathcal{S}, \{\mathcal{A}^i\}_{i \in \mathcal{N}}, \{\mathcal{R}^i\}_{i \in \mathcal{N}}, \mathcal{P}, \gamma \rangle$, where $\mathcal{N} = \{1, \dots, N\}$ denotes the set of $N > 1$ agents, $\mathcal{S}$, a finite set of environment states, $\mathcal{A}^i$, agent's i set of possible actions. Let $\mathcal{A} = \mathcal{A}^1 \times \dots \times \mathcal{A}^N$ be the set of agents' possible joint actions. Then $\mathcal{R}^i$ denotes agent's i reward function $\mathcal{R}^i : \mathcal{S} \times \mathcal{A} \times \mathcal{S} \rightarrow \mathbb{R}$ that defines the immediate reward earned by agent i given a transition from state $s \in \mathcal{S}$ to state $s' \in \mathcal{S}$ after a combination of actions $a \in \mathcal{A}$; $\mathcal{P}$, a transition function $\mathcal{P} : \mathcal{S} \times \mathcal{A} \times \mathcal{S} \rightarrow [0,1]$ that defines the probability of transitioning from state $s \in \mathcal{S}$ to state $s' \in \mathcal{S}$ after a combination of actions $a \in \mathcal{A}$; and $\gamma \in [0,1]$, a discount factor on agents future rewards [32].

5   Centralized Norm Enforcement in MARL

Here, we propose a norm-enhanced Markov Game (neMG) for governing mixed-motive MGs by making use of an RL regulator agent and some added normative concepts. The proposal builds upon regular mixed-motive MGs. It involves enhancing the environment's states with the ADICO information introduced in Sect. 3. The regulator is then able operate within this new ADICO information, which is also available for other agents in the game and can be considered for decision-making.

The method comprises two types of RL agents: $N > 1$ *players* and one *regulator*. Players are simple RL agents, analogous to the ones that interact with regular versions of MARL environments. These agents could be modeled as average self-interested RL agents with off-the-shelf architectures such as A2C [21]—which facilitates the engineering side.

The regulator, in turn, is able to operate on the environment's norms represented by the ADICO five dimensions; it can modify one or more dimensions at every period—a period consists of m time steps, m being a predefined integer value. This agent senses the state of the environment through a social metric—i.e. a system-level diagnostic—and the efficacy of its actions is signaled back by the environment based on the social outcome of past institutions. The regulator can also be modeled as a self-interested agent with off-the-shelf RL architectures.

Definition 1. A norm-enhanced Markov Game (neMG) can be formally defined by a 11-tuple $\langle \mathcal{N}_p, \mathcal{S}_p, \{\mathcal{A}_p^i\}_{i \in \mathcal{N}_p}, \{\mathcal{R}_p^i\}_{i \in \mathcal{N}_p}, \mathcal{P}_p, \gamma_p, \mathcal{S}_r, \mathcal{A}_r, \mathcal{R}_r, \mathcal{P}_r, \gamma_r \rangle$, with $\mathcal{N}_p, \mathcal{S}_p, \mathcal{A}_p^i, \mathcal{R}_p^i, \mathcal{P}_p, \gamma_p$ being the players' original MG as per defined in Sect. 4.2. $\mathcal{S}_r$, denotes the regulator's set of states; $\mathcal{A}_r$, the regulator's set of actions; $\mathcal{R}_r$, the regulator's reward function $\mathcal{R}_r : \mathcal{S}_r \times \mathcal{A}_r \times \mathcal{S}_r \to \mathbb{R}$ that determines the immediate reward earned by the regulator following a transition from state $s_r \in \mathcal{S}_r$ to $s_r' \in \mathcal{S}_r$ after an action $a \in \mathcal{A}_r$; $\mathcal{P}_r$, the regulator's transition function $\mathcal{P}_r : \mathcal{S}_r \times \mathcal{A}_r \times \mathcal{S}_r \to [0, 1]$ that defines the environment's probability of transitioning from state $s_r \in \mathcal{S}_r$ to state $s_r' \in \mathcal{S}_r$ after an action $a_r \in \mathcal{A}_r$; and $\gamma_r \in [0, 1]$, the regulator's discount factor.

In these settings, a neMG could be run following two RL loops; an outer one relative to the regulator, and an inner one relative to the players. Algorithm 1 exemplifies how these could be implemented.

Algorithm 1: neMG Pseudocode

---

algorithm parameters: number of players n, steps per period m;
initialize policy and/or value function parameters;
foreach *episode* **do**
    initialize environment (set initial states s_{r0} and s_{p0});
    foreach *period* **do**
        regulator sets norm by consulting its policy π_r in state s_r;
        for m/n **do**
            foreach *player* **do**
                player acts based on its policy π_p in state s_p, state transitions to
                s_p', player observes its reward r_p, and updates its policy π_p;
            end foreach
        end for
        regulator observes next state s_r', its reward r_r and updates its policy π_r;
    end foreach
end foreach

---

6 Tragedy of the Commons Experiment

The method was tested on a mixed-motive environment that emulates the tragedy of the commons problem described by Hardin (1968) [14]. The tragedy of the commons describes a situation wherein a group of people shares a common resource that replenishes at a given rate. Every person has the own interest to consume the resource as much as possible, but if the consumption rate consistently exceeds the replenishment rate, the common soon depletes.

6.1   A neMG of a Tragedy of the Commons Environment

The environment built closely resembles that of Ghorbani et al. (2021) [12] and was built using both the OpenAI gym [3] and pettingzoo [30] frameworks. An episode begins with an initial quantity R_0 of the common resource. Every n simulation steps—n being the number of agents; five for this simulation—the resource grows by a quantity given by the logistic function $\Delta R = rR(1 - \frac{R}{K})$, with ΔR being the amount to increase; r, the growth rate; R, the current resource quantity; and K, the environment's carrying capacity—an upper bound to resources. For this experiment, r was set to 0.3, R_0 is sampled from a uniform distribution $U(10000, 30000)$, and K was set to 50000.

The environment also encodes the ADICO variables as described in Sect. 5. The A, D, and I dimensions remain fixed for this experiment since $a)$ the norm applies to all players, $b)$ the norm always defines a forbidden action, and $c)$ players have only one action to choose from—they can only decide how much of the resource to consume and their rewards are proportional to their consumption. The C and O dimensions, on the other hand, may be changed by the regulator agent; i.e., every 100 steps the regulator may change how much of the resource a player is allowed to consume (l)—sampled at the beginning of each episode from a normal distribution $N(375, 93.75)$—and the fine applied to those who violate this condition ($f(c, l, \lambda)$)—by setting the value of λ, which is sampled at the beginning of each episode from a normal distribution $N(1, 0.2)$. Thus the ADICO information that enhances this environment is made up of:

- A: all players;
- D: forbidden;
- I: consume resources;
- C: when consumption is greater than l_i;
- O: pay a fine of $f = (c_i - l_i) \times (\lambda + 1)$, with c_i being the agent's consumption in step i; l_i the consumption limit in step i; and λ, a fine multiplier.

The fine is subtracted from the violator's consumption in the same step the norm is violated.

Before a new institution is set, the regulator can evaluate the system-level state of the environment by observing how much of the resource is left, and a short-term and long-term sustainability measurement, given by $S = \sum_{j=t-p}^{t} \frac{rp_j}{c_j}$ defined for $c_j > 0$ and $p \geq 0$, with p being the number of periods considered as short-term and long-term—respectively one and four for this simulation —; rp_j, the total amount of resources replenished in period j; c_j, the total consumption in period j; and t, the current period. At the end of the period, the success of past norms is feed-backed to the regulator by the environment as a reward value directly proportional to the last period's total consumption.

At every simulation step, players in the environment can observe R_i, l_i, and λ_i, and can choose how much of the resource to consume. An agent's consumption may vary from 0 to c_{max}, where c_{max} is a consumption limit that represents a physical limit in an analogous real-world scenario. Here, this value was set to 1500. An episode ends after 1000 simulation steps or when resources are depleted.

Agents in this simulation were built using traditional RL architectures—SAC [13] for the regulator and A2C [21] for the players—using the Stable Baselines 3 framework [28], and players were trained on a shared policy. The learning rates for all agents were set to 0.00039. A summary with all environment related variables used in this experiment and their values is presented in Table 1.

Table 1. Summary of the variables used in the experiment, their abbreviations, and values.

Variable name	Description	Value
n	Number of players	5
m	Number of steps in a period	100
R_0	Initial quantity of common resource	$U(10000, 30000)$
R	Current quantity of common resource	var
K	Environment's carrying capacity (resources upper bound)	50000
r	Resources growth rate	0.3
ΔR	Replenishment amount at a single step	var
l	Norm-set consumption limit	var
c	Single player consumption	var
λ	Norm-set fine multiplier	var
S	Sustainability metric	var
p	Number of periods considered for calculating S	1, 4
c	Player(s) consumption	var
c_{max}	Players max consumption (hard limit)	1500
rp	Period's total replenishment	var

6.2   Results and Discussion

Figure 1 shows the average total consumption per episode over a 10 simulation run with and without the regulator agent acting on the environment. As predicted by the Nash equilibrium, we notice there isn't much hope for generalized cooperation in case selfish agents are left playing the game by themselves—i.e. resources quickly deplete in the beginning of each episode.

Conversely, this is not the case when the regulator is put in place. After a short period of randomness at the beginning of the simulation, players learn not to consume from the resource since they frequently get punished when doing so. Around episode 300, players progressively learn to consume around as much of the resource as the set limit and the regulator increasingly learns to adjust such limit so as to keep resources at a sustainable level. A comparison between an episode at the beginning of a simulation and one at the end is shown in Fig. 2.

Every once in a while, the regulator overshoots by setting too big of a limit at the beginning of the episode and players quickly deplete the resource. This explains in parts the total consumption variation depicted in Fig. 1.

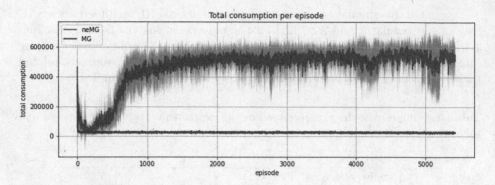

Fig. 1. The total consumption per episode average over a 10 simulation run for the tragedy of the commons experiment. The green line shows the total consumption for when the regulator is active and the blue line for when it is inactive. The green shaded area covers the region one standard deviation above and below the mean for the simulation with the active regulator. (Color figure online)

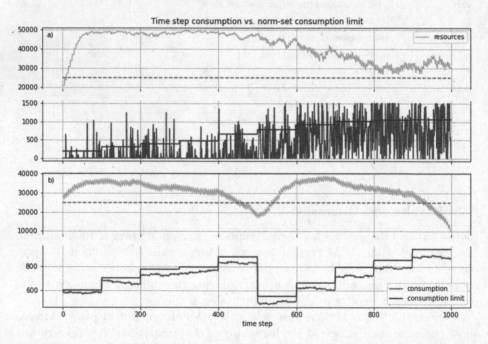

Fig. 2. Time step consumption vs. consumption limit set by the regulator at an earlier episode *a)* and at a later episode *b)*. The orange line shows the resource level at all time steps and the dotted red line shows the resource level in which the replenishment rate is greatest (25000). In *a)* players and the regulator act somewhat randomly and, for this reason, resources are kept at a sustainable range but consumption is sub-optimal. Players in *b)* learn to approximate their consumption to the norm-set consumption limit and the regulator learns to decrease such limit at times when resources are lower and increase it when resources are higher. Resources in this episode are still kept at a sustainable range and consumption sharply increases in comparison to *a)*. (Color figure online)

Note the system gets relatively close to an upper consumption benchmark by the end of the simulation—when agents' combined consumption equals the maximum replenishment in every iteration. We can calculate this value by multiplying the maximum replenishment (3750) by the maximum count of replenishments in a given episode (200). In this case, the value is 750000 units of resource.

7   Conclusion

Delegating norm enforcement to an external central authority might seem counter-intuitive at first, as we tend to associate distributed solutions with robustness. It also might seem to go against the findings of Elinor Ostrom [25,26], who showed that the collective action problem could be solved without the need of a regulatory central authority and for that, won the nobel prize in economics in 2009[5].

That being said, central regulation is still an important mechanism to govern complex systems. Many of the world's modern social and political systems use it in some form or shape. With this work, we try to show that central regulation is also a tool that could be useful in governing MAS and MARL, especially when it is not desirable for actors in the system to punish each other.

Still, centralized norm enforcement brings about many other challenges that are not present in decentralized norm enforcement. For instance, if poorly designed (purposefully or not) the regulator himself, through the imposition norms and sanctions, may drive the system to socially bad outcomes. What if the designer behind the regulator does not have the good incentives? Constraints as such must be taken into consideration when judging the applicability of centralized norm enforcement in MASs.

As further work, we plan to test this very same method in other mixed-motive MARL environments.

Acknowledgements. This research is being carried out with the support of *Itaú Unibanco S.A.*, through the scholarship program of *Programa de Bolsas Itaú* (PBI), and it is also financed in part by the Coordenação de Aperfeiçoamento de Pessoal de Nível Superior (CAPES), Finance Code 001, Brazil.

References

1. Bou, E., López-Sánchez, M., Rodríguez-Aguilar, J.A., Sichman, J.S.: Adapting autonomic electronic institutions to heterogeneous agent societies. In: Vouros, G., Artikis, A., Stathis, K., Pitt, J. (eds.) OAMAS 2008. LNCS (LNAI), vol. 5368, pp. 18–35. Springer, Heidelberg (2009). https://doi.org/10.1007/978-3-642-02377-4_2
2. Bou, E., López-Sánchez, M., Rodríguez-Aguilar, J.A.: Towards self-configuration in autonomic electronic institutions. In: Noriega, P., Vázquez-Salceda, J., Boella, G., Boissier, O., Dignum, V., Fornara, N., Matson, E. (eds.) COIN 2006. LNCS (LNAI), vol. 4386, pp. 229–244. Springer, Heidelberg (2007). https://doi.org/10.1007/978-3-540-74459-7_15

---

[5] https://www.nobelprize.org/prizes/economic-sciences/2009/ostrom/facts/.

3. Brockman, G., et al.: OpenAI Gym. arXiv preprint arXiv:1606.01540 (2016)
4. Cardoso, H.L., Oliveira, E.: Adaptive deterrence sanctions in a normative framework. In: Proceedings of the 2009 IEEE/WIC/ACM International Joint Conference on Web Intelligence and Intelligent Agent Technology, pp. 36–43. IEEE Computer Society (2009)
5. Castelfranchi, C.: Engineering social order. In: Omicini, A., Tolksdorf, R., Zambonelli, F. (eds.) ESAW 2000. LNCS (LNAI), vol. 1972, pp. 1–18. Springer, Heidelberg (2000). https://doi.org/10.1007/3-540-44539-0_1
6. Conte, R.: Emergent (info)institutions. Cogn. Syst. Res. **2**(2), 97–110 (2001). https://doi.org/10.1016/S1389-0417(01)00020-1
7. Crawford, S.E.S., Ostrom, E.: A grammar of institutions. Am. Polit. Sci. Rev. **89**(3), 582–600 (1995). https://doi.org/10.2307/2082975
8. Dawes, R.M.: Social dilemmas. Annu. Rev. Psychol. **31**(1), 169–193 (1980). https://doi.org/10.1146/annurev.ps.31.020180.001125
9. Eccles, T., Hughes, E., Kramár, J., Wheelwright, S., Leibo, J.Z.: Learning reciprocity in complex sequential social dilemmas (2019)
10. Esteva, M., de la Cruz, D., Rosell, B., Arcos, J.L., Rodríguez-Aguilar, J., Cuní, G.: Engineering open multi-agent systems as electronic institutions. In: Proceedings of the 19th National Conference on Artificial Intelligence, AAAI 2004, pp. 1010–1011. AAAI Press (01 2004)
11. Esteva, M., Rodríguez-Aguilar, J.-A., Sierra, C., Garcia, P., Arcos, J.L.: On the formal specification of electronic institutions. In: Dignum, F., Sierra, C. (eds.) Agent Mediated Electronic Commerce. LNCS (LNAI), vol. 1991, pp. 126–147. Springer, Heidelberg (2001). https://doi.org/10.1007/3-540-44682-6_8
12. Ghorbani, A., Ho, P., Bravo, G.: Institutional form versus function in a common property context: the credibility thesis tested through an agent-based model. Land Use Policy **102**, 105237 (2021). https://doi.org/10.1016/j.landusepol.2020.105237. https://www.sciencedirect.com/science/article/pii/S0264837720325758
13. Haarnoja, T., Zhou, A., Abbeel, P., Levine, S.: Soft actor-critic: off-policy maximum entropy deep reinforcement learning with a stochastic actor. In: Dy, J., Krause, A. (eds.) Proceedings of the 35th International Conference on Machine Learning. Proceedings of Machine Learning Research, vol. 80, pp. 1861–1870. PMLR, 10–15 July 2018. https://proceedings.mlr.press/v80/haarnoja18b.html
14. Hardin, G.: The tragedy of the commons. Science **162**(3859), 1243–1248 (1968). https://doi.org/10.1126/science.162.3859.1243. https://science.sciencemag.org/content/162/3859/1243
15. Hughes, E., et al.: Inequity aversion improves cooperation in intertemporal social dilemmas. In: Bengio, S., Wallach, H., Larochelle, H., Grauman, K., Cesa-Bianchi, N., Garnett, R. (eds.) Advances in Neural Information Processing Systems, vol. 31. Curran Associates, Inc. (2018). https://proceedings.neurips.cc/paper/2018/file/7fea637fd6d02b8f0adf6f7dc36aed93-Paper.pdf
16. Jones, A.J.I., Sergot, M.: On the characterization of law and computer systems: the normative systems perspective, pp. 275–307. Wiley, Chichester (1994)
17. Kollock, P.: Social dilemmas: the anatomy of cooperation. Annu. Rev. Sociol. **24**(1), 183–214 (1998). https://doi.org/10.1146/annurev.soc.24.1.183
18. Lerer, A., Peysakhovich, A.: Maintaining cooperation in complex social dilemmas using deep reinforcement learning (2018)
19. Littman, M.L.: Markov games as a framework for multi-agent reinforcement learning. In: Proceedings of the Eleventh International Conference on International Conference on Machine Learning, ICML 1994, pp. 157–163. Morgan Kaufmann Publishers Inc., San Francisco (1994)

20. McKee, K.R., Gemp, I., McWilliams, B., Duèñez Guzmán, E.A., Hughes, E., Leibo, J.Z.: Social diversity and social preferences in mixed-motive reinforcement learning. In: Proceedings of the 19th International Conference on Autonomous Agents and MultiAgent Systems, AAMAS 2020, pp. 869–877. International Foundation for Autonomous Agents and Multiagent Systems, Richland (2020)
21. Mnih, V., et al.: Asynchronous methods for deep reinforcement learning. In: Balcan, M.F., Weinberger, K.Q. (eds.) Proceedings of The 33rd International Conference on Machine Learning. Proceedings of Machine Learning Research, vol. 48, pp. 1928–1937. PMLR, New York, 20–22 June 2016. https://proceedings.mlr.press/v48/mniha16.html
22. Nardin, L.G.: An adaptive sanctioning enforcement model for normative multiagent systems. Ph.D. thesis, Universidade de São Paulo (2015)
23. Neufeld, E., Bartocci, E., Ciabattoni, A., Governatori, G.: A normative supervisor for reinforcement learning agents. In: Platzer, A., Sutcliffe, G. (eds.) CADE 2021. LNCS (LNAI), vol. 12699, pp. 565–576. Springer, Cham (2021). https://doi.org/10.1007/978-3-030-79876-5_32
24. Olson, M.: The Logic of Collective Action: Public Goods and the Theory of Groups. Harvard Economic Studies, vol. 124, p. 176. Harvard University Press, Cambridge (1965). https://www.hup.harvard.edu/catalog.php?isbn=9780674537514
25. Ostrom, E.: Coping with tragedies of the commons. Annu. Rev. Polit. Sci. $\mathbf{2}$(1), 493–535 (1999). https://doi.org/10.1146/annurev.polisci.2.1.493
26. Ostrom, E.: Collective action and the evolution of social norms. J. Econ. Perspect. $\mathbf{14}$(3), 137–158 (2000). https://doi.org/10.1257/jep.14.3.137
27. Pérolat, J., Leibo, J.Z., Zambaldi, V., Beattie, C., Tuyls, K., Graepel, T.: A multi-agent reinforcement learning model of common-pool resource appropriation. In: Guyon, I., et al. (eds.) Advances in Neural Information Processing Systems, vol. 30. Curran Associates, Inc. (2017). https://proceedings.neurips.cc/paper/2017/file/2b0f658cbffd284984fb11d90254081f-Paper.pdf
28. Raffin, A., Hill, A., Gleave, A., Kanervisto, A., Ernestus, M., Dormann, N.: Stable-baselines3: reliable reinforcement learning implementations. J. Mach. Learn. Res. $\mathbf{22}$(268), 1–8 (2021). http://jmlr.org/papers/v22/20-1364.html
29. Sutton, R.S., Barto, A.G.: Reinforcement Learning: An Introduction, 2nd edn. The MIT Press, Cambridge (2018)
30. Terry, J.K., et al.: PettingZoo: a standard API for multi-agent reinforcement learning. In: Advances in Neural Information Processing Systems (2021). https://proceedings.neurips.cc//paper/2021/file/7ed2d3454c5eea71148b11d0c25104ff-Paper.pdf
31. Ullmann-Margalit, E.: The Emergence of Norms. Oxford University Press, Oxford (1977)
32. Zhang, K., Yang, Z., Başar, T.: Multi-agent reinforcement learning: a selective overview of theories and algorithms. In: Vamvoudakis, K.G., Wan, Y., Lewis, F.L., Cansever, D. (eds.) Handbook of Reinforcement Learning and Control. SSDC, vol. 325, pp. 321–384. Springer, Cham (2021). https://doi.org/10.1007/978-3-030-60990-0_12
33. Zheng, S., et al.: The AI economist: improving equality and productivity with AI-driven tax policies (2020)

Supporting the Reasoning About Environmental Consequences of Institutional Actions

Rafhael R. Cunha[1,2]([✉]) [iD], Jomi F. Hübner[2] [iD], and Maiquel de Brito[3] [iD]

[1] Federal Institute of Education, Science and Technology of Rio Grande do Sul (IFRS), Campus Vacaria, Vacaria, Brazil
[2] Automation and Systems Department, Federal University of Santa Catarina, Florianópolis, Brazil
rafhael.cunha@posgrad.ufsc.br, jomi.hubner@ufsc.br
[3] Control, Automation, and Computation Engineering Department, Federal University of Santa Catarina, Blumenau, Brazil
maiquel.b@ufsc.br

Abstract. In this paper we are considering multi-agent systems (MAS) with agents that have both goals and anti-goals. Goals represent environment states that agents want to achieve and anti-goals represent environment states they want to avoid. To achieve their goals, agents perform some actions that may have institutional consequences. Which could potentially change the environment towards as a counter effect. Since these consequences are institutional, they should be explicitly specified so that agents are able take them into consideration in their decision process. However, existing models of artificial institutions do not consider such consequences. Considering this problem, this paper proposes to extend the institutional specification making explicit the implications of the institutional actions in the environment. The proposal is presented, discussed and implemented using the JaCaMo framework, highlighting its advantages for agents while reasoning about the consequences of their action both in the institution and the environment.

Keywords: Purposes · Status-functions · Artificial institutions

1 Introduction

The achievement of the goals of an agent may depend on some status assigned to the actions that it performs instead of depending on the actions themselves. Consider a scenario where an agent called *sBob* has the goal of *conquering a new territory*. The agent knows from some available guidelines that the goal is achieved by performing a digital action (e.g. sending a message, posting on a webservice) that has the status (or *counts as*) *commanding an attack*. This action is supposed to produce in the environment the effects corresponding to such status (e.g. destroying buildings, killing opponents, etc.). However, these

N. Ajmeri et al. (Eds.): COINE 2022, LNAI 13549, pp. 134–147, 2022.
https://doi.org/10.1007/978-3-031-20845-4_9

effects may not be explicit to the agent. It can choose the action to perform based solely on its status.

Inspired by human societies, some works propose models and tools to manage the assignment of *statuses* to the elements involved in the Multi-Agent System (MAS) [15]. In this paper, the element of the system in charge of managing the assignment of status is called *institution*. Through the institution, agents may have the status of *soldiers*, while some of their digital actions may have the status of *commanding an attack*. These works focus on assigning status to the elements that compose the MAS in a process called constitution. However, they do not address the effects in the environment[1] of such statuses. For example, a digital action with the assigned status of *commanding an attack* can trigger a series of consequences in the environment such as *killing a soldier from allied base*, *killing innocent people*, etc. that may be unknown/unwanted to agents and that would not happen if the action did not have the status.

There are some drawbacks of not specifying the consequences in the environment of actions that have a status (see more in [9]). This work focuses on actions whose status leads to a goal achievement but whose effects in the environment are undesirable for the agent. For example, consider an institutional specification stating that *sending a broadcast message has the status of commanding an attack*. In this case, *sBob* can use this specification to discover how to achieve its goal, i.e., by broadcasting a message. However, if the institutional specification does not express the effects in the environment of commanding an attack, *sBob* can not rely on this specification to discover the consequences of broadcasting the message. If *sBob* has the principle of not killing a soldier from the allied base but commanding an attack can make this consequence possible, *sBob* may violate its principle if not aware of these consequences.

Regarding these issues, the main contribution of this paper is a proposal of a mechanism that allows agents to discover what are the consequences in the environment of performing an action that has a status. This proposal is inspired by the Construction of the social reality by John Searle [22,23] theory that seems to be fundamental for comprehending the social reality.

This paper is organized as follows: Sect. 2 introduces the main background concepts necessary to understanding our proposal and its position in the literature. It includes philosophical theory and related works. Section 3 presents the proposed model, its definitions and functions and algorithms to use of the model. Section 4 illustrates how the use of artificial institutions and purposes facilitates the development of agents capable of reasoning about the implications of status actions in the environment. Finally, Sect. 5 presents some conclusions about this work and suggests future works.

---

[1] In this paper, *environment* refers to the set of physical and digital resources which the agents perceive and act upon [26].

2   Artificial Institutions

The problem described in the introduction is rooted in the fact that concrete elements of MAS may have statuses that are not necessarily related to their design features. In MAS, these statuses are managed by Artificial Institutions. Artificial Institutions are inspired by John Searle's theory [22,23], which claims that the social reality where human beings are immersed arises from the concrete world (i.e., the environment) based on some elements, including status-functions and constitutive rules. *Status-functions* are *status* that assign *functions* to the concrete elements [22,23]. These functions cannot be explained through their physical virtues. For example, the status *buyer* assigns to an agent some functions such as perform payments, take loans, etc. *Constitutive rules* specify the assignment of status-functions to concrete elements with the following formula: X count-as Y in C. For example, a piece of paper count-as money in a bank, where X represents the concrete element, Y the status-function, and C the context where that attribute is valid. The attribution of status-functions through constitutive rules to environment elements is called constitution and creates institutional facts. The set of institutional facts gives rise to institutions [22]. Artificial Institutions (or simply *institutions*) are the component of the MAS that is responsible for defining the conditions for an agent to become a *buyer*, or an action to become a *payment* [22,23].

Works on Artificial Institutions are usually inspired by the theory of John Searle [22,23]. Some works present functional approaches, relating brute facts to normative states (e.g., a given action counts as a violation of a norm). These works do not address ontological issues, and, therefore, it becomes even more difficult to support the meaning of abstract concepts present in the institutional reality. Other works have ontological approaches, where brute facts are related to concepts used in the specification of norms (e.g., sending a message counts as a bid in an auction). However, these works have some limitations.

Some approaches allow the agents to reason about the constitutive rules [1, 6,8,10,11,25]. However, generally the *status-function* (Y) is a label assigned to the concrete element (X) that is used in the specification of the regulative norms. Therefore, Y does not seem to have any other purpose than to serve as a basis for the specification of stable regulative norms [1,24]. Some exceptions are (i) in [11–14] where Y represents a class formed with some properties as roles responsible for executing actions, time to execute them, condition for execution, etc.; (ii) in [24] where Y is a general concept, and X is a sub-concept that can be used to explain Y. Although the exceptions contain more information than just a label in the Y element, these data are somehow associated with regulative norms.

In short, existing works in artificial institutions are mainly concerned with specifying and managing the constitution. However, the constitution is based on facts occurring in the environment that may even produce further environmental consequences. While the constitution is explicit, *it is implicit in these works the environmental states that can be reached because an action constitutes a status-function*. In the previous example, while the constitutive rule specifies how to constitute *commanding an attack*, the effects in the environment of commanding an attack are not explicit. Some agent cannot rely on the institutional specification to evaluate the effects in the environment of achieving a goal that depends on the constitution of a status-function. Designers make this association between the constitution of a status-function and its environmental consequences in an ad-hoc manner. The main disadvantage of an ad-hoc association is that the agent works only in scenarios foreseen by the developer.

The limitation discussed indicates the need to develop a model that explains the purposes of status-functions belonging to institutional reality. Aguilar et al. [21] corroborate this conclusion by stating that institutions have not yet considered how to help agents in decision-making, helping them to achieve their own goals. The modeling of purposes of status-functions, described in the next section, is a step to fill this open gap.

3 The Purposes of Status-Functions

The mentioned issues are associated with the relationship between constitutions of status-functions and their consequences in the environment. While works on MAS ignore these relations, Searle addresses them under the notion of *Purpose* [22,23]. Functions related to statuses are called agentive functions because they are assigned from the practical interests of agents [23, p.20]. These practical interests of agents are called *purposes* [22, p.58]. Thus, the purposes point to the consequences in the environment of the constitution of status-functions that are aligned with the agents' interests. For example, someone has a goal of *inhabiting a piece of land* when he broadcasts a message that institutionally is considered as *commanding an attack*. In this example, *inhabiting a piece of land* represents a state of the world that is pointed by a purpose. This state is enabled (and will probably happen) when the status-function *commanding an attack* is constituted. The states must reflect the interest of the agents involved in that context. Moreover, the agents involved in the interaction should have a common understanding of these facts and purposes and consider them in their deliberation. Otherwise, none of them achieve their social goal[2].

The essential elements of the proposed model are *agents*, *states*, *institutions*, and *purposes*, depicted in the Fig. 1. *Agents* are autonomous entities that pursue their goals in the MAS [28]. The literature presents several definitions of *goal* that are different but complementary to each other (see more in [3,16–18,20,27]). In this work, *goals* are something that agents aim to achieve (e.g. a certain state, the performance of an action. According to Aydemir, et al. [2], *anti-goal* is an undesired circumstance of the system. In this work, *anti-goal* represents states that the agent does not wish to reach for ethical reasons, particular values, prohibition by some regulative norm, etc. Moreover, agents can perform actions that trigger events in the MAS. If this action produces events that may constitute some status-function, this action is an *institutional action*. *States* are formed by

---

[2] In this paper, a social goal is an goal that depends on other agents acting on the system.

one or more properties that describe the characteristics of the system at some point of its execution [7].

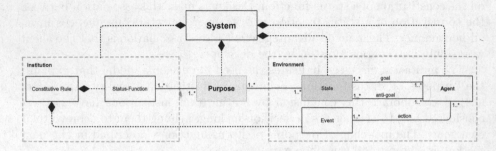

Fig. 1. Overview of the model.

Institutions provide the social interpretation of the environmental elements of the MAS as usually proposed in the literature. This social interpretation occurs through the interpretation of constitutive rules that assign status to environmental elements, as described in Sect. 2. It is beyond the scope of this paper to propose a model of artificial institution. Rather, it considers this general notion of the institution as the entity that constitutes status-functions, that is adopted by several models in the field of MAS.

While *agents*, *states* and *institutions* are known concepts, *purposes* are introduced in this model. The functions associated with status-functions can satisfy the practical interests of agents. From the institution's perspective, these interests are called *Purposes*. From the agents' perspective, these interests are their goals or anti-goals. Then, we claim that (i) *the goals or anti-goals of the agents match with the purposes of the status-functions* and (ii) *goals, anti-goals and purposes point to environmental states related to the status-functions*. For example, in the war scenario, an agent that performs an action that counts as *commanding an attack* triggers intermediate events that bring the system to states such as *conquer a new territory* (i.e., the agent goal) or *killing a soldier from the allied base* (i.e., the agent anti-goal). The intermediate events (e.g. shoot someone) between the constitution of the status-functions and the environmental states reached are ignored in our proposal, since we consider that the agent is only interested in the states that can be reached after the status-functions is constituted.

Shortly, this model provides two relationships: (i) between purposes and status-functions and (ii) between purposes and agent goals and anti-goals. Thus, if (i) there is a constitutive rule specifying how a status-function is constituted, (ii) a purpose associated with that status-functions, and (iii) an agent that has a goal or anti-goal that matches with the states pointed to by the purpose, then it is explicit how the agent should act to achieve its goal or avoid an anti-goal. In the previous example, *sBob* can know that if it constitutes the status-function *commanding an attack* to satisfy its goal of *conquering a new territory*, some other states will be reached such as *killing a soldier from the allied base, killing innocent people*, which may be undesirable to the agent.

3.1 Definitions

This section formally[3] describes the model by specifying (i) the purposes associated with the status-functions and (ii) the purposes associated with the consequences in the environment of constituting status-functions. These consequences are states of the world that agents want to reach or prefer to avoid. Although the concept of purpose is independent, it is used in conjunction with the states, agents and institutions that make up the MAS.

Definitions 1 to 5 represent the MAS states, events, agents, agents goals and anti-goals, and the relationships that exist between these concepts. These definitions express the environmental elements that belong to the MAS (expressed in the Environment rectangle in the Fig. 1). Definitions 6 and 7 are imported from the Situated Artificial Institution (SAI) model [5,10] and represent the elements that make up the institution and its connection with the environmental elements (expressed in the Institution rectangle in the Fig. 1). The Definitions 8 to 11 represent the purposes and the relationships that exist between them and the institution and between purpose and the states of the world that agents wish to achieve or avoid (expressed in the Purpose rectangle and its relations in the Fig. 1).

Definition 1 (States). *Properties are characteristics of the system at some point of its execution. The set of all properties that the system can present is represented by $\mathcal{T}$. The state of the system at some point of its execution is the set of all the standing properties. $\mathcal{S} = 2^{\mathcal{T}}$ is the set of all the possible states of the MAS. For example, the sets* s1 = {*territory conquered*} *and* s2 = {*killed from allied base*} *define states that exist in the MAS, where* s1 $\in \mathcal{S}$ *and* s2 $\in \mathcal{S}$.

Definition 2 (Events). *Event is an instantaneous occurrence within the system [7]. Events may be both triggered by actions of the agents (e.g. sending of a message) and spontaneously produced by some non autonomous element (e.g. a clock tick). The set of all events that may happen in the system is represented by $\mathcal{E}$. Each event is represented by an identifier. For example, the set $\mathcal{E}$ =* {*broadcast a message*} *defines the event that can happen in the MAS.*

Definition 3 (Agents). *The set of all agents that can act in the MAS is represented by $\mathcal{A}$. Each agent is represented by an identifier. For example, the set $\mathcal{A}$ =* {*sBob*} *defines the agent that exists in the MAS.*

---

[3] We formalize the model to make it more accurate and facilitate the development of algorithms that can be used to improve the agents' decision process.

Definition 4 (Relationship between Agents and their goals). *In this work, agents goals are states of the world that agents desire to reach[4]. The set of the goals of the agents acting in the system is given by $\mathcal{G} \subseteq \mathcal{A} \times \mathcal{S}$. For example, the pair $\langle sBob, territory\ conquered \rangle \in \mathcal{G}$ means that the agent sBob has the goal territory conquered.*

Definition 5 (Relationship between Agents and their anti-goals). *Anti-goals are states in the MAS that agents desire to avoid. The set of the anti-goals of the agents is given by $\overline{G} \subseteq \mathcal{A} \times \mathcal{S}$. For example, the pair $\langle sBob, soldier\ killed from\ allied\ base \rangle \in \overline{G}$ means that the agent sBob has the anti-goal "soldier killed from allied base". From a general point of view, there is no difference between an anti-goal and the denial of a goal (the negation of a goal). However, to avoid the addition of negated goals in the model, we opted to have explicit anti-goals. The intersection between agent goal and anti-goal should be empty ($\mathcal{G} \cap \overline{G} = \emptyset$).*

Definition 6 (Status-Functions). *A status is an identifier that assigns to the environmental elements an accepted position, especially in a social group. It allows the environmental elements to perform functions (associated with the status) that cannot be explained through its physical structure [22, p.07]. For simplicity, in this formalization we only consider statuses assigned to events. The set of all the event-status-functions of an institution is represented by $\mathcal{F}$. For example, the set $\mathsf{f} = \{command\ an\ attack\}$ defines a status that exists in the MAS, where $\mathsf{f} \subseteq \mathcal{F}$.*

Definition 7 (Constitutive rules). *Constitutive rules specify the constitution of status-functions from environmental elements. Searle proposes to express these rules as X count-as Y in C, explained in Sect. 2. Since the process of constitution is beyond the scope of this paper, the element C can be ignored. For simplicity, a constitutive rule is hereinafter expressed as X count-as Y. The set of all constitutive rules of an institution is represented by $\mathcal{C}$. A constitutive rule $c \subseteq \mathcal{C}$ is a tuple $\langle x, y \rangle$, where $x \in \mathcal{E}$ and $y \in \mathcal{F}$, meaning that x count-as y. For example, the set $c = \{\langle broadcast\ a\ message, command\ an\ attack \rangle\}$ defines a constitutive rule related to the scenario.*

Definition 8 (Purposes). *The purposes are related to the agents' practical interests. We assume that the set of all purposes is represented by $\mathcal{P}$. Each purpose is represented by an identifier. For example, the set $\mathcal{P} = \{new\_territory\}$, define the unique purpose that exists in the MAS.*

Definition 9 (Relationship between status-functions and purposes). *We define that purposes can be satisfied through the constitution of status-functions. Thus, there must be a relationship between these two concepts. This relation is represented by $\mathcal{F}_P \subseteq \mathcal{F} \times \mathcal{P}$. For example, $\{\langle command\ an\ attack,\ new\_territory \rangle\} \in$*

---

[4] We focus on declarative goals (i.e., goals that describe desirable situations) because we are interested in the effects of the constitution of status-functions that may even produce further environmental consequences (i.e., new states of the world). There are some other types of goals (e.g. procedural goal) that focus on the execution of the action and therefore are not compatible with the concept of purpose.

$\mathcal{F}_P$ means that the constitution of the status-function command an attack satisfies the purpose new territory.

Definition 10 (Relationship between purposes and agent's goals and anti-goals). *The relationship between purpose and agent goal and anti-goal considers that a purpose point to one or more states in the MAS that matches the agents goals and anti-goals. The relationship $\mathcal{G}_P$ is a tuple $\langle p, a_{gag} \rangle$ where $p \in \mathcal{P}$ and $a_{gag} \in 2^{\mathcal{G} \cup \overline{G}}$. For example, the set $\mathcal{G}_P = \{\langle new\_territory, \{territory\ conquered\}, \{soldier\ killed\ from\ allied\ base\} \rangle\}$ defines the relation that exists between the purpose and the states of the world that it points that match with agents' goal or anti-goal.*

Definition 11 (Model). *The model is a tuple $\langle S, \mathcal{E}, \mathcal{A}, \mathcal{A}_{GA}, \mathcal{F}, \mathcal{C}, \mathcal{P}, \mathcal{F}_P, \mathcal{G}_P \rangle$, where S is the set of states that may be maintained in the MAS, $\mathcal{E}$ is the set of events happen that may happen in the MAS, $\mathcal{A}$ is the set of agents that can act in the MAS, $\mathcal{A}_{GA}$ is the set of goals and anti-goals of agents (i.e., $\mathcal{A}_{GA} = \mathcal{G} \cup \overline{G}$), $\mathcal{F}$ is the set of status-functions, $\mathcal{C}$ is the set of constitutive-rules that may exists in the MAS, $\mathcal{P}$ is the set of purposes, $\mathcal{F}_P$ is set that expresses the relationship between the $\mathcal{F}$ and $\mathcal{P}$ sets and $\mathcal{G}_P$ is the set that represents the relationship between $\mathcal{P}$ and $\mathcal{A}_{GA}$.*

3.2 Functions and Algorithms

In this section we formalize some functions that can be used by an agent to discover the environmental effects of performing an institutional action. For that, we need the status-functions related to the events produced by an action (Definition 14), the purposes of these status-functions (Definition 12), and the states of these purposes (Definition 13). In the example of this paper, *sBob* knows by doing *broadcast a message* that it satisfies its goal. With the proposed functions, it can discover that this action has other consequences (e.g., someone being killed) which are among its anti-goals. It may thus avoid that action to achieve its goal.

Definition 12 (Mapping status-functions to purposes). *Given a set $\mathcal{F}$ of status-functions and a set $\mathcal{P}$ of purposes, the set of purposes that are enabled when a status-function is constituted is given by the function $fp : \mathcal{F} \rightarrow 2^{\mathcal{P}}$ s.t. $fp(f) = \{p \mid \langle f, p \rangle \in \mathcal{F}_P\}$.*

For example, if $\mathcal{F}_P = \{\langle command\ an\ attack,\ new\_territory \rangle\}$, then $fp(command\ an\ attack) = \{new\_territory\}$.

Definition 13 (Mapping purposes to states). *Given a set $\mathcal{P}$ of purposes and a set $\mathcal{A}_{GA}$ ($\mathcal{A}_{GA} = \mathcal{G} \cup \overline{G}$) of agents goals and anti-goals, the set of agents goals and anti-goals that are pointed by a purpose is given by the function $fsw : \mathcal{P} \rightarrow 2^{\mathcal{A}_{GA}}$ s.t. $fsw(p) = \{a_{ga} \mid \langle p, a_{ga} \rangle \in \mathcal{G}_P\}$.*

For example, if $\mathcal{G}_P = \{\langle new\_territory, \{territory\ conquered\}, \{soldier\ killed\ from\ allied\ base\} \rangle\}$, then $fsw(new\_territory) = \{\{territory\ conquered\}, \{soldier\ killed\ from\ allied\ base\}\}$.

Definition 14 (Mapping events to status-functions). *Given a set $\mathcal{F}$ of status-functions and a set of events $\mathcal{E}$, the status-functions that are constituted by an event are given by the function $fc : \mathcal{E} \to 2^{\mathcal{F}}$ s.t. $fc(e) = \{f \mid \langle e, f \rangle \in \mathcal{C}\}$.*

For example, if $\mathcal{C} = \{\langle broadcast\ a\ message, command\ an\ attack\ \rangle\}$, then $fc(broadcast\ a\ message) = \{command\ an\ attack\}$.

Definition 15 (Mapping status-functions to events). *Given a set $\mathcal{F}$ of status-functions and a set of events $\mathcal{E}$, the events that constitute the status-functions are given by the function $fca : \mathcal{F} \to 2^{\mathcal{E}}$ s.t. $fca(f) = \{e \mid \langle e, f \rangle \in \mathcal{C}\}$.*

For example, if $\mathcal{C} = \{\langle broadcast\ a\ message, command\ an\ attack\ \rangle\}$, then $fca(command\ an\ attack) = \{broadcast\ a\ message\}$.

From these functions, the Algorithm 1 can be used by the agent to find out which are the environmental effects if some action is executed in an institutional context. The algorithm can be summarized in some steps: (1) verify whether the action is an institutional action, i.e., it its events constitutes something in the institution (lines 4 and 5), if true, go to the next step, otherwise returns the empty set (line 12); (2) consider all status-functions related to the action (line 6); (3) consider all purposes of such status-functions (line 7); and (4) for each purpose, looks for the states it points to and add them in the answer of the algorithm.

Algorithm 1. Find the effects of an action in the environment

---

```
 1: Input: an action ac
 2: Output: the set of possible states after ac
 3: s ← {}
 4: e ← event produced by action ac
 5: if fc(e) ≠ {} then          ▷ if the event e may constitute a status-functions
 6:     for f ∈ fc(e) do        ▷ f is the set of status-functions that e count-as
 7:         for p ∈ fp(f) do     ▷ p is the set of purposes that are associated with f
 8:             s ← s ∪ fsw(p)              ▷ add states pointed to by p
 9:         end for
10:     end for
11: end if
12: return s
```

To verify if some action can produce some state considered as an anti-goal, we developed Algorithm 2. To illustrate it, in the case of *sBob* considering the action *broadcast a message* to achieve some goal, the execution of the algorithm for this action returns *true*, meaning that the action can also produce effects considered as an anti-goal.

Algorithm 2. Verifies whether some action can produce states considered as anti-goals.

1: **Input:** $\overline{G}$, ac
2: **Output:** returns true if ac implies anti-goals and false otherwse
3: se ← algorithm 1(ac)   ▷ se is the set of states pointed to by ac
4: **return** $\exists_{ag \in \overline{G}}$ ag ∈ se   ▷ checks whether anti goals are included in se

---

4   Implementing the Purpose Model

To illustrate the use of this model, we recall the example introduced at the beginning of this paper: the scenario where *sBob* desires to reach its goal of *territory conquered*. To this end, *sBob* knows that to achieve *territory conquered*, it needs to perform an (institutional) action that count-as *commanding an attack*. From the constitutive rule — *broadcast a message count-as commanding an attack* — it knows that it needs to *broadcast a message* to achieve its goal. The purpose model it is possible to specify that the status-function *commanding an attack* is associated with the purpose *new_territory*, which, on its turn, is associated with a state with the following properties: *territory conquered* and *soldier killed from the allied base*. Thus, *sBob* is now able to reason about the consequences of performing the action *broadcast a message* in the institutional context. Such an institution could include other status-functions but, for simplicity, we focus only on those essential to illustrate the main features of the model proposed in Sect. 3.

The example is implemented through the components depicted in Fig. 2. The agent *sBob* is programmed in Jason [4] and the environment in CArtAgO [19]. To implement the artificial institution, we use an implementation of the Situated Artificial Institution model (SAI) model [10]. It provides means to specify status-functions and constitutive rules and to manage the constitution process. The purpose model is implemented through an ontology encapsulated in a CArtAgO artifact which is accessible to the agents. The query and persistence of data in the ontology are enabled by the MasOntology[5], a set of tools developed in CArtAgO to interact with ontologies[6].

Figure 3 depicts the agent program. Line 1 specifies an anti-goal of *sBob*. *sBob* goal can be achieved by the plan illustrated in lines 3–11. This plan creates subgoals `alg1` and `alg2` that can be achieved by plans in lines 13–22, which are the Jason implementation of Algorithms 1 and 2. Regarding the plan for `alg1`, if the `Action` does not constitute a status-function, the `States` are empty (line 17). Otherwise, some operations are used to retrieve the list of `States` related to the action in lines 14 and 15. Regarding the plan for `alg2`, it simply gets the list of states from `alg1` and tests if some anti-goal is member of this list. The result is unified with variable R. The value of R is then used to decide whether to

---

[5] https://github.com/smart-pucrs/MasOntology.
[6] An initial implementation of this platform can be found in https://github.com/rafhaelrc/psf_model.

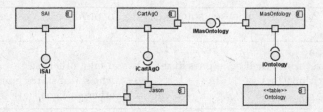

Fig. 2. Component diagram with the systems used to compose the example.

```
1 anti_goal(kill_soldier_from_allied_base).
2
3 +!territory_conquered
4     <- // broadcasting_a_message is the action that achieves the goal territory_conquered
5         !alg2(broadcasting_a_message, R);
6         if(R){
7           .fail;
8         }
9         else{
10          broadcasting_a_message;
11        }.
12
13 +!alg1(Action,States) : constitutive_rule(Action,Status_Functions,_,_)
14     <- getPurposeOfStatusFunctions(Status_Functions, NamePurposes);
15        getStatesOfPurposes(NamePurposes, States).
16
17 +!alg1(Action,[]). // if there is no constitutive rule
18
19 +! alg2(Action, R)
20    <-
21        !alg1(Action, States);
22        R = (anti_goal(AG) & .member(Ag,States)).
```

Fig. 3. Plan of the agent *sBob*.

execute **broadcasting_a_message**, if R is **false** it means that the action does not promote some of the agent anti-goals.

The code snippet depicted in Fig. 3 illustrates how the algorithms and the model proposed in this work can be used by the agent to check if the action to be performed can constitute a status-functions and enable new states in the system and verify if these new states are unwanted by the agent. We can notice that the code from lines 6 to 11 are just an example of how the proposed model and algorithms can be used. Of course, more complex solutions could be developed for other applications.

5   Conclusions and Future Work

The problem motivating this paper is some difficulty for agents to reason about the consequences in the environment when performing an action that has an institutional interpretation (i.e., it has a status-function). To help agents with this issue, we introduce the notion of *purpose* in artificial institutions. Purposes connect two concepts: *status-functions* in the institutional side and *goals and anti-goals* in the agent side. While status-functions represent how the environment changes the institution, purposes represent how the institution can potentially change the environment. From an agent perspective, their goals and anti-goals are also considered in the proposal: purposes point to states of the world that are of interest to the agents. Thus, the model connects institutional facts with the interests of the agents.

The main advantage of purposes in MAS regards the agents. We have an improvement in agent decision-making, since it has more information available to help it to decide whether to achieve its goals or avoid its anti-goals. With the proposed model, agents can access and reason about the consequences of institutional actions and adapt themselves to different scenarios. They can notice that (a) some purposes point to states that are similar to their interests and therefore useful to reach their goals or (b) avoid these purposes because they point to states that are similar to their anti-goals. In both cases, the agent has more information while deciding whether a particular action will help it or not. This kind of reasoning is important for advances in agents autonomy [21].

As future work, we plan to explore additional theoretical aspects related to the proposal, such as (i) investigations about how other proposed institutional abstractions (e.g. social functions) fit on the model, and (ii) check if the purposes related to status must be further detailed. We plan to also address more practical points such as (i) the modeling of a status-functions purposes based on a real scenario, (ii) the implementation of the proposal in a computer system (iii) its integration in an computational model that implements the constitution of status-functions in an MAS platform and (iv) evaluate the application of the model in scenarios that involve ethical reasoning of agents.

Acknowledgments. This study was supported by the Federal Institute of Education, Science and Technology of Rio Grande do Sul (IFRS). We thank the reviewers for the valuable contributions that allowed this work to evolve.

References

1. Aldewereld, H., Álvarez-Napagao, S., Dignum, F., Vázquez-Salceda, J.: Making norms concrete. In: Proceedings of the 9th International Conference on Autonomous Agents and Multiagent Systems: volume 1, vol. 1, pp. 807–814. International Foundation for Autonomous Agents and Multiagent Systems (2010)
2. Aydemir, F.B., Giorgini, P., Mylopoulos, J.: Multi-objective risk analysis with goal models. In: 2016 IEEE Tenth International Conference on Research Challenges in Information Science (RCIS), pp. 1–10. IEEE (2016)
3. Boissier, O., Bordini, R.H., Hubner, J., Ricci, A.: Multi-Agent Oriented Programming: Programming Multi-agent Systems Using JaCaMo. MIT Press, Cambridge (2020)
4. Bordini, R.H., Hübner, J.F., Wooldridge, M.: Programming Multi-Agent Systems in AgentSpeak Using Jason, vol. 8. Wiley, Hoboken (2007)
5. de Brito, M., et al.: A model of institucional reality supporting the regulation in artificial institutions. Ph.D. thesis, Universidade Federal de Santa Catarina (2016)
6. Cardoso, H.L., Oliveira, E.: Institutional reality and norms: specifying and monitoring agent organizations. Int. J. Coop. Inf. Syst. **16**(01), 67–95 (2007). https://doi.org/10.1142/s0218843007001573

7. Cassandras, C.G., Lafortune, S.: Introduction to Discrete Event Systems. Springer, New York (2008). https://doi.org/10.1007/978-0-387-68612-7
8. Cliffe, O., De Vos, M., Padget, J.: Specifying and reasoning about multiple institutions. In: Noriega, P., et al. (eds.) COIN 2006. LNCS (LNAI), vol. 4386, pp. 67–85. Springer, Heidelberg (2007). https://doi.org/10.1007/978-3-540-74459-7_5
9. Cunha, R.R., Hübner, J.F., de Brito, M.: Coupling purposes with status-functions in artificial institutions. arXiv preprint arXiv:2105.00090 (2021)
10. De Brito, M., Hübner, J.F., Boissier, O.: Situated artificial institutions: stability, consistency, and flexibility in the regulation of agent societies. Auton. Agents Multi-Agent Syst. **32**(2), 219–251 (2018)
11. Fornara, N.: Specifying and monitoring obligations in open multiagent systems using semantic web technology. In: Elçi, A., Koné, M.T., Orgun, M.A. (eds.) Semantic agent systems. SCI, vol. 344, pp. 25–45. Springer, Heidelberg (2011). https://doi.org/10.1007/978-3-642-18308-9_2
12. Fornara, N., Colombetti, M.: Ontology and time evolution of obligations and prohibitions using semantic web technology. In: Baldoni, M., Bentahar, J., van Riemsdijk, M.B., Lloyd, J. (eds.) DALT 2009. LNCS (LNAI), vol. 5948, pp. 101–118. Springer, Heidelberg (2010). https://doi.org/10.1007/978-3-642-11355-0_7
13. Fornara, N., Colombetti, M.: Representation and monitoring of commitments and norms using owl. AI Commun. **23**(4), 341–356 (2010)
14. Fornara, N., Tampitsikas, C.: Using OWL artificial institutions for dynamically creating open spaces of interaction. In: AT, pp. 281–295 (2012)
15. Fornara, N., Viganò, F., Colombetti, M.: Agent communication and artificial institutions. Auton. Agents Multi-Agent Syst. **14**(2), 121–142 (2007). https://doi.org/10.1007/s10458-006-0017-8
16. Hindriks, K.V., de Boer, F.S., van der Hoek, W., Meyer, J.-J.C.: Agent programming with declarative goals. In: Castelfranchi, C., Lespérance, Y. (eds.) ATAL 2000. LNCS (LNAI), vol. 1986, pp. 228–243. Springer, Heidelberg (2001). https://doi.org/10.1007/3-540-44631-1_16
17. Hübner, J.F., Bordini, R.H., Wooldridge, M.: Declarative goal patterns for AgentSpeak. In: Proceedings of the Fifth International Joint Conference on Autonomous Agents and Multiagent Systems (AAMAS 2006) (2006)
18. Nigam, V., Leite, J.: A dynamic logic programming based system for agents with declarative goals. In: Baldoni, M., Endriss, U. (eds.) DALT 2006. LNCS (LNAI), vol. 4327, pp. 174–190. Springer, Heidelberg (2006). https://doi.org/10.1007/11961536_12
19. Ricci, A., Piunti, M., Viroli, M.: Environment programming in multi-agent systems: an artifact-based perspective. Auton. Agents Multi-Agent Syst. **23**(2), 158–192 (2011)
20. van Riemsdijk, B., van der Hoek, W., Meyer, J.J.C.: Agent programming in dribble: from beliefs to goals using plans. In: Proceedings of the Second International Joint Conference on Autonomous Agents and Multiagent Systems, pp. 393–400 (2003)
21. Rodriguez-Aguilar, J.A., Sierra, C., Arcos, J.L., Lopez-Sanchez, M., Rodriguez, I.: Towards next generation coordination infrastructures. Knowle. Eng. Rev. **30**(4), 435–453 (2015). https://doi.org/10.1017/S0269888915000090
22. Searle, J.: Making the Social World: The Structure of Human Civilization. Oxford University Press, Oxford (2010)
23. Searle, J.R.: The Construction of Social Reality. Simon and Schuster, New York (1995)

24. Vázquez-Salceda, J., Aldewereld, H., Grossi, D., Dignum, F.: From human regulations to regulated software agents' behavior. Artif. Intell. Law **16**(1), 73–87 (2008)
25. Vigano, F., Colombetti, M.: Model checking norms and sanctions in institutions. In: International Workshop on Coordination, Organizations, Institutions, and Norms in Agent Systems pp. 316–329 (2007)
26. Weyns, D., Omicini, A., Odell, J.: Environment as a first class abstraction in multiagent systems. Auton. Agents Multi-Agent Syst. **14**(1), 5–30 (2007)
27. Winikoff, M., Padgham, L., Harland, J., Thangarajah, J.: Declarative and procedural goals in intelligent agent systems. In: International Conference on Principles of Knowledge Representation and Reasoning. Morgan Kaufman (2002)
28. Wooldridge, M.: An Introduction to Multiagent Systems. Wiley, Chichester (2009)

Social Motives and Social Contracts in Cooperative Survival Games

Matthew Scott[1] , Mathieu Dubied[1,2] , and Jeremy Pitt[1(✉)]

[1] Imperial College London, London SW7 2BX, UK
{mss2518,md1721,jpitt}@ic.ac.uk
[2] ETH Zürich, 8092 Zürich, Switzerland

Abstract. Cooperative survival games are a sub-class of resource competition games wherein self-interest appears to be the rational choice in the short-term, but if every 'player' always acts out of self-interest, extinction is guaranteed in the long-term. The situation is dramatised in the film *The Platform* (*El Hoyo*); in this paper, we implement a self-organising multi-agent system that approximately recreates the cooperative survival game depicted in this film. In a series of experiments, we investigate how communication, a pre-existing tendency to sociality (characterised by social motives) and a capacity for social construction (characterised by social contracts) enables a collective of random individuals to establish a stable institution that increases their overall life expectancy. The experimental results provide some insight into how a pro-social personality and the ability to bootstrap institutions enable a random collective to find a psychologically and sociologically plausible solution to what is effectively a cooperative survival game merged with Rawl's *Veil of Ignorance*.

Keywords: Multi-agent system · Social contracts · Collective action

1 Introduction

Cooperative survival games are a sub-class of iterative resource competition games wherein self-interest appears to be the rational choice in the short-term, but if every 'player' always acts out of self-interest, elimination or extinction is inevitable in the long-term. The players need to maintain a critical mass that can gather sufficient resources to survive this iteration to ensure that there are sufficient players to survive the next iteration. Dropping below a certain threshold means that "if one is lost, all are lost".

Cooperative survival games are a popular form of entertainment in low- or zero-stakes entertainment, as seen in board games (e.g. *Ravine*) and computer games (e.g. *Don't Starve*, *Rust* and *Minecraft*), and have been analysed extensively in anthropological studies of collective behaviour in extreme environmental conditions [3,12]. Addressing anthropogenic climate change can be seen as a

Supported by Imperial College London and the Swiss Study Foundation.

high-stakes cooperative survival game on a planetary scale with nation states as the players.

Ostrom has shown how collectives have solved the common-pool resource management (CPR) problem by using self-governing institutions [15], i.e. sets of mutable, mutually-agreed conventional rules which the members voluntarily regulate their behaviour. Considering a cooperative survival games as a form of extreme, high-stakes CPR problem where any one individual maximising self-interest or free-riding is an existential hazard to all, this paper addresses the question of how to bootstrap the formation of such an institution from a starting position of complete ignorance. In this initial situation, the players have no knowledge of the other players, and there are no rules, no social network, and no external authority. The players only have their personal psychological characteristics (which we call *social motives*) and an ability for the social construction [2] of social contracts (which we call *treaties*).

Accordingly, this paper is structured as follows. In Sect. 2, we first present a scenario, which is based on the film *The Platform* (*El Hoyo*), and related work that provides the background to the multi-agent simulator developed in Sect. 3, and the social motives for agents specified in Sect. 4. Section 5 presents the experimental results which show how communication, a pre-existing tendency to sociality (characterised by social motives) and a capacity for social construction (characterised by social contracts or treaties) enables a collective of random individuals to establish a stable institution that increases their overall life expectancy. Finally, Sect. 6 concludes with some observations on how pro-social behaviour and the ability to bootstrap institutions enable a collective to find a psychologically and sociologically plausible solution to what is effectively a cooperative survival game merged with Rawl's *Veil of Ignorance* [18].

2   Scenario and Related Work

For this paper, we consider the social dilemma presented the 2019 film 'The Platform' (*El Hoyo*). This film envisions a tower consisting of N floors with a pair of prisoners on each floor.

A platform laden with food descends through a central shaft in the tower, starting from floor 1, at the very top, and stopping at consecutive floors. The prisoners are allowed to eat as much as they want while the platform has stopped on their floor, but cannot save food "for later". At the beginning of each day, the platform is replenished with food and descends again, always starting at the top of the tower.

Obviously it is advantageous to be on a low-numbered (upper) floor to have first access to the food on the platform; however there is a 'reshuffle' after D days, with all the agents are randomly re-assigned to new floors, and with no knowledge of which floor they will be re-assigned. When an agent dies due to the lack of food, it is replaced by a new agent. The exact rules that our simulator follows to replace the agents are introduced in Sect. 3.

It has been shown that by taking an approach inspired by moral philosophy there are solutions to the *social contract design problem* [5]. This means that, for any non-cooperative game, it is theoretically feasible to define a social contract which produces a modified game that optimises for a moral imperative. In our paper, we distance ourself from the game-theoretic setting used in [5], and rather focus on the effects of specific social contracts in our scenario.

Ostrom's work, as previously mentioned [15], provides empirical evidence that it is practically possible for groups of people to resolve collective action situations through the social construction of self-governing institutions. Effectively, this is identifying the institutions, understood as a set of rules, as the social contract, and sustainability of the common-pool resource as the moral imperative.

The studied setting of this paper can be classified as an iterative game of Rawl's *Veil of Ignorance* [18]. Rawls' Veil of Ignorance is a thought experiment intended to expose the principles, preferences and thought processes that inform the structure of a society. The experiment imagines asking someone, that if they started from a blank slate and no knowledge beforehand of their eventual position in a society, what sort social structures, form of governance, etc., would be selected for such a society. The thought experiment is in many ways analogous to the situation presented in the platform: if the players have no idea beforehand to which tower level they will be assigned, then what sort of principles would they prefer to manage access to the food on the platform.

The question addressed in this paper is under what conditions is it practically possible for groups of *agents* to resolve a collective action situation, specifically that posed by *The Platform* scenario. In this scenario, we presume that the motivation for creating a social contract comes from an abstraction of the psychological concept of *social motives* [14,19], which Folmer describes as "the psychological processes that drive people's thinking, feeling and behavior in interactions with other people." Social motives are further identified as a potential source of conflict, with Folmer also claiming that "the actions that are dictated by one individual's motives are incompatible with, or even harmful to, the interests of others," creating what is termed a 'social dilemma.' In other words, the social contract must not only solve this social dilemma, but must also resolve any residual tension between potentially conflicting social motives.

Although, without loss of generality, we make some modifications to the scenario from the film – for example, we assume one prisoner per floor rather than a pair (although that is only required for dramatic effect), no movement between floors, and direct communication allowed between adjacent floors only (although a message may be propagated along multiple floors, assuming that the prisoners are willing to cooperate). We are assuming strict constraints of no prior knowledge, no pre-existing social network and no external authority, with the additional complications of a dynamic population, where 'new' prisoners are 'injected' into the tower after death, and periodic floor re-assignment. The challenge is then to determine whether, despite the combination of limited communication and varied social motives, a propensity for social construction enables the agents to 'find' a social contract which is a solution to the current formulation of the game and perpetuates across subsequent re-formulations.

3   Simulator Design

To simulate *The Platform*, we implement a self-organising, multi-agent system. This system consists of a set of agents connected by a social network; each link in the social network is associated with a weight. The social network is iteratively constructed by proximity on adjacent levels of the tower through a predefined communication language (not further discussed here). These agents are stored inside a 'tower' data structure which acts a server, handling agent interactions over the network and containing the setup parameters for the simulation.

External to the basic representation of agents in the tower, we further represent the infrastructure of the simulator by modelling the agents' health, global utility, and treaties.

3.1   Health Modelling

All agents have a health value that exists on a continuous spectrum with three additional discrete levels of *criticalLevel*, *weakLevel* and *maxHP*. An agent is considered to have critical health if it falls between the *criticalLevel*, the minimum possible health, and *weakLevel*, the cutoff for the critical region. An agent process is terminated if they remain in this region for N days, equal to *maxDaysCritical*.

An agent's health is updated through two mechanisms: agents eating food (appropriating resources), which causes a positive change, and the cost of living, which causes a negative change.

Mathematically, the mapping between food intake and health is parameterised as follows:

$$newHP = currentHP + w(1 - e^{\frac{-foodTaken}{\tau}}) \tag{1}$$

with τ offered as a tuning parameter to either increase or decrease the magnitude of health change from one unit of food and w a variable to represent the width of the gap between the *weakLevel* and *maxHP*. This function is chosen similarly to a step response function to replicate 'diminishing returns' and prevent rapid changes in health. An agent in the critical region has a slightly different update function:

$$newHP = currentHP + \min\left\{HPReqCToW, w(1 - e^{\frac{-foodTaken}{\tau}})\right\} \tag{2}$$

to ensure that a critical agent must first transition to weak, before applying Eq. (1). Hence, *HPReqCToW* represents the change in health required to transition from the critical region to the weak level.

To offset an agent's health gain, its health will also decay at the end of each day according to the equation:

$$newHP = currentHP - [b + s(currentHP - WeakLevel)] \tag{3}$$

where b and s are parameters that are set constant for all the simulations of this paper. The agent's health is subsequently bounded to the range [*criticalLevel*, *maxHP*]. We note that critical agents are affected differently by health decay. If an agent is unable to achieve *HPReqCToW*, they will be reset to the *criticalLevel*. Conversely, if they do appropriate this food, they will be reset to the *weakLevel*.

3.2   Global Utility

To assess the performance of the agents in the tower as a group, we investigate their *social welfare*, based on each agent's individual utility [16].

In this scenario, each agent $i \in \{1, \ldots, N\}$ carries out four actions at each iteration $t \in \{1, \ldots, \infty\}$: it first determines the resources it has on the platform (g_i), then its need for resources (q_i). After this, it receives an allocation of resources (r_i) from the treaties it has formed and finally makes an appropriation of resources (r_i'). Since agents are programmed to be *honest*, we assert that $r_i' = r_i$.

The need for resources q_i, looks to reward agents who take food only when necessary. Hence:

$$q_i = \frac{numberDaysInCriticalState}{maxDaysInCriticalState} \tag{4}$$

The total resources accrued at the end of an iteration, R_i, is then defined as:

$$R_i = r_i' + g_i \tag{5}$$

which gives the utility per agent:

$$u_i = \begin{cases} \alpha_i q_i + \beta_i(R_i - q_i) & \text{if } R_i \geq q_i \\ \alpha_i R_i - \gamma_i(q_i - R_i) & \text{else} \end{cases} \tag{6}$$

where α_i, β_i and γ_i are tuning parameters that follow the rule $\alpha_i > \gamma_i > \beta_i$. In our work, we use the values $\alpha_i = \alpha = 0.2$, $\beta_i = \beta = 0.1$, and $\gamma_i = \gamma = 0.18$.

Finally, we use (6) to compute an average global utility, which corresponds to the social welfare SW divided by the number of agents:

$$U = \frac{\sum_i^N u_i}{N} = \frac{SW}{N} \tag{7}$$

3.3   Treaties

To successfully handle treaties, an agent must be able to propose, evaluate, and propagate treaties. In addition, we enforce the agents act *honestly*, and therefore comply with the treaties to which they agree. This section aims to describe the general structure of treaties, whereas the actions related to the treaties (proposal, acceptance, etc.) are described in Sect. 4.3.

Treaties are codified as data structures with three main parts: a condition, a request concerning the amount of food to be "taken" or "left" and a duration. Whilst the condition for the validity of the treaty can be any variable, for this paper only the health of the agent is concerned. One such example of a treaty is: "if *currentHP* $\geq$ 60, take $\leq$ 5 food for 5 days.". They serve as an extension of message passing, wherein a treaty is proposed verbally either 1 floor above or below the floor of the proposer. Such proposals happen *asynchronously* in the tower and are implemented with concurrent channels, meaning that all agents can send treaties simultaneously. When a treaty is proposed, it enters the receiver's 'inbox' to be processed.

Table 1. Parameters held in the *Treaty* data structure.

Parameter	Range
Condition	*HP*
ConditionValue	*int*
Request	*[Leave, Take]*
RequestValue	*int*
ConditionOp	$[>, \geq, =, \leq, <]$
RequestOp	$[>, \geq, =, \leq, <]$
SignatureCount	*int*
Duration	*int*
TreatyID	*UUID*
ProposerID	*UUID*

An agent may compile a treaty with $newTreaty(t_1, t_2, \ldots t_n)$, which packages the different treaty parameters, t_i, into the data structure discussed in Table 1 to be subsequently sent as a proposal to an agent. Upon agreeing with a treaty, both agents involved will place this data into their respective *activeTreaties* arrays. The treaties in this array are then processed iteratively to find constraints on the agents' consumption.

4   Agent Design

The N agents in the tower forms a group of agents we name $\mathcal{A}$. Each agent $i \in \mathcal{A}$ are implemented as a data structure with parameterisation to participate in the various communication methods $c \in C$, resulting in a set of interactions defined by $I = <\mathcal{A}, C>$. Each agent inherits from the *baseAgent* structure and also contains the fields contained in Table 2. We note only the most relevant fields for quantifying the agent have been included.

Table 2. The *Config* (left) and *Agent* (right) data structures.

Parameter	Range	Parameter	Range
BaseBehaviour	$int \in [0,10]$	Config	*config{}*
Stubbornness	$float \in [0,1]$	CurrBehaviour	*int*
MaxBehaviourSwing	$int \in [0,10]$	MaxFloorGuess	*int*
ParamWeights	{ *HPW:int, FW:int* }	AverageFoodIntake	*int*
FloorDiscount	$float \in [0,1]$	ShortTermMemory	*[int]*
MaxBehaviour	$int = 10$	LongTermMemory	*[int]*
		ActiveTreaties	*[Treaty]*

4.1   Social Motives

Social Motives Spectrum. The agent's behaviour revolves around the concept of social motives [14], which Folmer defines as "the psychological processes that drive people's thinking, feeling and behavior in interactions with other people" [19]. This in turn leads to a "mixed-motive" setting [20] in the tower. From this concept, we abstract 4 distinct social motives:

Altruist: The disinterested and selfless concern for the well-being of others. An altruist then acts in a way that purely benefits others, even if it means harming themselves.

Collectivist: The practice or principle of giving a group priority over each individual in it. A collectivist then acts in a way that benefits the group, themselves included, over purely the individual.

Selfish: Being concerned excessively or exclusively with oneself. A selfish agent will act in a way to satisfy themselves, but not necessarily with the intent to harm the other agents.

Narcissist: An excessive interest or admiration of oneself. A narcissistic agent will act in a way that not only benefits themselves, but also hinders the collective.

For this implementation, we assert that all agents' social motives can be defined on a spectrum, with one end corresponding to pure altruism, and the other to pure narcissism, which we codify as a continuous value between 0.0 and 10.0 respectively. Figure 1 illustrates the spectrum of social motives.

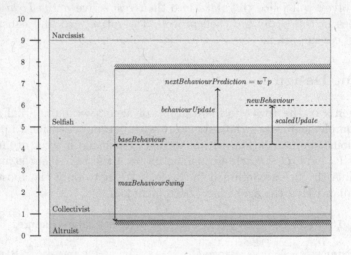

Fig. 1. Illustration of a change in social motive.

Changing Social Motives. This paper proposes that it is both limiting and unrealistic for an agent to express one social motive for its entire lifespan. For this reason, agents are able to dynamically update their initially assigned social motive to reflect the duality of "nature vs nurture" [11]: an agent's genotype does not necessarily match the agent's phenotype.

To codify this idea, we use a 'predictor' that calculates a *behaviourUpdate* from the feature transformations of the 1) current health of the agent (8) and 2) floor that the agent is located on (9). These feature transformations map their respective features to a range $[0, 1]$, with poorer performances (low health, low floor) tending towards 1 to represent a skew towards narcissistic behaviour:

$$hpScore = 1 - \frac{currentHP}{maxHP} \tag{8}$$

Agents forecast the $maxFloor$ by keeping track of the lowest floor they have visited. The lower down the floor, the faster Eq. (9) tends to 1. This is to have the agents tend towards narcissism faster as they reach lower floors. We take λ as the $floorDiscount$ variable from Table 2 to 'tune' the function.

$$floorScore = \frac{e^{\frac{\lambda \cdot currentFloor}{maxFloor}}}{e^{\lambda}} \tag{9}$$

The predictor then weights these feature transformations with the 'HP weight,' HPW and 'floor weight,' FW variables from Table 2 to yield a value in the range $[0, 10]$:

$$p = [hpScore, floorScore]^{\top}, \quad w = [HPW, FW]^{\top}$$
$$nextBehaviourPrediction = w^{\top}p \tag{10}$$

and we construct a vector illustrating the change in social motive as:

$$behaviourUpdate = nextBehaviourPrediction - currentBehaviour \tag{11}$$

This paper further asserts that agents are unlikely to rapidly change their social motive, instead requiring multiple similar experiences to alter their phenotype. We hence offer a concept of $stubbornness$, which limits the vectorial change in $behaviourUpdate$:

$$scaledUpdate = behaviourUpdate \cdot (1 - stubbornness) \tag{12}$$
$$newBehaviour = currentBehaviour + scaledUpdate \tag{13}$$

With the new social motive defined as the movement from the current behaviour using the $scaledUpdate$ vector. Finally, we propose that a genotypically altruistic agent, say, is unlikely to make a severe transition in personality to full narcissism. This is solved by introducing a $maxBehaviourSwing$, which bounds the total change in social motive that an agent can experience.

Agents are also able to dynamically update the weights in Eq. (10) in order to make more permanent shifts towards narcissism if one of the parameters is constantly evaluated poorly. If the agent's health is below 20, we increase HPW by 0.05 and decrease FW by 0.05. Alternatively, if the agent's average food intake is less than 1 per turn, we decrease HPW by 0.1 and increase FW by 0.1. After this update, we ensure that the weights remain in the range $[0, 1]$.

4.2   Food Consumption

Resources are conditionally appropriated depending on both the social motive and environmental factors such as commitments to messages and treaties. The baseline behaviours exhibited by the different social motives are as follows:

Altruist: An altruistic agent always takes 0 food, as it is only concerned for the well-being of others with a total disregard for itself.

Collectivist: A collectivist agent consume the food required to survive, and consumes no food when not in danger of dying. To codify this, agents randomly choose a day in the range [1, *maxDaysCritical*] and take food once they have remained at critical health for this period. This has the effect of staggering when collectivists are able to take food, to prevent the entire tower simultaneously depleting resources.

Selfish: A selfish agent always aims to stay at the *healthyLevel*. This means that it will always appropriate the food required to reach this point.

Narcissist: A narcissistic agent takes maximum amount of food consumable, since it is purely be concerned for its own well-being whilst sabotaging the others.

4.3   Handling Treaties

Evaluating Treaties. It is through the agents interacting with one another that a social network is formed. Agents use techniques from risk assessment, forecasting and utility theory to handle the acceptance or rejection of treaties.

Risk assessment is performed by agents evaluating the link weights against a predefined threshold to decide whether or not to reject a treaty. This is a rudimentary form of 'trust' which represents, in this simulation, an agent's willingness to expose itself to the risk from accepting or rejecting a treaty. Richer computational models of trust are possible [17], but this is not primary focus of the agent's decision-making process.

Given that treaties do not have any immediate effect, but instead influence the future consumption of an agent, agents forecast to assess the present value of a treaty. This is codified by using two separate arrays corresponding to long-term and short-term memory and storing the amount of food received each day (Fig. 2), with the short-term memory reset after each reshuffle. The reason for having two memory types is to allow agents to separately look at the current reshuffle period and total experience in the tower, which aligns with the core assumption in cognitive psychology that there are separate systems for long- and short-term memory [13].

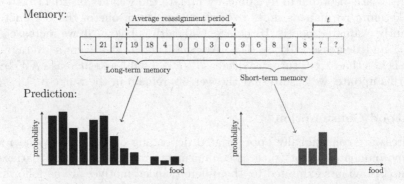

Fig. 2. Illustration of different agent memory types.

Since the reshuffle period is unknown to agents, they forecast this information by averaging over all previous reshuffling periods.

Agents must also contrast the effect that a treaty will have on the *future* food intake to assess if it is beneficial or not. Since the satisfaction of gaining or losing wealth is non-linear [7], utility functions can account for this by mapping the monetary value of a good or service to an individual's preference [6].

Therefore, an agent calculates the expected utility both with and without a treaty and subsequently maximises the estimated future benefit. The utility of gaining an uncertain amount of food per turn, x_i with probability p_i (based on past experience), is computed with:

$$E[U(x)] = p_1 \times U(x_1) + p_2 \times U(x_2) + ... + p_n \times U(x_n) \qquad (14)$$

Prospect theory [10] is a well-established model of how a change in value is perceived or, alternatively, how much utility is gained or lost from a change in value. This model comprises four main principles:

Greediness: Agents are generally greedy, meaning that more of a resource is at least beneficial. Utility functions are hence generally increasing.

Diminishing sensitivity: Marginal returns are strictly decreasing, thus the greater the personal wealth of an agent, the less they value the resource.

Risk aversion: Agents generally try to avoid risk. With risk aversion, the amount of food the agent perceives as equivalent to a random distribution (its *certainty equivalent C*) is hence less than its mean.

$$U(C) = E[U(x)] < U(E[x]) \qquad (15)$$

Loss aversion: Losing some amount of food is generally perceived as worse than gaining that same amount. Agents hence weight loss higher than gain

Using these concepts, we identify a *gain (g)* and *cost (c)* associated with each unit of food received *(x)*, as well as the *risk aversion (r)* to define the utility of receiving a unit of food. The amount of food that the collectivist and selfish agents would need to consume in order to maximise their utility varies depending on the current health level. The peak of its total utility function thus needs to be able to vary too. We account for this by introducing a scaling factor a as:

$$a = \frac{1}{z} \left(\frac{cr}{g} \right)^{\frac{r}{1-r}} \qquad (16)$$

yielding:

$$U(x) = g(ax)^{\frac{1}{r}} - cax \qquad (17)$$

with z being the desired food intake, falling at the maximum of this function.

The utility calculation for each different social motive has been parameterised according to three insights: 1) the more selfish an agent is, the greedier it is, 2) the more an agent cares for the greater good, the greater its social cost associated with consumption and 3) more narcissistic people are generally less risk-averse [4]. The resulting utility functions are shown in Fig. 3.

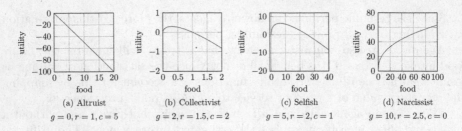

Fig. 3. Different utility functions used to rate treaties according to the social motive of the agents.

Agents also use the proportion of estimated days before the next reshuffle period in order to weight how much they should focus on the short term. To optimise survivability, agents ignore the expected long-term utility when their health is on a critical level.

Let b_{short} and b_{long} be the estimated short and long term benefit of a treaty, respectively. Also, let the estimated days remaining on the current level be given by $d_{current}$ and the duration of a treaty by d_{treaty}. The total benefit, b_{tot} is then:

$$b_{tot} = \frac{d_{current}}{d_{treaty}} \times b_{short} + (1 - \frac{d_{current}}{d_{treaty}}) \times b_{long} \tag{18}$$

Overall, the algorithm that agents follow when considering treaties is summarised as follows:

1. Check if the link weight with the *proposing* agent is above a threshold
2. Check that the treaty does not conflict with treaties the agent already signed[1]
3. Calculate the expected short- and long-term utility according to Eq. (14)
4. Amplify the utility if it is negative to simulate loss-aversion.
5. Calculate the utility of the food it can feasibly take under the treaty
6. Compute the estimated benefits of signing the treaty as U(sign) − U(don't sign)
7. Choose to focus on the long- or short-term benefit according to Eq. (18)
8. Sign the treaty if its overall benefit is positive

Proposing and Propagating Treaties. Altruist agents wish to sacrifice themselves by taking 0 food and narcissist agents wish to sacrifice others by taking all the food. This means that these agent types will never sign treaties, as it goes against their strategy. The collectivist and selfish agents are therefore the two social motives that propose treaties. These proposed treaties are taken from a list of possible treaties, following the structure introduced in Table 1. For this paper, we consider the three following treaties:

- T1: "If *currentHP* > 0.6 × *maxHP*, take 0 food."

---

[1] It is, for example, not possible for an agent to sign a treaty asking it to take 5 food, when it has already signed a treaty requesting it to take 0 food.

- T2: "If *currentHP* ≥ *weakLevel*, take 0 food."
- T3: "If *currentHP* < *weakLevel*, take ≤ 2 food."

T1 can be proposed by the selfish agents, whereas T2 and T3 can be proposed by the collectivist agents. The three treaties are valid for a period of $2D$ days, where D is the 'reshuffling period' as introduced in Sect. 2.

Once a treaty has been accepted or rejected, it is possible for the agent to re-propose the same treaty to its neighbour. Logically, the best possible strategy is to propagate one single treaty throughout the tower and have all agents behave uniformly. Narcissist agents act to avoid this, hoping for the downfall of the collective and hence refuse to propagate treaties. All other agents, however, propagate the treaty five floors above and below if these floors exist.

5 Experimental Results and Discussion

In this section, we use the simulator and agent designs introduced in Sect. 3 and Sect. 4 to assess the performance of the studied system.

We divide the simulations into 4 groups (A to D) characterised by having different initialisation parameters. Table 3 summarises the simulations parameters for each simulation. The percentages of each social motive (first four rows of the table) correspond to the initial distribution of the agents' 'types'. If not explicitly mentioned, we run experiments using 100 agents, with 100 food initially on the platform for 60 days and with a reshuffle period D of 30 days. As mentioned in Sect. 2, the agents are replaced upon death, following the distribution given in Table 3. Our simulations results are given as the average over 30 repeated simulations.

Table 3. Summary of the experiments.

	A1	A2	A3	A4	B1	B2	C1	C2	C3	D1	D2
% Altruist	100	0	0	0	10	0	10	10	10	100	100
% Collectivist	0	100	0	0	40	80	40	40	40	0	0
% Selfish	0	0	100	0	40	20	40	40	40	0	0
% Narcissist	0	0	0	100	10	0	10	10	10	0	0
Stubbornness	–	–	–	–	–	–	0.2	0.2	0.2	0.8	0.8
MaxBehaviourSwing	0	0	0	0	0	0	8	8	8	6	6
Treaties	T1–2	T1–2	T1–2	T1–2	T1–2	T1–2	T1–2	–	T1–3	T1–2	T1–3

In addition, the treaties used in cases C3 and D2 are slightly different, including all three treaties (T1, T2, T3) introduced in Sect. 4.3. C2 does not use any treaty. The other cases use treaties T1 and T2.

5.1   Simulation A

The first set of simulations we analyse are simulations that include agents that all have the same social motive. Moreover, these agents do not have the ability to change their social motive. The simulations results are shown in Fig. 4.

We observe that a system containing purely altruists (Fig. 4 (a)) effectively self-destructs, since by acting purely selflessly, these agents never take any resources. As the agents all die at the same time and are replaced by a new group of altruists, we see a step pattern in the number of deaths over time.

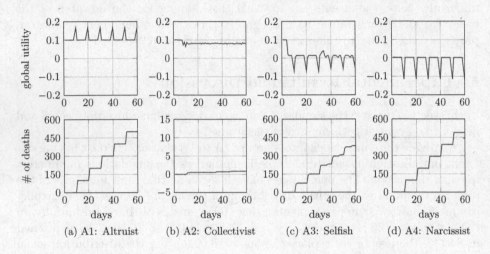

Fig. 4. Simulation results for a group of agents with uniform fixed social motive.

Similar to the altruist agents, the narcissists have a large number of deaths among them every 10 days (Fig. 4 (d)). This is due to the agents on the upper floors of the tower taking all of the food, leaving none for the agents below.

The main difference between the altruist and the narcissist agents can be seen in their corresponding global utility. The patterns can be explained by (6), which yields positive values only for A1, but leads to negative spikes for A4.

As a compromise between the two systems, a system including only selfish agents present a lower number of deaths and a better global utility than A4 (Fig. 4 (c))

Finally, the collectivists instantaneously achieve a stable society in which (almost) none of the agents die (Fig. 4 (b)). We also note a uniformly positive curve for global utility over time that is smoother than for the other social motives. This reflects the increased social cohesion between the agents and identifies the almost perfect allocation of resources, leading to no wasted utility.

5.2   Simulation B

Having assessed groups of agents of each social motive individually in Sect. 5.1, we increase the complexity of the system by having agents with different *fixed* social motives in the tower. The inability for these agents to change their social motive with time leads to the simulation results shown in Fig. 5.

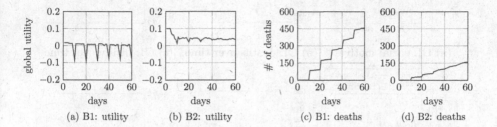

(a) B1: utility   (b) B2: utility   (c) B1: deaths   (d) B2: deaths

Fig. 5. Simulation results for a group of agents with different fixed social motives.

Through comparing B1 to B2, we see that the system comprising a larger amount of collectivists (B2) outperforms the system with a comparatively smaller amount of collectivists (B1). This is to be expected, as the more collectivist agents there are, the more similar to Fig. 4 (b) the system will be.

A second result illustrated by this simulation is that the action of introducing treaties (Sect. 4.3) is not always relevant. The collectivist agents sign the collectivist and selfish treaty (the collectivist one being more restrictive), but the selfish agents *only* sign the selfish treaty. This way, the two agent types are following their natural strategy concerning food intake (Sect. 4.2). Knowing this, the system shows similar results with and without treaties, hence we only show the results where communication is allowed.

5.3 Simulation C

This set of simulations builds on top of the framework set by simulation B, instead investigating the behaviour of a system comprising different distributions of *fluid* social motives. We utilise different levels of communication and treaties to contrast the results using the treaties introduced in Sect. 4.3 (Fig. 6 (a–c)). We simulate the system under two other configurations: without considering any form of communication (Fig. 6 (d–f)), and by restricting the agents' actions further through the additional use of the treaty T3 (Fig. 6 (g–i)).

The treaty T3 restricts the amount of food its members can take when their health drops below the *weakLevel*: "if *currentHP* < *weakLevel*, take ≤ 2 food."

The overarching comment to draw from this set of results is the impact of specific treaties on the global utility. Although thought to improve the global utility, treaties might have a negative effect on it: the results C1, using the collectivist treaty as introduced Sect. 4.3, are worst than the ones obtained without communication (C2).

As the agents' health falls, their social motives tend to change toward narcissist. Instead of following the natural decision of this social motive, the agents have to follow the treaties they signed (T1 and T2 for case C1). The moment

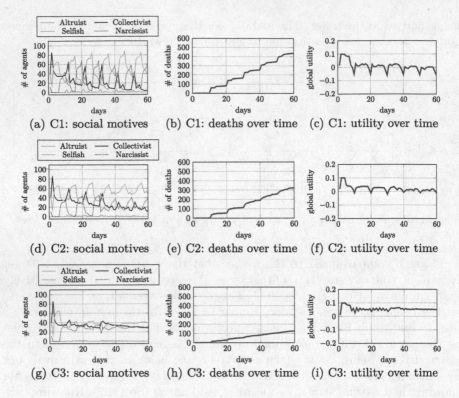

Fig. 6. Simulation results for case C. C1 and C3 include communication, but C2 does not. C3 includes a more restrictive treaty.

their health falls below the *weakLevel*, these treaties no longer apply and they will follow their natural food intake rule defined in Sect. 4.2. However, this leads to a lot of wasted resources at this critical health level. Notably, each food intake greater than 2 will not offer additional utility to agents whose health falls below the *weakLevel*: any food intake greater than or equal to 2 upgrades the agents health to the *weakLevel*. The waste of common pool resources can also be visualised in Fig. 6 (c), where the global utility becomes strongly negative every 10 days.

This waste of common resources induced by agents following the collectivist treaty is arguably due to a poor treaty design. To contrast these results, we can consider the addition of a different, more effective treaty. Simulation C3 introduced the treaty T3 that applies when the agents HP is below the *weakLevel*. As can be seen in Fig. 6 (h) and (i), this treaty allows for better performance of the system.

5.4   Simulation D

In these experiments, we initialise the tower's population with collectivist agents only, but with the possibility for them to change their social motive over time.

The goal of these experiments is to evaluate if a society comprised solely of collectivists is able to remain stable over time. In addition, we investigate the effect of treaties on such a system. The simulation results are shown in Fig. 7.

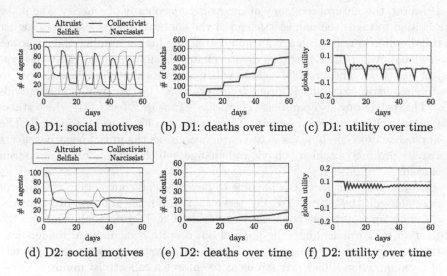

(a) D1: social motives   (b) D1: deaths over time   (c) D1: utility over time

(d) D2: social motives   (e) D2: deaths over time   (f) D2: utility over time

Fig. 7. Simulation results different treaties acceptances.

The results of D1 are similar to the ones of C1 in terms of (high) number of deaths and (low) global utility. The replacement of terminated agents by collectivist agents leads to an oscillatory behaviour between 2 quasi-stable states, with convergence to both a high concentration of collectivists and selfish agents in inverse proportions. We hence deem this experiment as 2-phase polystable [1].

Using the more restrictive treaty T3 on a system initially composed solely of collectivist agents leads to an impressive performance (Fig. 7 (e) and (f)). In addition, the use of this treaty also allows for a stable distribution of the social motives across the tower (Fig. 7 (d)). This stability can also be seen in Fig. 6 (g). Despite the presence of selfish (and even narcissistic) agents in the tower, they all follow the rule dictated by the treaties they signed whilst being collectivist.

In addition, we can also see the effect of the reshuffle period on the social motives distribution in Fig. 7 (d). The reshuffle period is 30 days in this case and we see a global shift toward collectivism at that moment.

6   Summary and Conclusions

6.1   Summary

Our first set of experiments shows the natural strategies taken by agents of different (fixed) social motives, and therefore gives us a baseline (A). The collectivist strategy is by far the one achieving the highest global utility. Consequently, the more collectivist agents in the tower, the higher the global utility (B).

However, the natural tendency of agents in an economy of scarcity is to make a transition towards the narcissistic end of the spectrum. This leads to a higher overall distribution of selfish agents, and therefore a higher number of deaths and lower global utility (C, D). Such a drastic change is supported by the Conservation of Resources Theory (COR) [8,9], which suggests that "individuals seek to create circumstances that will protect and promote the integrity of the individual." This behaviour also parallels 'Thorndike's Law of Effect,' [21] which states that actions that produce a favourable outcome are likely to be repeated. The agents' behaviours combine these two observations, as the initial negative effects of scarcity produce a selfish behavioural change, which persists until narcissism is reached.

To counteract this fact, it is possible to design social contracts in the form of treaties between the agents. Treaties serve as a stabilising self-organising mechanism, with appropriately constrictive treaties (C3, D2) even allowing for the integration of narcissists into the population, despite their natural tendency to destabilise a system. Treaties may also change a polystable system into a purely stable system, when sufficiently strong as to enforce a collectivist mindset. Oscillatory distributions of social motives can be brought to a static distribution using this mechanism (D1, D2). However, designing treaties that lead to a high global utility is not a trivial task; agents using poorly designed treaties may even perform worse than agents only following their natural strategy without using any sort of communication (C1, C2).

6.2   Future Work

Our future work would focus around adapting the ways in which we model the agents' changes in social motives. One such way is to make agents tend towards altruism, rather than narcissism, when faced with adversarial conditions. This could be interpreted as an understanding of the agent's environment and the long-term improvement of the individual utility through a short-term sacrifice, thus bringing the system back to an equilibrium.

Furthermore, we might imagine a randomly distributed assignment of behavioural weights (Table 2) across different agents. This would illustrate how different agents react to their condition, from which the concept of agent personality could be derived. For example, some agents may encounter a comfortable situation (high HP, high floor) and take advantage of it by acting selfishly, while another agent may encounter the same situation and take the opportunity to make a positive impact for their fellow agents below by acting altruistically.

The physical arrangement of the tower can also be investigated and leans into the possibility of having different non-linear topologies. This would allow for fully-connected graphs, where all agents can communicate with all other agents or planar lattices, with connections between the four or eight closest neighbouring agents, for example.

Finally, we want to analyse the effects of a larger number of treaties on global utility. The choice of treaties which lead to an increase in the global utility is not straightforward. Since treaties are expressed in a generic way, it may be possible to tune the treaty parameters to find optimal treaties in a given scenario.

6.3   Conclusion

In conclusion, we observe that the scenario demands that the prisoners in the tower are effectively faced with an iterated version of Rawls' Veil of Ignorance: they have to decide repeatedly what sort of society they would prefer if they did not know what position they would occupy in such a society. This work shows that even with limited communication and a population with diverse social motives, the ability to construct social contracts leads to a stable society which perpetuates across generations, arguably showing that there is some psychological and sociological plausibility to Rawls' theory, although there is still work to be done on establishing whether or not, even if our agents establish a stable and self-perpetuating social contract, it is the 'best' social contract.

Acknowledgements. We are particularly grateful to the three anonymous reviewers whose many insightful comments helped to revise and improve the presentation of this work. The experiments reported in this paper have used the Imperial College London 2021–22 SOMAS Cohort's engine, and many thanks to everyone involved in the creation of this platform (sic).

References

1. Ashby, W.: Design for a Brain; The Origin of Adaptive Behavior - Scholar's Choice Edition, Chap. 4–5. Creative Media Partners, LLC (2015)
2. Berger, P., Luckmann, T.: The Social Construction of Reality. Penguin Books, Harmondsworth (1966)
3. Briggs, J.: Never in Anger: Portrait of an Eskimo Family. Harvard University Press, Cambridge (1970)
4. Campbell, W.K., Goodie, A.S., Foster, J.D.: Narcissism, confidence, and risk attitude. J. Behav. Decis. Mak. **17**(4), 297–311 (2004)
5. Davoust, A., Rovatsos, M.: Social contracts for non-cooperative games. In: AIES 2020: Proceedings of the AAAI/ACM Conference on AI, Ethics, and Society, pp. 43–49. Association for Computing Machinery, New York (2020)
6. Fishburn, P.C.: Utility theory for decision making. Technical report, Research Analysis Corp McLean VA (1970)
7. Fishburn, P.C.: Nonlinear Preference and Utility Theory, p. 2. Johns Hopkins University Press, Baltimore (1988)

8. Hobfoll, S.E.: Conservation of resource caravans and engaged settings. J. Occup. Organ. Psychol. **84**(1), 116–122 (2011)
9. Hobfoll, S.E., Shirom, A., Golembiewski, R.: Conservation of resources theory. In: Handbook of Organizational Behavior, pp. 57–80 (2000)
10. Kahneman, D., Tversky, A.: Prospect theory: an analysis of decision under risk, pp. 99–127. World Scientific (2013)
11. Kong, A., Thorleifsson, G.: The nature of nurture: effects of parental genotypes. Science **359**(6374), 424–428 (2018)
12. Norberg-Hodge, H.: Ancient Futures: Learning from Ladakh. Sierra Club Books, San Francisco (1991)
13. Norris, D.: Short-term memory and long-term memory are still different. Psychol. Bull. **143**(9), 992 (2017)
14. Oppenheimer, O.: The origin of social motives. Educ. Theory **4**(2), 95–104 (1954)
15. Ostrom, E.: Governing the Commons. Cambridge University Press, Cambridge (1990)
16. Pitt, J.: Self-Organising Multi-Agent Systems, pp. 149–151. World Scientific, Singapore (2021)
17. Ramchurn, S., Huynh, T., Jennings, N.: Trust in multi-agent systems. Knowl. Eng. Rev. **19**, 1–25 (2004)
18. Rawls, J., Kelly, E.: Justice as Fairness: A Restatement. Belknap Press, Cambridge (2001)
19. Reinders Folmer, C.: Social motives. In: The SAGE Encyclopedia of Theory in Psychology. pp. 886–890. SAGE (2016)
20. Schelling, T.C.: The strategy of conflict prospectus for a reorientation of game theory. J. Conflict Resolut. **2**(3), 203–264 (1958)
21. Thorndike, E.L.: The law of effect. Am. J. Psychol. **39**(1/4), 212–222 (1927)

Evaluating Human and Agent Task Allocators in Ad Hoc Human-Agent Teams

Sami Abuhaimed[✉] and Sandip Sen

Tandy School of Computer Science, The University of Tulsa, Tulsa, USA
{saa8061,sandip}@utulsa.edu

Abstract. With accelerated progress in autonomous agent capabilities, mixed human and agent teams will become increasingly commonplace in both our personal and professional spheres. Hence, further examination of factors affecting coordination efficacy in these types of teams are needed to inform the design and use of effective human-agent teams. Ad hoc human-agent teams, where team members interact without prior experience with teammates and only for a limited number of interactions, will be commonplace in dynamic environments with short opportunity windows for coordination between diverse groups. We study virtual ad-hoc team scenarios pairing a human with an agent where both need to assess and adapt to the capabilities of the partner to maximize team performance. In this work, we investigate the relative efficacy of two human-agent coordination protocols that differ in the team member responsible for allocating tasks to the team. We designed, implemented, and experimented with an environment in which virtual human-agent teams repeatedly coordinate to complete heterogeneous task sets.

Keywords: Human-agent coordination · Team performance · Task allocation

1 Introduction

Recent intelligent agent applications assume traditionally human roles in human-agent teams, e.g., tutor [35] and trainer [22]. Agents can also coordinate with people in critical tasks, including guiding emergency evacuations [33] and disaster relief [32]. New environments have been developed recently to enable group activities or coordination between people and agents, such as crowd-work and multiplayer online games. Human and agent teams are increasingly commonplace where they play different team roles. Since human-agent teams are being recognized as a routine and functionally critical important component of our societies, researchers have been studying the interactions and dynamics within these teams to understand and improve on their design [13]. Such human-agent teams have been studied in physical (robotic) and virtual settings [34].

We are studying ad hoc coordination scenarios where humans start coordinating with agents in a new environment with no prior interaction experience with the agent. The agent also does not have prior knowledge about its human partners' abilities and preferences. Such coordination environments correspond to *ad hoc teams*: *An ad hoc team setting is one in which teammates must work together to obtain a common goal, but without any prior agreement regarding how to work together* [11]. Coordination in ad hoc teams is more challenging because of absence of prior knowledge and established relationships. Ad hoc human-agent coordination also raises critical new issues compared to ad hoc agent teams.

In this paper, we consider ad hoc teams trying to accomplish a set of tasks chosen from diverse task types. We assume that different human users will have different competence and expertise over various task types. We use a fixed agent expertise distribution (simulated) over the task types. To optimize the performance of a given human-agent team, therefore, it is necessary to have different task allocation distributions to the team members based on the expertise of the human team member. The allocation problem is exacerbated by the fact that a team member does not know the expertise levels of its partner *a priori*. While we allow for human and agent partners to share their estimated expertise over different task types, the accuracy and consistency of such expressed estimates by humans are unreliable [17].

Repeated interaction allows partners to refine the initial estimates provided, but such opportunities are few due to (i) only a limited number of repeated teamwork episodes and (ii) allocation decisions that determine what task types are performed by a partner in an episode. The success of such ad hoc human-agent teams in completing assigned team tasks, therefore, will critically depend on effective adaptability in the task allocation process.

Task allocation have been studied extensively in agent teams [27] as well as in human team and organizations literature [31]. However, we are not aware of prior examination of autonomous agents with task allocation roles, compared to humans, in virtual and ad hoc human-agent teams.

Some critical questions on task allocation decisions and human-agent ad hoc team efficacy that we study in this paper are:

- Is the performance of human-agent teams influenced by who allocates the tasks? If so, who produce higher team performance?
- How is the performance of human-agent teams affected by over/under-confidence of humans in their performance on different task types?
- How quickly can the task allocator in an ad hoc human-agent team learn about the relative capabilities of team members to optimize allocation of tasks?

We designed a new human-agent team coordination framework for task allocation and performance analysis: the Collaborative Human-Agent Taskboard (CHATboard). We use CHATboard for ad hoc human-agent team coordination, for repeated team task allocation scenarios, with human workers recruited from the Amazon Mechanical Turk (MTurk) platform. We present some conjectures as hypotheses about human confidence level in their expertise, about the relative effectiveness of human and agent task allocators, about the ability of agents to learn about human capabilities and adapt task allocations, and the ability of agents to harness human potential. We ran experiments involving repeated coordination using the Human and Agent Allocation protocols. We present the results and our analysis to confirm our hypotheses and identify interesting phenomena that suggests future research tasks.

2 Related Work

Human-agent teams have been studied in different domains such as space robotics [13], therapy [1], deception-detection [20], programming [23] and decision-making [3]. The focus has been on agents who play supportive roles to human teammates [20], and they have been studied in robotic and simulation settings [34].

We, however, focus on an ad hoc environment, whereas studies, such as [13], incorporate training or interaction sessions with the agent and environment prior to the study. We are also interested in agents that are autonomous; DeChurch and Larson view an autonomous agent as a "team member fulfilling a distinct role in the team and making a unique contribution" [21].

Task allocation has been studied extensively in multi-agent teams [12,14,18, 27,28]. In agent teams, the focus is on designing efficient mechanisms for agents to distribute tasks within their society; current approaches include integer programming [9], genetic [29], consensus and auction algorithms [6], and markets [8], and in domains such as Search and Rescue [37]. There is a recent focus on ad hoc environments [5] in which agents coordinate without pre-coordination. The majority of agent teams work is focused on simulation and robotic environments, and few have studied task allocation in ad hoc human-agent teams. Moreover, there is a general lack of investigating environments that include human teammates; including humans in same agent teams may require new approaches, as we do not know If the same mechanisms would produce similar results.

Task allocation is also studied in humans' team and organization literature. The mechanism of task allocation, which includes capabilities identification, role specification, and task planning, is considered an important component of teamwork [10,24,25]. Any organization needs to solve four universal problems, including task allocation, to achieve its goals [31]. In human teams, the focus is on understanding human team characteristics to design the best possible task allocation mechanism; however, there is little investigation of autonomous agents' effects on human teams when they are included in teams' allocation mechanisms.

Thus, the study of task allocation with combined human and agent team members is promising [4,34]. The few existing work examine different dimensions. [34] and [32] investigate an agent assisting humans' control of robots in a simulation and experiments; the focus is supporting operators. Some of this work do not empirically investigate the area, focused on industrial settings, configure the agent in supporting roles, and it is unclear whether human participants received training prior to experiments, which means that the scenario not ad hoc.

In summary, studies that investigate task allocation within teams composed of humans and autonomous agents in ad hoc environments over repeated interactions are limited. We, therefore, study task allocation in ad hoc human-agent teams while being informed by potential human miscalibration tendencies.

3 Hypotheses Development

We now motivate and present a number of research hypotheses related to ad hoc human-agent team task allocation and team performance that we will be experimentally evaluating in this paper. We study two task allocation protocols that govern the human-agent teamwork: Human Allocator Protocol and Agent Allocator Protocol. The former assigns task allocator role to human teammate, and the later to agent teammate (Section 5 presents more details).

We assume there is considerable variability in ability to complete tasks amongst average citizens. If this was not the case, human expertise in tasks can be gauged offline, and optimal task allocation can be performed, i.e., ad hoc teams would be no different than teams with significant prior working experience.

Hypothesis 0a (H0a): *Different human participants have different perception and actual performance for different task types.*

We also assume that humans are unable to accurately estimate or express their performance (confidence levels) on different, somewhat routine task types. If this was not the case, then again, we could simply ask the human about their expertise levels for different task types and use that accurate information for task allocation, i.e., ad hoc teams would be no different than teams with significant prior working experience.

Hypothesis 0b (H0b): *Human's average confidence levels on task types are not consistent with their performance on those task types.*

We conjecture that the agent allocator has several advantages over the human allocator for effectively allocating team tasks: (a) lack of personal bias or preference for task types that is not performance motivated (for example, humans may like to do certain tasks even though they may not be good at it), (b) agents will have better estimates of their capabilities on known task types whereas humans typically over or under-estimate their expertise or performance on task types, (c) agents can consistently follow optimal allocation procedures given confidence levels over task types, (d) agents can more consistently learn from task performance of teammates in early episodes to update confidence level estimates and adapt task allocation to improve performance. This lack of bias may also result in the agent allocator allocating tasks such that together with higher team performance we also observe better performance of the human team member, i.e., better realize the human potential, compared to when the humans allocate tasks between team members! When the agent is assigned allocator role, it follows an allocation strategy that search for allocations that maximize total performance while learning about actual human performances (See Sect. 5.2 for more details). We believe that agent allocation strategies that effectively embody advantages (a)–(d) above will conform to following set of hypotheses:

Hypothesis 1 (H1): *Agent Allocator Protocol produces higher teamwork overall performance than Human Allocator Protocol.*

Hypothesis 2 (H2): *Agent Allocator can learn from ad hoc teamwork experience to quickly improve team performance through adaptation.*

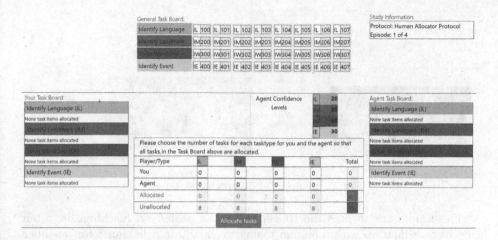

Fig. 1. CHATboard showing allocation phase of human allocation protocol.

Hypothesis 3 (H3): *Agent allocator will engender higher Human potential realization compared to the Human Allocator.*

4 Collaborative Human-Agent Taskboard (CHATboard)

For systematic experimentation to evaluate the above hypotheses, we needed a domain that encapsulates the following characteristics:

- The team tasks used should be such that there would be significant variation in expertise level in the general populace. Larger variability would allow for more space for team adaptation and for human satisfaction with teamwork. We should also have the latitude to easily and believably configure varying agent capability distribution over the task types.
- The domain should allow an agent to be perceived as autonomous and playing a distinct peer role in the team.
- The domain should not require significant prior knowledge or training for human participants and should be accessible to non-experts for effectively operating in an ad hoc team setting.
- There should be flexibility in sharing team information, including task allocations and completions, with team members. The environment should be configurable between perfect and imperfect information scenarios as necessitated by the research question being investigated.

We developed CHATboard, an environment that facilitates human-agent, as well as human-human, team coordination. CHATboard contains a graphical interface that supports human-agent team coordination to complete a set of tasks (see Fig. 1). CHATboard allows for displaying the task sets to be completed, supports multiple task allocation protocols, communication between team members for expressing confidence levels, displaying task allocations and performance by team members on assigned tasks, etc.

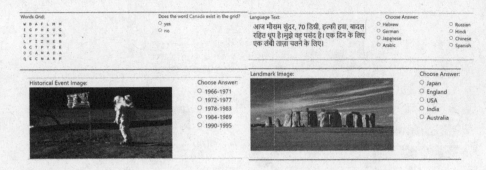

Fig. 2. Instances of different task types.

The framework utilizes the concept of tasks posted on blackboards, often used in coordination within human teams, to facilitate a human team member perceiving an agent as a distinct team member. Blackboards have also been effectively used in agent teams as a common repository for information sharing between agents [16]. Figure 1 shows the shared taskboad on top, which includes the set of team tasks organized by type, and two other boards respectively for the tasks assigned to the human and the agent team member. Figure 2 presents examples of task types. These task boards facilitate coordination, and act as easily navigable repositories for team information allowing team members to share and view information through these boards.

We define a set of n team members N: $\{p_1, p_2, ..., p_n\}$, a set of m task types M: $\{y_1, y_2, ..., y_m\}$, a set of r tasks, T_{jr}: $\{t_{j1}, t_{j2}, ..., t_{jr}\}$, for each task type y_j. Team member i can share their confidence levels $p_i(y_j)$ over task types y_j. The set C_i: $\{p_i(y_1), p_i(y_2), ..., p_i(y_m)\}$ represent confidence levels for different task types for team player, p_i. The team members will interact over E episodes, where episode numbers range from $1 ... E$. $A_{i,e}$ denotes the set of tasks allocated to player i in episode e and we assume that all available tasks are exhaustively allocated, i.e., $\bigcup_i A_{i,e} = \bigcup_j T_{jr}$. The performance of player p_i for a task t_{jk} in episode e is referred to as $o_{ijke} \in \{0, 1\}$. We define the performance of p_i on task type y_j in episode e as $\mu_{i,y_j,e} = \sum_{t_{jk} \in A_{i,e}} o_{ijke}$.

5   Methodology

We present details about the team interaction protocol, agent behavior, evaluation metrics, and experiment design in this section.

5.1   Interaction Protocols

We describe the protocols that govern the human-agent ad hoc teamwork. Two interaction protocols have been designed to guide task allocation process in an ad hoc environment: (i) the Human Allocator Protocol and (ii) the Agent Allocator Protocol. The former assigns the task allocator role to the human teammate, and is illustrated as follows:

1. *The protocol asks agent teammate for its task types confidence levels.*
2. *The protocol passes the agent's confidence levels to the human.*
   The following steps comprise an episode and are repeated N times
   Episode starts: $e \leftarrow 1$
3. *The protocol asks Human to provide task allocations for the team.*
4. *Allocated tasks are assigned to the team members.*
5. *The protocol receives human and agent task performance measures and computes statistics.*
6. *The protocol displays team overall team performance as well as individual team member performances for the episode on their respective task boards.*
   Episode ends
   $e \leftarrow e + 1$; *if (e < N), Go to step 3*

The Agent Allocator Protocol is the flip side of the coin and assigns the task allocator role to the agent. Team members repeatably interact over different stages in both protocols: Task Allocation, Task Completion, and Taskwork results (see Though these protocols provide a framework for team interaction and task allocation, they do not dictate the allocation strategy used by the allocator. For the current study, we use a perfect information scenario, where all team information, such as set of team tasks, task assignments to team members, and the task performance is fully observable for all team members.

5.2 Agent Characteristics

Expertise: We configure an agent team member with a fixed expertise profile that has different expertise level for different task types, represented as a vector of probabilities for successful completion of task types[1]. **Agent Allocator Strategy:** In the current paper, we also use the following additional constraints within the CHATboard framework that informs the allocator strategy. We assume each task is allocated to and performed by a single team member and does not require work from multiple individuals, i.e., $A_{i,e} \cap A_{j,e} = \phi$. We additionally required that the total number of tasks assigned to each team member be the same, i.e., $\forall x, y, |A_x| = |A_y|$. Different number of tasks can however be assigned to two team members for different task types.

The primary allocation goal is to maximize utilization of the available team capacity given the expertise of the team. Additionally, agent should account for the constraint that team members have to do equal number of task items. Instead of using *task items* for task division, the agent uses *task types*. The agent stores and uses estimates of on task completion rates by task types for the human team member in the allocation procedure.

$$Max \sum_{y \in M} (x_y a(y) + (1 - x_y)h(y)); s.t. \forall y, x_y \in 0, 1$$

---

[1] Agent expertise is simulated in our experiments: given a expertise (confidence) level P_t of the agent for task type t, a task of type t is considered successfully completed if a coin flipped with probability P_t returns head; else failure is reported on the task.

Algorithm 1. Agent Allocator Strategy

Input: $N = \{p_h, p_g\}$, $M = \{y_1, \ldots, y_m\}$, E

1: **for** $e = 1....E$ **do**
2:     **if** $e = 1$ **then**
3:         $Q_{i,y_j} \leftarrow p_i(y_j)$, $\forall p_i \in N, y_j \in M$
4:         each T_{y_j} is partitioned into n equal size subsets, which are randomly allocated to agent i to form $A_{i,1}$, for each $p_i \in N$
5:     **else**
6:         $A_{i,e} \leftarrow$ getAllocations$(Q_{i,e})$
7:     **end if**
8:     **if** y_j is allocated to p_i **then**
9:         $Q_{i,y_j} \leftarrow (1 - \alpha) \cdot Q_{i,y_j} + \alpha \cdot \mu_{i,y_j,e}$
10:    **end if**
11: **end for**

$$\sum_{y \in M} x_y = \sum_{y \in M} (1 - x_y) = \frac{|M|}{2}.$$

In the above equations, x_y is binary variable indicating whether a task type, y, is assigned to human or agent, based on the current performance estimate of the human, $h(y)$, and agent, $a(y)$, on that task type. As per requirement, each team member is assigned exactly half of the task types. This is an *unbalanced assignment problem*, as number of task types is greater than number of team members $(m > n)$. It can be solved by transforming it into a *balanced* formulation, e.g., adding dummy variables, and running, e.g., Hungarian algorithm [19]. We utilize the SCIP mixed integer programming solver [30], represented by getAllocations() procedure in Line 6 of Algorithm 1, to find the allocation that maximizes utilization of team's confidence levels.

In many task allocation formulations, e.g., matching markets, assignment problems, and others, participants' preferences or confidence levels are assumed to be accurately known [36]. In our formulation, however, learning is needed as we believe human participant's estimates of their capabilities can be inaccurate. The second goal that agent's strategy should account for is related to learning and adaptation. Since this is an ad hoc environment, the second goal of our agent is to quickly learn about its partner's expertise levels and quickly adapt the allocations accordingly for improved team performance. After each interaction, e, the agent updates the capability model, Q_{i,y_j}, of team member, p_i, for each task type, y_j, from the observed performances, $\mu_{i,y_j,e}$, as follows: $Q_{i,y_j} \leftarrow (1 - \alpha) \cdot Q_{i,y_j} + \alpha \cdot \mu_{i,y_j,e}$. In the first episode, however, the agent allocator explores team member's capabilities by partitioning task items within each task type, T_{y_j}, equally among team members, as shown in Line 4 in Algorithm 1.

5.3   Evaluation Metrics

Human Teammate Miscalibration and Variability Trends: In our experiments, human teammates coordinate with agent to accomplish tasks items from

m task types (we have used $m = 4$ in our experiments). We measure the variability, over task types, of the difference between the human teammates' stated confidence levels and their actual performance.

The confidence levels shared by a human teammate for each task type are used as estimated probability of success for the respective task types. The agent maintains a moving average over the episodes of the team member's performance on a task type as the percentage of tasks of that type that the human successfully completes. We measure miscalibration for a human player i for task type y_j, based on the stated confidence level, $p_i(y_j)$, and actual average performance on that task type over all episodes, $\mu_{i,y_j} = \frac{1}{E} \sum_{e=1}^{E} \mu_{i,y_j,e}$, as squared error: $Miscalibration_{i,y_j} \leftarrow (p_i(y_j) - \mu_{i,y_j})^2$.

Team Performance: Human and agent collaborate as a team to complete the set of tasks. We consider boolean task completion: a task allocated to a team member is either successfully completed or a failure is reported. Team overall performance is measured as the percentage of successful completion of assigned tasks over all episodes: Unweighted Team Performance is measured as the average team performance over episodes, $\frac{1}{E} \sum_{e=1}^{E} R_{team,e}$, where $R_{team,e}$ is the team performance in episode e, which is the average performance, μ, of all team members over all task types in that episode $R_{team,e} \leftarrow \frac{1}{mn} \sum_{i=1}^{n} \sum_{j=1}^{m} \mu_{i,y_j,e}$.

Team Improvement and Learning: Since our scenario is ad hoc, it requires quick learning and improvements in team performance from task allocators. We investigate the differences in mean performance between episodes to gauge improvements. We also measure the ability to improve as the weighted team performance over episodes, with the performance of latter episodes are weighted more than the earlier ones: Weighted Team Performance $\leftarrow \frac{1}{E} \sum_{e=1}^{E} z_e \cdot R_{team,e}$, where z_e is the weight for episode e.

Potential Realization: An effective allocator will better utilize the capacity of the team and realize as much of their teammate's potential as possible. Potential realization can be measured through the difference between available capacity and utilized capacity. We have perfect knowledge of the agent's capacity, which is fixed at design time. We do not know, however, know of the available capacity of human team members. We compare the difference in the capacity utilized by human and agent allocators. We measure utilized capacity of humans as the individual performance level within the team. The performance (success rate) of an agent i over all episodes, referred to as Potential Realization of i, is $S_i = \sum_{e=1}^{E} \sum_{y_j \in M} \mu_{i,y_j,e}$. We designate by S_i^h and S_i^a the performance (potential realization) of agent i under human and agent allocator protocol respectively.

Weighted Likeability: The human-agent team is expected to accomplish m task types over the interaction episodes. At the end of the study, we ask human participants how much they liked each task type by asking them to rate their likeability of each task type on a 10-point Likert scale. For each participant, p_i, we compute the weighted likeability over all allocated tasks as $\sum_{y_j \in M} l_{i,y_j} \sum_{e=1}^{E} |A_{i,y_j,e}|$, where $A_{i,y_j,e}$ is the set of tasks of type y_j allocated to player p_i in episode e and l_{i,y_j} is the human player p_i's stated likeability of task type y_j.

5.4 Experimental Configurations

We conduct experiments with teams of one human and one agent $(n = 2)$, i.e., $N = \{p_a, p_h\}$. We use four task types $(m = 4)$, i.e., M: $\{y_1, y_2, y_4, y_4\}$, which are *Identify Language, Solve WordGrid, Identify Landmark*, and *Identify Event* (examples of these task types shown in Fig. 2). The task types in this paper are selected so that, for each type, sufficient expertise variations in recruited human subjects are likely. For example, *Identify Language* is a task type in which team are asked to identify the language, e.g. Japanese, in a text message from a number of options, e.g., Japanese, German, Hebrew, Arabic.

We created 32 $(r = 8)$ task item instances for each episode, and the total number of interactions is four, $E = 4$. The confidence levels are stated in a $[1, 100]$ range, which are then scaled by the agent internally into a $[0, 1]$ to be interpreted as probabilities of completing tasks of that type. Also, we configure the agent strategy with $\alpha = 0.4$ since Ad hoc situations require allocation strategies to quickly learn about team's capabilities. Additionally, for the weighted performance measure, we have used the following vector of weights over episodes: $z = [0.15, 0.20, 0.30, 0.35]$; it assign more value to performance on latter episodes (any weights that does that would qualitatively produce similar results).

We recruited 130 participants from Amazon Mechanical Turk, 65 for each condition, as is recommended for a medium-sized effect [7]. We use a between-subject, and each team is assigned randomly to one protocol or the other. After participants agree to the Informed Consent Form, they read a description of the study, and then start the first episode. Each episode contains three phases: taskwork allocation, taskwork completion, and taskwork results. After each episode, the results are displayed to both human and agent teammates, which include overall and per-type performance levels. Once participants complete all four episodes, they are asked to complete a survey including their satisfaction on various aspects of teamwork and their likeability for task types. We incorporate random comprehension attention checks to ensure result fidelity [15]. Participants receive a bonus payment based on team performance.

6 Experimental Results

Human Variability and Miscalibration: We analyze human variability and task type perceptions in their stated confidence levels and their performance. We first analyze human variability in their stated confidence levels using one-way ANOVA. We find that confidence level between task types ($M_A = 63.27, SD_A = 23.16, M_B = 57.01, SD_B = 21.45, M_C4 = 77.64, SD_C = 19.06, M_D = 41.49, SD_D = 21.70$) are significantly different, F=31, p < 0.001. We similarity evaluate variability in humans' actual performances and find that actual performance levels between task types ($M_A = 77.52, SD_A = 17.01, M_B = $

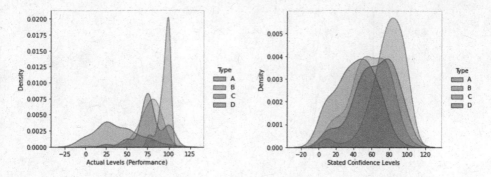

Fig. 3. Human variability in stated confidence (right) and actual performance (Left).

Table 1. Stated levels and performances for task types.

Task Type	Level			
	Stated		Actual	
	Mean	SD	Mean	SD
Identify Language (**A**)	63.27	23.16	77.52	17.01
Identify Landmark (**B**)	57.01	21.45	75.87	16.28
Solve WordsGrid (**C**)	77.64	19.06	95.0	6.4
Identify Event (**D**)	41.49	21.70	37.30	25.43

75.87, $SD_B = 16.28.45, M_C4 = 95.0, SD_C = 6.4, M_D = 37.30, SD_D = 25.43$) are significantly different, F=123, p < 0.001. As Fig. 3 and Table 1 show, humans are exhibiting variability and different perceptions toward the task types. **H0a** *is supported.*

We analyze confidence levels estimates stated by human teammates in the Agent Allocator Protocol for the different task types: A, B, C, and D. We analyze the average squared error of the difference between the stated confidence level and actual performance over all task types, 0.08, and was found to be significantly different from zero, t = 7.4, p < 0.001. We then compute the squared error for each task type ($M_A = 0.07$, $SD_A = 0.13$, $M_B = 0.08$, $SD_B = 0.13$, $M_C = 0.06$, $SD_C = 0.12$, $M_D = 0.12$, $SD_D = 0.14$), and find that it is significantly different from zero, $t_A = 4.37$, $p_A < 0.001$, $t_B = 5.28$, $p_B < 0.001$, $t_C = 4.16$, $p_C < 0.001$, $t_D = 7.11$, $p_D < 0.001$ (See Fig. 4). Thus, human teammates are showing miscalibration tendencies in all task types. **H0b** *is supported.*

To determine whether human teammates are over- or under-estimating their stated confidence levels in different task types, relative to actual performance, we run non-parametric Sign Tests. We found that, on average, human tend to underestimate their capabilities relative to actual performance ($S_{avg} = 18$, $p_{avg} = 0.001$). We then run Sign Test for each task type, and find that human teammates are significantly underestimating their capabilities for task type A, B, and C ($S_A = 15$, $p_A < 0.001$, $S_B = 13$, $p_B < 0.001$, $S_C = 7$, $p_C < 0.001$),

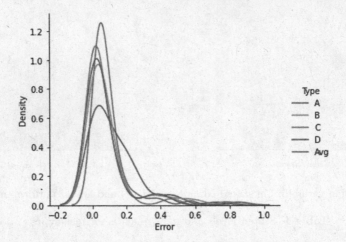

Fig. 4. Density of squared estimation error for task types.

and over-estimating for task type D ($S_D = 38$, $p_D = 0.018$). We analyze task type characteristics, and found that task type A, B, and C share one common trait in which they are more general and familiar to typical human teammates, whereas task type D, *Identify Event*, is more specialized [2].

Team Performance: The teams using Agent Allocator Protocol (M = 0.75, SD = 0.04) compared to ones using Human Allocator Protocol (M = 0.69, SD = 0.09) demonstrated significantly higher team performance, t = 4.4, p < 0.001, with a large size effect, cohen's d = 0.86 (See Table 2). **H1** *is supported.*

Learning and Improvement: Since the teams are working in an ad hoc environment, task allocators need to quickly learn about team capabilities and increase team performance. First, we investigate if team performances over episodes is different in each protocol. We find that it is significantly different for the Agent Allocator Protocol ($M_{eps1} = 0.59, SD_{eps1} = 0.10, M_{eps2} = 0.76, SD_{eps2} = 0.11, M_{eps3} = 0.82, SD_{eps3} = 0.10, M_{eps4} = 0.83, SD_{eps4} = 0.11$), $F_a = 167.17$, $p_a < 0.001$. We also find that it is significantly different for the Human Allocator Protocol ($M_{eps1} = 0.66, SD_{eps1} = 0.10, M_{eps2} = 0.67, SD_{eps2} = 0.13, M_{eps3} = 0.71, SD_{eps3} = 0.12, M_{eps4} = 0.71, SD_{eps4} = 0.12$), $F_h = 3.17$, and $p_h = 0.024$.

The agent allocator starts has lower performance, $M_{eps1} = 0.59$, than human allocator, $M_{eps1} = 0.66$ in the first episode. This is due to the agent strategy of exploration during the first episode. However, the agent improves quickly, and outperforms human in the second, third, and fourth episodes. The agent improves team performance by a significant margin going from episode 1 to episode 2, and then by smaller margins going from episode 2 to episode 3, and episode 3 to episode 4. The improvements over episodes by the Human allocator is less pronounced.

Table 2. Team performance (*p < 0.001).

Performance	Allocator				t
	Human		Agent		
	Mean	SD	Mean	SD	
Unweighted	0.69	0.09	**0.75**	0.04	4.4*
Weighted	0.70	0.10	**0.78**	0.04	5.8*

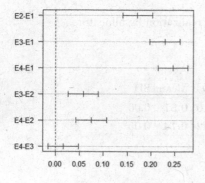 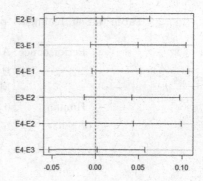

Fig. 5. Tukey's HSD Test: differences in mean levels of four episodes (E1 to E4). Left: Agent, Right: Human.

Moreover, we run Post hoc analysis, using Tukey's HSD Test, to evaluate the performance differences between episodes (See Fig. 5). When Human is allocating, we find no significant mean differences between the episodes, $E2 - E1 = 0.007, p = 0.98, E3 - E1 = 0.05, p = 0.10, E4 - E1 = 0.05, p = 0.08, E3 - E2 = 0.04, p = 0.20, E4 - E2 = 0.42, p = 0.17, E4 - E3 = 0.001, p = 0.99$. We do, however, find significant mean differences between episodes with the Agent Allocator, except for E4-E3, $E2 - E1 = 0.17, p < 0.001, E3 - E1 = 023, p < 0.001, E4 - E1 = 0.25, p < 0.001, E3 - E2 = 0.06, p < 0.001, E4 - E2 = 0.08, p < 0.001, E4 - E3 = 0.02, p = 0.52$. This shows that the agent is, indeed, improving after each experience. One possible interpretation between the small difference between episode 3 and 4, relative to the larger differences from episodes E1 to E2, and from E2 to E3, is that the agent is getting close to the optimal allocation of tasks based on the team member capabilities.

We also note that performance of teams using the Agent Allocator Protocol $(M = 0.78, SD = 0.04)$ are better than teams using the Human Allocator Protocol $(M = 0.70, SD = 0.10)$ in weighted performance, $t = 5.8, p < 0.001$. In other words, the agent is showing better learning of its teammate's capabilities and adapting the task allocations accordingly to further improve team performance in latter rounds. since weighted performance measures overall team performance over the latter, rather than, earlier episodes. The agent allocator significantly outperforms the human allocator using the weighted performance measures (See Table 2). **H2** *is supported.*

Potential Realization: We compared teams based on how allocators realize potential of teammates and themselves. The pertinent question is: which allocator utilizes human capacity better? We find that teams who have agents as task allocators (M = 0.87, SD = 0.06) realize significantly more human potential than Human Allocator (M = 0.81, SD = 0.10), t = 2.2, p = 0.02. **H3** *is supported.*

Table 3. Self, teammate potential realization by allocators.

Performance	Allocator			
	Human		Agent	
	Mean	SD	Mean	SD
Human	0.81	0.10	**0.87**	0.06
Agent	0.59	0.12	**0.74**	0.05

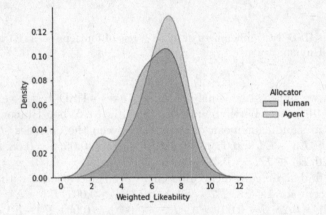

Fig. 6. Weighted likeability density for human and agent protocols.

We also analyze how team allocators effectively utilize agent capacity. We find that agent capacity utilization or performance is significantly higher in teams who have agents as task allocators (M = 0.74, SD = 0.05) compared to teams with Human allocators (M = 0.59, SD = 0.12), t = 5.02, p < 001. Thirdly, we investigate which allocator utilizes the capacity of their teammate better. We find that teams who Agent allocators (M = 0.87, SD = 0.06) significantly realize more performance from their teammates than Human Allocator (M = 0.59, SD = 0.12), t = 13.4, p < 0.001.

We do not analyze self-realization between human and agent allocators since human capacity in the Human Allocator Protocol is unknown. We also define the level of agent capacity or confidence level structure prior to the interaction;

thus, we cannot compare self-realization of human and agent allocators. We posit, however, when allocators are agents, they realize more potential in the team; both in themselves and in the human team member (See Table 3)[2].

Weighted Likeability: To understand the performance differences between the Human and Agent Allocator Protocols, we analyze the task types allocated to human teammates. Do humans allocate more tasks of types they like to themselves? We find that Agent allocators ($M_a = 6.77, SD_a = 1.51$) allocate more items of liked task types to the human team member than does the human allocator ($M_h = 6.07, SD_h = 1.80$), $t_{like} = 2.3, p_{like} = 0.01$ (See Fig. 6).

7 Discussion and Future Work

We introduced CHATboard, a flexible task allocation framework between human and agent team members for ad hoc scenarios. While CHATboard can be configured to support larger teams and more complex constraints between tasks, such as multiple workers per task, in this paper we showed its efficacy in supporting coordination between one human and one autonomous agent.

To understand team dynamics with respect to task allocation within human-agent teams, we presented two interaction protocols and team designs in which task allocator role is either assigned to human or agent team member: Human and Agent Allocator Protocols. We ran experiments with these team designs and showed human teammates often exhibit miscalibration, where they either over- or under-estimate their capabilities.

We demonstrated that agent task allocators generally increase the quality of team with respect to team performance and realizing potential of team compared to human allocators. The agent allocators learn quickly about team capabilities, and realize more potential in the team, both their own and of their human teammate. Our analysis of the experiments also confirms various hypotheses we had posed about such ad hoc human-agent team coordination.

Though finding the reason for the lower performance of human allocators is beyond scope of this paper, we conjectured that it might be due to humans allocating more tasks they like to themselves, even though they may not be good at it. We find, however, that the agent is allocating more likeable tasks to the human teammate. The lower performance might be explained by biases identified in behavioral economics, such as prospect theory, in which they perceive performance gains or success differently than losses or failure rate. We leave this line of investigation to future work.

While our work provides interesting insights into effective task allocation protocols and strategies in human-agent teams, our current work has some limitations. The first is concerned with the types of tasks the team allocates. The team only allocates intellective tasks, and it is unclear how the results would generalize if the team is responsible for other classifications of task types [26]. In

---

[2] Humans outperform agents for both allocators as agents are endowed with medium-level capabilities. Increasing agent expertise will change relative performances.

addition, in the current study the protocol is configured to allow for only task sharing. We do not know the effect of removing this constraint.

As future work, we will evaluate the effect of different agent expertise distributions on team performances. We also plan to experiment with different environment and protocol configurations, including those where the constraint of equal division of tasks is relaxed, and where allocator role is shared. Lastly, we plan to study how the dynamics of human-agent teams change when the team consists of more than two members.

References

1. Abdulrahman, A., Richards, D., Bilgin, A.A.: Reason explanation for encouraging behaviour change intention. In: Proceedings of the 20th International Conference on Autonomous Agents and MultiAgent Systems, pp. 68–77 (2021)
2. Adams, P.A., Adams, J.K.: Confidence in the recognition and reproduction of words difficult to spell. Am. J. Psychol. **73**, 544–552 (1960)
3. Anderson, A., Kleinberg, J., Mullainathan, S.: Assessing human error against a benchmark of perfection. ACM Trans. Knowl. Disc. Data (TKDD) **11**(4), 1–25 (2017)
4. Athey, S.C., Bryan, K.A., Gans, J.S.: The allocation of decision authority to human and artificial intelligence. In: AEA Papers and Proceedings, vol. 110, pp. 80–84 (2020)
5. Barrett, S., Stone, P., Kraus, S.: Empirical evaluation of ad hoc teamwork in the pursuit domain. In: AAMAS, pp. 567–574 (2011)
6. Binetti, G., Naso, D., Turchiano, B.: Decentralized task allocation for surveillance systems with critical tasks. Robot. Auton. Syst. **61**(12), 1653–1664 (2013)
7. Brinkman, W.P.: Design of a questionnaire instrument. In: Handbook of Mobile Technology Research Methods, pp. 31–57. Nova Publishers (2009)
8. Dias, M.B., Zlot, R., Kalra, N., Stentz, A.: Market-based multirobot coordination: a survey and analysis. Proc. IEEE **94**(7), 1257–1270 (2006)
9. Ernst, A., Jiang, H., Krishnamoorthy, M.: Exact solutions to task allocation problems. Manag. Sci. **52**(10), 1634–1646 (2006)
10. Fisher, D.M.: Distinguishing between taskwork and teamwork planning in teams: relations with coordination and interpersonal processes. J. Appl. Psychol. **99**(3), 423 (2014)
11. Genter, K., Agmon, N., Stone, P.: Role-based ad hoc teamwork. In: Proceedings of the Plan, Activity, and Intent Recognition Workshop at the Twenty-Fifth Conference on Artificial Intelligence (PAIR 2011), August 2011
12. Gerkey, B.P., Matarić, M.J.: A formal analysis and taxonomy of task allocation in multi-robot systems. Int. J. Robot. Res. **23**(9), 939–954 (2004)
13. Gervits, F., Thurston, D., Thielstrom, R., Fong, T., Pham, Q., Scheutz, M.: Toward genuine robot teammates: improving human-robot team performance using robot shared mental models. In: AAMAS, pp. 429–437 (2020)
14. Gunn, T., Anderson, J.: Effective task allocation for evolving multi-robot teams in dangerous environments. In: 2013 IEEE/WIC/ACM International Joint Conferences on Web Intelligence (WI) and Intelligent Agent Technologies (IAT), vol. 2, pp. 231–238. IEEE (2013)
15. Hauser, D., Paolacci, G., Chandler, J.: Common concerns with MTurk as a participant pool: evidence and solutions (2019)

16. Hayes-Roth, B.: A blackboard architecture for control. Artif. Intell. **26**(3), 251–321 (1985)

17. Kahneman, D.: Thinking, Fast and Slow. Macmillan, London (2011)

18. Korsah, G.A., Stentz, A., Dias, M.B.: A comprehensive taxonomy for multi-robot task allocation. Int. J. Robot. Res. **32**(12), 1495–1512 (2013)

19. Kuhn, H.W.: The Hungarian method for the assignment problem. Naval Res. Logist. Q. **2**(1–2), 83–97 (1955)

20. Lai, V., Tan, C.: On human predictions with explanations and predictions of machine learning models: a case study on deception detection. In: Proceedings of the Conference on Fairness, Accountability, and Transparency, pp. 29–38 (2019)

21. Larson, L., DeChurch, L.A.: Leading teams in the digital age: four perspectives on technology and what they mean for leading teams. Leadersh. Q. **31**(1), 101377 (2020)

22. Lin, R., Gal, Y., Kraus, S., Mazliah, Y.: Training with automated agents improves people's behavior in negotiation and coordination tasks. Decis. Support Syst. (DSS) **60**, 1–9 (2014)

23. Lott, C., McAuliffe, A., Kuttal, S.K.: Remote pair collaborations of CS students: leaving women behind? In: 2021 IEEE Symposium on Visual Languages and Human-Centric Computing (VL/HCC), pp. 1–11. IEEE (2021)

24. Mathieu, J.E., Hollenbeck, J.R., van Knippenberg, D., Ilgen, D.R.: A century of work teams in the Journal of Applied Psychology. J. Appl. Psychol. **102**(3), 452 (2017)

25. Mathieu, J.E., Rapp, T.L.: Laying the foundation for successful team performance trajectories: The roles of team charters and performance strategies. J. Appl. Psychol. **94**(1), 90 (2009)

26. McGrath, J.E.: Groups: Interaction and Performance, vol. 14. Prentice-Hall, Englewood Cliffs (1984)

27. Mosteo, A.R., Montano, L.: A survey of multi-robot task allocation. Technical report, Instituto de Investigacin en Ingenierła de Aragn (I3A) (2010)

28. Nunes, E., Manner, M., Mitiche, H., Gini, M.: A taxonomy for task allocation problems with temporal and ordering constraints. Robot. Auton. Syst. **90**, 55–70 (2017)

29. Patel, R., Rudnick-Cohen, E., Azarm, S., Otte, M., Xu, H., Herrmann, J.W.: Decentralized task allocation in multi-agent systems using a decentralized genetic algorithm. In: 2020 IEEE International Conference on Robotics and Automation (ICRA), pp. 3770–3776. IEEE (2020)

30. Perron, L., Furnon, V.: OR-tools. https://developers.google.com/optimization/

31. Puranam, P., Alexy, O., Reitzig, M.: What's "new" about new forms of organizing? Acad. Manag. Rev. **39**(2), 162–180 (2014)

32. Ramchurn, S.D., et al.: HAC-ER: a disaster response system based on human-agent collectives. In: Proceedings of the 2015 International Conference on Autonomous Agents and Multiagent Systems, pp. 533–541. International Foundation for Autonomous Agents and Multiagent Systems, Richland (2015)

33. Robinette, P., Wagner, A.R., Howard, A.M.: Building and maintaining trust between humans and guidance robots in an emergency. In: AAAI Spring Symposium: Trust and Autonomous Systems, Stanford, CA, pp. 78–83, March 2013

34. Rosenfeld, A., Agmon, N., Maksimov, O., Kraus, S.: Intelligent agent supporting human-multi-robot team collaboration. Artif. Intell. **252**, 211–231 (2017)

35. Sanchez, R.P., Bartel, C.M., Brown, E., DeRosier, M.: The acceptability and efficacy of an intelligent social tutoring system. Comput. Educ. **78**, 321–332 (2014)

36. Shoham, Y., Leyton-Brown, K.: Multiagent Systems: Algorithmic, Game-Theoretic, and Logical Foundations. Cambridge University Press, Cambridge (2008)
37. Zhao, W., Meng, Q., Chung, P.W.: A heuristic distributed task allocation method for multivehicle multitask problems and its application to search and rescue scenario. IEEE Trans. Cybern. **46**(4), 902–915 (2015)

FLEUR: Social Values Orientation for Robust Norm Emergence

Sz-Ting Tzeng[1]([✉]), Nirav Ajmeri[2], and Munindar P. Singh[1]

[1] North Carolina State University, Raleigh, NC 27695, USA
{stzeng,mpsingh}@ncsu.edu
[2] University of Bristol, Bristol BS8 1UB, UK
nirav.ajmeri@bristol.ac.uk

Abstract. By regulating agent interactions, norms facilitate coordination in multiagent systems. We investigate challenges and opportunities in the emergence of norms of prosociality, such as vaccination and mask wearing. Little research on norm emergence has incorporated social preferences, which determines how agents behave when others are involved.

We evaluate the influence of preference distributions in a society on the emergence of prosocial norms. We adopt the Social Value Orientation (SVO) framework, which places value preferences along the dimensions of self and other. SVO brings forth the aspects of values most relevant to prosociality. Therefore, it provides an effective basis to structure our evaluation.

We find that including SVO in agents enables (1) better social experience; and (2) robust norm emergence.

Keywords: Agent-based simulation · Norm adherence · Preferences · Social value orientation · Ethics

1 Introduction

What makes people make different decisions? Schwartz [23] defined ten fundamental human values, and each of them reflects specific motivations. Besides values, preferences define an individual's tendency to make a subjective selection among alternatives. Whereas values are relatively stable, preferences are sensitive to context and constructed when triggered [25].

In the real world, humans with varied weights of values evaluate the outcomes of their actions subjectively and act to maximize their utility [23]. In addition to values, an individual's social value orientation (SVO) influences the individual's behaviors [30]. Whereas values define the motivational bases of behaviors and attitudes of an individual [23], social value orientation indicates an individual's preference for resource allocation between self and others [8]. Specifically, social value orientation provides stable subjective weights for making decisions [17]. When interacting with others is inevitable, one individual's behavior may affect another. SVO revises an individual's utility function by assigning different weights to itself and others. Here is an example of a real-world case of SVO.

N. Ajmeri et al. (Eds.): COINE 2022, LNAI 13549, pp. 185–200, 2022.
https://doi.org/10.1007/978-3-031-20845-4_12

Example 1. **SVO.**

During a pandemic, the authorities announce a mask-wearing regulation and claim that regulation would help avoid infecting others or being infected. Although Felix tests positive on the pandemic and prefers not to wear a mask, he also cares about others' health. If he stays in a room with another healthy person, Elliot, Felix will put the mask on.

An agent is an autonomous, adaptive, and goal-driven entity [22]. Whereas many works assume agents consider the payoff of themselves, humans may further consider social preferences in the real world. e.g., payoffs of others or social welfare [5]. When humans are in the loop along with software, there are emerging need to consider human factors when building modern software and systems. These systems should consider human values and be capable of reasoning over humans' behaviors to be realistic and trustworthy.

In a multiagent system, social norms or social expectations [2,21] are societal principles that regulate our behavior towards one another by measuring our perceived psychological distance. Humans evaluate social norms based on human values. Most previous works related to norms do not consider human values and assume regimented environments. However, humans are capable of deliberately adhering to or violating norms. Previous works on normative agents consider human values and theories on sociality [4,31] in decision-making process. SVO as an agent's preference in a social context has not been fully explored.

Contributions. We investigate the following research question.

RQ_{SVO}. How do the preferences for others' rewards influence norm compliance?

To address RQ_{SVO}, we develop FLEUR, an agent framework that considers values, personal preferences, and social norms when making decisions. Our proposed framework FLEUR combines world model, cognitive model, emotion model, and social model. Since values are abstract and need further definition, we start with social value orientations, the stable preferences for resource allocation, in this work. Specifically, FLEUR agents take into account social value orientation in utility calculation.

Findings. We evaluate FLEUR via an agent simulation of a pandemic scenario designed as an iterated single-shot and intertemporal social dilemma game. We measure compliance, social experiences, and invalidation during the simulation. We find that the understanding of SVO helps agents to make more ethical decisions.

Organization. Section 2 presents the related works. Section 3 describes the schematics of FLEUR. Section 4 details the simulation experiments we conduct and the results. Section 5 presents our conclusion and directions for future extensions.

2   Related Works

Griesinger and Livingston Jr. [8] present a geometric model of SVO, the social value orientation ring as Fig. 2. Van Lange [30] proposes a model and interprets prosocial orientation as enhancing both joint outcomes and equality in the outcomes. Declerck and Bogaert [6] describe social value orientation as a personality trait. Their work indicates that prosocial orientation positively correlates with adopting others' viewpoints and the ability to infer others' mental states. On the contrary, an individualistic orientation shows a negative correlation with these social skills. FLEUR follows the concepts of social preferences from [8].

Szekely et al. [26] show that high risk promotes robust norms, which have high resistance to risk change. de Mooij et al. [15] build a large-scale data-driven agent-based simulation model to simulate behavioral interventions among humans. Each agent reasons over their internal attitudes and external factors in this work. Ajmeri et al. [3] show that robust norms emerge among interactions where deviating agents reveal their contexts. This work enables agents to empathize with other agents' dilemmas by revealing contexts. Instead of sharing contexts, values, or preferences, FLEUR approximates others' payoff with observation. Serramia et al. [24] consider shared values in a society with norms and focus on making ethical decisions that promote the values. Ajmeri et al. [4] propose an agent framework that enables agents to aggregate the value preferences of stakeholders and make ethical decisions accordingly. This work takes other agents' values into account when making decisions. Mosca and Such [16] describe an agent framework that aggregates the shared preferences and moral values of multiple users and makes the optimal decisions for all users. Kalia et al. [10] investigate the relationship between norm outcomes and trust and emotions. Tzeng et al. [29] consider emotions as sanctions. Specifically, norm satisfaction or norm violation may trigger self-directed and other-directed emotions, which further enforce social norms. Dell'Anna et al. [7] propose a mechanism to regulate a multiagent system by revising the sanctions at runtime to achieve runtime norm enforcement. Agrawal et al. [1] provide and evaluate explicit norms and explanations. Winikoff et al. [33] construct comprehensible explanations with beliefs, desires, and values. Kurtan and Yolum [11] estimate privacy values with existing shared images in a user's social network. Tielman et al. [27] derive norms based on values and contexts. However, these works do not consider the differences between agents and the influences of an individual's behavior on others. Mashayekhi et al. [13] model guilt based on inequity aversion theory for an individual perspective on prosociality. In addition, they consider justice from a societal perspective on prosociality. Whereas Mashayekhi et al. [13] assume agents may be self-interested and their decisions may be affected by others' performance, FLEUR investigates the influence of social value orientations.

Table 1 summarizes related works on ethical agents. Adaptivity describes the capability of responding to different contexts. Empathy defines the ability to consider others' gain. The information share indicates information sharing among agents. The information model describes the applied models to process information and states. Among varied information models, contexts describe the situation in which an agent stands. Emotions are the responses to internal or external events or objects. Guilt is an aversive self-directed emotion. Explicit norms state causal normative information, including antecedents and consequences. Values and preferences both define desirable or undesirable states.

Table 1. Comparisons of works on ethical agents with norms and values.

Research	Adaptivity	Empathy	Information share	Information model
FLEUR	✓	✓	✗	Preferences & Emotions & Contexts
Agrawal et al. [1]	✓	✗	✓	Explicit norms
Ajmeri et al. [3]	✓	✓	✓	Contexts
Ajmeri et al. [4]	✓	✓	✓	Values & Value preference & Contexts
Kalia et al. [10]	✓	✗	✗	Trust & Emotions
Kurtan and Yolum [11]	✓	✗	✗	Values
Mashayekhi et al. [13]	✓	✓	✓	Guilt
Mosca and Such [16]	✓	✓	✓	Preferences & Values
Serramia et al. [24]	✓	✗	✗	Values
Tielman et al. [27]	✓	✗	✓	Values & Contexts
Tzeng et al. [29]	✗	✗	✗	Emotions
Winikoff et al. [33]	✓	✗	✗	Values & Beliefs & Goals

3   FLEUR

We now discuss the schematics of FLEUR agents.

Figure 1 shows the architecture of FLEUR. FLEUR agents consists of five main components: cognitive model, emotion model, world model, social model, and a decision module.

3.1   Cognitive Model

Cognition relates to conscious intellectual activities, such as thinking, reasoning, or remembering, among which human values and preferences are essential. Specifically, values and preferences may change how an individual evaluates an agent, an event, or an object. In FLEUR, We start with including human preferences. While preferences are the attitudes toward a set of objects in psychology [25], individual and social preferences provide intrinsic rewards. For instance, SVO provides agents with different preferences over resource allocations between themselves and others. Figure 2 demonstrates the reward distribution of different SVO types. The horizontal axis measures the resources allocated to oneself, and the vertical axis measures the resources allocated to others.

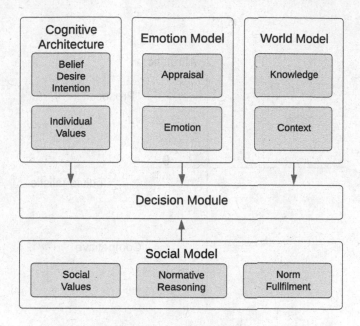

Fig. 1. FLEUR architecture.

Let $\overrightarrow{R} = (r_1, r_2, \ldots, r_n)$ represent the reward vector for a group of agents with size n. The reward for agent i considering social aspect is:

$$reward_i = r_i \cdot \cos \theta + r_{-i} \cdot \sin \theta \qquad (1)$$

where r_i represents the reward for agent i and r_{-i} is the mean reward of all other agents interacting with agent i. Here we adopt the reward angle in [14] and represent agents' social value orientation with θ. We define $\theta \in \{90°, 45°, 0°, -45°\}$ as SVO $\in$ {altruistic, prosocial, individualistic, competitive}, respectively. With the weights provided by SVO, the presented equation enables the accommodation of social preferences.

In utility calculation, we consider two components: (1) extrinsic reward and (2) intrinsic reward. Whereas extrinsic rewards come from the environment, intrinsic rewards stem from internal stats, e.g., human values and preferences.

We extend the Belief-Desire-Intention (BDI) architecture [20]. An agent forms beliefs based on the information from the environment. The desire of an agent represents having dispositions to act. An agent's intention is a plan or action to achieve a selected desire.

Take Example 1 for instance. Since Felix has an intention to maximize the joint gain with Elliot, he may choose a strategy to not increase his payoff at the cost of others' sacrifice.

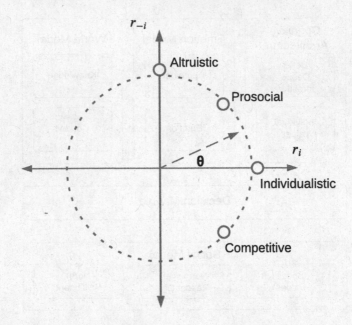

Fig. 2. Representation of Social Value Orientation [8,14]. r_i denotes outcome for oneself and r_{-i} denotes outcomes for others.

3.2   Emotion Model

We adopt the OCC model of emotions [19]. Specifically, our emotion model appraises an object, an action, or an event and then triggers emotions. We consider emotional valence and assume norm satisfaction or norm violation yields positive or negative emotions if self behaviors align with the norms.

3.3   World Model

The world model describes the contexts in which FLEUR agents stand and represents the general knowledge FLEUR agents possess. A context is a scenario that an agent faces. Knowledge in this model are facts of the world. In Example 1, the context is that an infected individual, Felix, seeks to maximize the collective gain of himself and a healthy individual, Elliot. In the meantime, Felix acknowledges that a pandemic is ongoing.

3.4   Social Model

The social model of an agent includes social values, normative reasoning, and norm fulfillment. Social values define standards that individuals and groups employ to shape the form of social order [28], e.g., fairness and justice. Agents use the normative-reasoning component to reason over states, norms, and possible outcomes of satisfying or violating norms. Norm fulfillment checks if a norm has been fulfilled or violated with the selected action. Sanctions may come after norm fulfillments or violations.

3.5   Decision Module

The decision module selects actions based on agents' payoffs and individual values. We apply Q-Learning [32], a model-free reinforcement learning algorithm that learns from trial and error, to our agents. Q-Learning approximates the action-state value $Q(s, a)$ (Q value), with each state and action:

$$Q'(s_t, a_t) = Q(s_t, a_t) + \alpha * (R_t + \gamma \max_{a'} Q(s_{t+1}, a) - Q(s_t, a_t)) \qquad (2)$$

where $Q'(s_t, a_t)$ represents the updated Q-value after performing action a at time t and s_{t+1} represents the next state. α denotes the learning rate in the Q-value update function, and R_t represents the rewards received at time t after acting a. γ defines the reward discount rate, which characterizes the importance of future rewards. Agents observe the environment, form their beliefs about the world, and update their state-value with rewards via interactions. By approximating the action-state value, the Q-Learning algorithm finds the optimal policy via the expected and cumulative rewards.

Algorithm 1 describes the agent interaction in our simulation.

Algorithm 1: Decision loop of a FLEUR agent

1 Initialize one agent with its desires D and preference P and SVO angle θ;
2 Initialize action-value function Q with random weights w;
3 **for** $t=1, T$ **do**
4   Pair up with another agent pn to interact with;
5   Observe the environment (including the partner and its θ) and form beliefs b_t;
6   With a probability ϵ select a random action a_t
           Otherwise select $a_t = argmax_a Q(b_t, a; w)$
7   Execute action a_t and observe reward r_t;
8   Observe the environment (including the partner) and form beliefs b_{t+1};
9   Activate norms N with beliefs b_t, b_{t+1}, and action a_t;
10   **if** $N != \varnothing$ **then**
11 | Sanction the partner based on a_t and its behavior;
12   **end**
13 **end**

---

4   Experiments

We now describe our experiments and discuss the results.

4.1   Experimental Scenario: Pandemic Mask Regulation

We build a pandemic scenario as an iterated single-shot and intertemporal social dilemma. We assume that the authorities have announced a masking regulation. In each game, each agent selects from the following two actions: (1) wear a mask, and (2) not wear a mask. Each agent has its inherent preferences and social value orientation. An agent forms a belief about its partner's health based on its observation. During the interaction, the decision an agent makes affects itself and others. The collective behaviors among agents determine the dynamics in a society. Each agent receives the final points from its own action and effects from others: $R_{sum} = P_{i\_self} + P_{i\_other} + S_j$. P_{i_self} denotes the payoff from the action that agent i selects considering the reward distribution in Fig. 2 and self-directed emotions. P_{i_other} is the payoff from the action that the other agent performs. S_j denotes the other-directed emotions from others towards agent i.

Table 2. Payoff for an actor and its partner based on how the actor acts and how its action influence others. Column Actors show the points from the actions of the actor. Column Partners display the points from the actions to the partner.

Health		Actions			
Actor	Partner	Mask		No mask	
		Actor	Partner	Actor	Partner
Healthy	Healthy	0.00	0.00	0.00	0.00
Healthy	Infected	1.00	0.00	−1.00	0.00
Infected	Healthy	0.00	1.00	0.00	−1.00
Infected	Infected	0.50	0.50	−0.50	−0.50

Table 3. Payoff for decisions on preferences

Type	Decisions	
	Satisfy	Dissatisfy
Preference	0.50	0.00

4.2   Experimental Setup

We develop a simulation using Mesa [12], an agent-based modeling framework in Python for creating, visualizing, and analyzing agent-based models. We ran the simulations on a device with 32 GB RAM and GPU NVIDIA GTX 1070 Ti.

We evaluated FLEUR via a simulated pandemic scenario where agents' behaviors influence the collective outcome of the social game. A game-theoretical setting may be ideal for validating the social dilemma with SVO and norms. However, real-world cases are usually non-zero-sum games where one's gain does not always lead to others' loss. In our scenario, depending on the context, the same

Table 4. Payoff for decisions on norms

Actor	Partner	
	Wear	Not-Wear
Wear	0.10	−0.10
Not-Wear	0.00	0.10

action may lead to different consequences for the agent itself and its partner. For instance, when an agent is healthy and its partner is infected, wearing a mask gives the agent a positive payoff from the protection of the mask but no payoff for its partner. Conversely, not wearing a mask leads to a negative payoff for the agent and no payoff for its partner. The payoff given to the agent and its partner corresponds to the X and Y axis in Fig. 2. When formalizing social interactions with SVO in game-theoretical settings, the payoffs of actions for an agent and others are required information.

We incorporated beliefs and desires, and intentions into our agents. An agent observes its environment and processes its perception, and forms its beliefs about the world. In each episode, agents pair up to interact with one another and sanction based on their and partners' decisions (Table 4).

Context. A context is composed of attributes from an agent and others and the environment as shown in Table 2. We frame the simulation as a non-zero-sum game where one's gain does not necessarily lead to the other parties' loss.

Preference. In psychology, preferences refer to an agent's attitudes towards a set of objects. In our simulation, we set 40% of agents to prefer to wear and prefer not to masks individually. The rest of the agents have a neutral attitude on masks. The payoffs for following the preferences are listed in Table 3.

Social Value Orientation. Social value orientation defines an agent's preference for allocating resources between itself and others. We consider altruistic, prosocial, individualistic, and competitive orientations selected from Fig. 2.

4.3   Hypotheses and Metrics

We compute the following measures to address our research question RQ_{SVO}.

Compliance. The percentage of agents who satisfy norms
Social Experience. The total payoff of the agents in a society
Invalidation. The percentage of agents who do not meet their preferences in a society

To answer our research question RQ_{SVO}, we evaluate three hypotheses that correspond to the specific metric, respectively.

$H_{Compliance}$: Preferences for others' rewards positively affect norm compliance with prosocial norms

$H_{Social\ Experience}$: The distribution of preferences for others' rewards positively affect social experiences in a society

$H_{Invalidation}$: Preferences for others' rewards negatively affect the tendency to meet personal preferences

4.4 Experiments

We ran a population of $N = 40$ agents in which we equally distributed our targeted SVO types: altruistic, prosocial, individualistic, and competitive. Since each game is a single-shot social dilemma, we consider each game as an episode. The training last for 500,000 episodes. In evaluation, we run 100 episodes and compute the mean values to minimize deviation from coincidence. We define our five societies as below.

Mixed society. A society of agents with mixed social value orientation distribution

Altruistic society. A society of agents who make decisions based on altruistic concerns

Prosocial society. A society of agents who make decisions based on prosocial concerns

Selfish society. A society of agents who make decisions based on selfish concerns

Competitive society. A society of agents who make decisions based on competitive concerns

We assume all agents are aware of a mask-wearing norm. Agents who satisfy the norm receive positive emotions from themselves and others, as in Table 4. Conversely, norm violators receive negative emotions. Table 5 summarizes results of our simulation.

Figure 3 displays the compliance, the percentage of agents who satisfy norms, in the mixed and baseline-agent societies. We find that the compliance in the altruistic and prosocial-agent society, averaging at 69.70% and 70.25%, is higher than in the mixed (63.34%) and agent societies have no positive weights on others' payoff (65.10% and 54.08% for selfish and competitive-agent societies, respectively). The differences in the results of altruistic and prosocial-agent societies are statistically significant with medium effect ($p < 0.001$; Glass' $\Delta > 0.5$). Conversely, the competitive-agent society has the least compliance, averaging at 54.08%, with $p < 0.001$ and Glass' $\Delta > 0.8$. The results of the selfish-agent society (65.10%) shows no significant difference with $p > 0.05$ and Glass' $\Delta \approx 0.2$.

There are 25% of agents in the mixed-agent society are competitive agents. Specifically, they prefer to minimize others' payoff. A competitive infected agent may choose not to wear a mask when interacting with other healthy agents in this scenario. In the meantime, the selfish agents would maximize their self utility without considering others. Therefore, the behaviors of selfish and competitive agents may decrease compliance in the mixed-agent society.

Table 5. Comparing agent societies with different social value orientation distribution on various metrics and their statistical analysis with Glass' Δ and p-value. Each metric row shows the numeric value of the metric after simulation convergence.

		Compliance	Social experience	Invalidation
S_{mixed}	Results	63.40%	0.4483	0.2960
	p-value	–	–	–
	Δ	–	–	–
$S_{altruistic}$	Results	69.70%	0.5543	**0.3340**
	p-value	< 0.001	< 0.001	< 0.001
	Δ	0.6602	0.6116	0.4635
$S_{prosocial}$	Results	**70.25%**	**0.5656**	0.3228
	p-value	< 0.001	< 0.001	< 0.05
	Δ	0.7178	0.6771	0.3263
$S_{selfish}$	Results	65.10%	0.4695	0.2690
	p-value	0.2180	0.4245	< 0.05
	Δ	0.1781	0.1221	0.3293
$S_{competitive}$	Results	54.08%	0.2208	0.2888
	p-value	< 0.001	< 0.001	0.5412
	Δ	0.9772	1.3131	0.0884

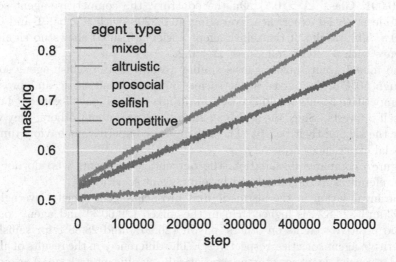

Fig. 3. Compliance in training phase: The percentage of norm satisfaction in a society.

Figure 4 compares the average payoff in the mixed and baseline-agent societies. The social experience in the altruistic and prosocial-agent society, averaging at 0.5543 and 0.5656, is higher than in the mixed (0.4483) and agent societies

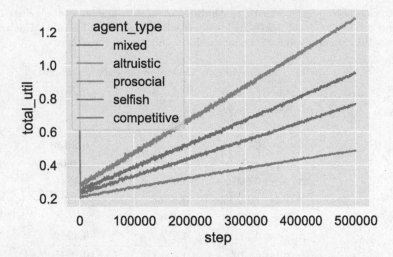

Fig. 4. Social Experience in training phase: The total payoff of the agents in a society.

have no positive weights on others' payoff (46.95% and 22.08% for selfish and competitive-agent societies, respectively). The differences in the results of altruistic and prosocial-agent societies are statistically significant with medium effect ($p < 0.001$; Glass' $\Delta > 0.5$). On the contrary, the competitive-agent society has the least social experience, averaging at 0.2208, with $p < 0.001$ and Glass' $\Delta > 0.8$. The results of the selfish-agent society (0.4695) shows no significant difference with $p > 0.05$ and Glass' $\Delta < 0.2$.

The mixed-agent society shows similar results as the selfish-agent society. Although 50% of the mixed-agent society agents are altruistic and prosocial, the competitive agents would choose to minimize others' payoff without hurting their self-interests. Since the selfish agents do not care about others, they would act for the sake of their benefit. The selfish and competitive behaviors diminish the social experiences in society.

Figure 5 compares invalidation, the percentage of agents who do not meet their preferences in the mixed and baseline-agent societies.

The invalidation in the altruistic and prosocial-agent society, averaging at 33.40% and 32.28%, is higher than in the mixed (29.60%) and agent societies have no positive weights on others' payoff (26.90% and 28.88% for selfish and competitive-agent societies, respectively). The differences in the results of altruistic and prosocial-agent societies are statistically significant with small or medium effect ($p < 0.001$; Glass' $\Delta > 0.2$). On the contrary, the selfish-agent society has the least invalidation, average at 26.90%, with $p < 0.05$ and Glass' $\Delta > 0.2$. The results of the competitive-agent society (28.88%) shows no significant difference with $p > 0.05$ and Glass' $\Delta < 0.2$.

While agents who consider others' rewards positively achieve better compliance and social experiences, these achievements are based on their sacrifice of

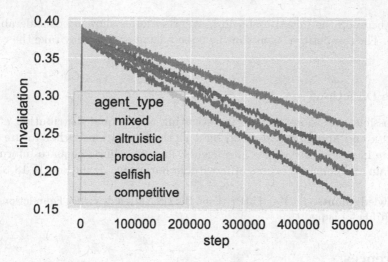

Fig. 5. Invalidation in training phase: The percentage of agents who do not meet their preferences in a society.

preferences. The altruistic and prosocial agent societies have the most percentage of agents who do not meet their preferences.

4.5   Threats to Validity

First, our simulation has a limited action space. Moreover, different actions may have the same payoff in some contexts. Other behaviors may better describe different types of SVO, yet our focus is on showing how SVO influences normative decisions.

Second, we represent actual societies as simulations. While differences in preference and SVO among people are inevitable, we focus on validating the influence of SVO.

Third, to simplify the simulation, we assume fixed interaction, whereas real-world interactions tend to be random. An agent may interact with one another in the same place many times or have no interaction. We randomly pair up all agents to mitigate this threat and average out the results.

5   Conclusions and Directions

We present an agent architecture that integrates cognitive architecture, world model, and social model to investigate how social value orientation influences compliance with norms. We simulate a pandemic scenario in which agents make decisions based on their individual and social preferences. The simulations show that altruistic and prosocial-agent societies comply better with the mask norm and bring out higher social experiences. However, altruistic and prosocial agents trade their personal preferences for compliance and social experiences. The results between the mixed and selfish-agent societies show no considerable difference. The competitive agents in the mixed-agent society may take the responsibility.

Future Directions

Our possible extensions include investigating an unequal distribution of SVO in FLEUR and applying real-world data in the simulation. Other future directions are incorporating values into agents, and revealing adequate information to explain and convince others of inevitable normative deviations [1,18,34].

Acknowledgments. STT and MPS thank the US National Science Foundation (grant IIS-2116751) for support.

References

1. Agrawal, R., Ajmeri, N., Singh, M.P.: Socially intelligent genetic agents for the emergence of explicit norms. In: Proceedings of the 31st International Joint Conference on Artificial Intelligence (IJCAI), pp. 1–7. IJCAI, Vienna (2022)
2. Ajmeri, N., Guo, H., Murukannaiah, P.K., Singh, M.P.: Arnor: modeling social intelligence via norms to engineer privacy-aware personal agents. In: Proceedings of the 16th International Conference on Autonomous Agents and MultiAgent Systems (AAMAS), pp. 230–238. IFAAMAS, São Paulo (2017). https://doi.org/10.5555/3091125.3091163
3. Ajmeri, N., Guo, H., Murukannaiah, P.K., Singh, M.P.: Robust norm emergence by revealing and reasoning about context: Socially intelligent agents for enhancing privacy. In: Proceedings of the 27th International Joint Conference on Artificial Intelligence (IJCAI), pp. 28–34. IJCAI, Stockholm (2018). https://doi.org/10.24963/ijcai.2018/4
4. Ajmeri, N., Guo, H., Murukannaiah, P.K., Singh, M.P.: Elessar: ethics in norm-aware agents. In: Proceedings of the 19th International Conference on Autonomous Agents and MultiAgent Systems (AAMAS), pp. 16–24. IFAAMAS, Auckland (2020). https://doi.org/10.5555/3398761.3398769
5. Charness, G., Rabin, M.: Understanding social preferences with simple tests. Q. J. Econ. **117**(3), 817–869 (2002)
6. Declerck, C.H., Bogaert, S.: Social value orientation: related to empathy and the ability to read the mind in the eyes. J. Social Psychol. **148**(6), 711–726 (2008). https://doi.org/10.3200/SOCP.148.6.711-726
7. Dell'Anna, D., Dastani, M., Dalpiaz, F.: Runtime revision of norms and sanctions based on agent preferences. In: Proceedings of the 18th International Conference on Autonomous Agents and MultiAgent Systems (AAMAS), pp. 1609–1617. IFAAMAS (2019). https://doi.org/10.5555/3306127.3331881
8. Griesinger, D.W., Livingston Jr., J.W.: Toward a model of interpersonal motivation in experimental games. Behav. Sci. **18**(3), 173–188 (1973). https://doi.org/10.1002/bs.3830180305
9. Huhns, M.N., Singh, M.P. (eds.): Readings in Agents. Morgan Kaufmann, San Francisco (1998). ISBN 9780080515809

10. Kalia, A.K., Ajmeri, N., Chan, K., Cho, J.H., Adalı, S., Singh, M.P.: The interplay of emotions and norms in multiagent systems. In: Proceedings of the 28th International Joint Conference on Artificial Intelligence (IJCAI), pp. 371–377. IJCAI, Macau (2019). https://doi.org/10.24963/ijcai.2019/53
11. Kurtan, A.C., Yolum, P.: Assisting humans in privacy management: an agent-based approach. Auton. Agents Multi-Agent Syst. **35**(1), 1–33 (2020). https://doi.org/10.1007/s10458-020-09488-1
12. Masad, D., Kazil, J.: MESA: an agent-based modeling framework. In: Proceedings of the 14th PYTHON in Science Conference, pp. 53–60 (2015)
13. Mashayekhi, M., Ajmeri, N., List, G.F., Singh, M.P.: Prosocial norm emergence in multiagent systems. ACM Trans. Auton. Adapt. Syst. (TAAS) **17**, 1–24 (2022)
14. McKee, K.R., Gemp, I.M., McWilliams, B., Duéñez-Guzmán, E.A., Hughes, E., Leibo, J.Z.: Social diversity and social preferences in mixed-motive reinforcement learning. In: Proceedings of the 19th International Conference on Autonomous Agents and Multiagent Systems (AAMAS), pp. 869–877. IFAAMAS, Auckland (2020). https://doi.org/10.5555/3398761.3398863
15. de Mooij, J., Dell'Anna, D., Bhattacharya, P., Dastani, M., Logan, B., Swarup, S.: Quantifying the effects of norms on COVID-19 cases using an agent-based simulation. In: Van Dam, K.H., Verstaevel, N. (eds.) MABS 2021. LNCS (LNAI), vol. 13128, pp. 99–112. Springer, Cham (2022). https://doi.org/10.1007/978-3-030-94548-0_8
16. Mosca, F., Such, J.M.: ELVIRA: an explainable agent for value and utility-driven multiuser privacy. In: Proceedings of the 20th International Conference on Autonomous Agents and Multiagent Systems (AAMAS), pp. 916–924. IFAAMAS, London (2021). https://doi.org/10.5555/3463952.3464061
17. Murphy, R.O., Ackermann, K.A.: Social value orientation: theoretical and measurement issues in the study of social preferences. Pers. Social Psychol. Rev. **18**(1), 13–41 (2014). https://doi.org/10.1177/1088868313501745
18. Murukannaiah, P.K., Ajmeri, N., Jonker, C.M., Singh, M.P.: New foundations of ethical multiagent systems. In: Proceedings of the 19th International Conference on Autonomous Agents and MultiAgent Systems (AAMAS), pp. 1706–1710. IFAAMAS, Auckland (2020). https://doi.org/10.5555/3398761.3398958, Blue Sky Ideas Track
19. Ortony, A., Clore, G.L., Collins, A.: The Cognitive Structure of Emotions. Cambridge University Press, New York (1988). https://doi.org/10.1017/CBO9780511571299
20. Rao, A.S., Georgeff, M.P.: Modeling rational agents within a BDI-architecture. In: Proceedings of the International Conference on Principles of Knowledge Representation and Reasoning, pp. 473–484 (1991). reprinted in [9]
21. Rummel, R.J.: Understanding Conflict and War: Vol. 1: The Dynamic Psychological Field. Sage Publications, Thousand Oaks (1975)
22. Russell, S., Norvig, P.: Artificial Intelligence: A Modern Approach, 3rd edn. Prentice Hall, Upper Saddle River (2010)
23. Schwartz, S.H.: An overview of the schwartz theory of basic values. Online Read. Psychol. Cult. **2**(1), 0919–2307 (2012). https://doi.org/10.9707/2307-0919.1116
24. Serramia, M., et al.: Moral values in norm decision making. In: Proceedings of the 17th Conference on Autonomous Agents and MultiAgent Systems (AAMAS), pp. 1294–1302. IFAAMAS, Stockholm (2018). https://doi.org/10.5555/3237383.3237891
25. Slovic, P.: The construction of preference. Am. Psychol. **50**(5), 364 (1995). https://doi.org/10.1037/0003-066X.50.5.364

26. Szekely, A., et al.: Evidence from a long-term experiment that collective risks change social norms and promote cooperation. Nat. Commun. **12**, 5452:1–5452:7 (2021). https://doi.org/10.1038/s41467-021-25734-w

27. Tielman, M.L., Jonker, C.M., Van Riemsdijk, M.B.: Deriving norms from actions, values and context. In: Proceedings of the 18th International Conference on Autonomous Agents and MultiAgent Systems, pp. 2223–2225 (2019). https://doi.org/10.5555/3306127.3332065

28. Tsirogianni, S., Sammut, G., Park, E.: Social Values and Good Living. Springer, Netherlands (2014). https://doi.org/10.1007/978-94-007-0753-5_3666

29. Tzeng, S.T., Ajmeri, N., Singh, M.P.: Noe: norms emergence and robustness based on emotions in multiagent systems. In: Pre-proceedings of the International Workshop on Coordination, Organizations, Institutions, Norms and Ethics for Governance of Multi-Agent Systems (COINE), London, pp. 1–17 (2021). https://arxiv.org/abs/2104.15034

30. Van Lange, P.A.M.: The pursuit of joint outcomes and equality in outcomes: an integrative model of social value orientation. J. Pers. Social Psychol. **77**(2), 337–349 (1999). https://doi.org/10.1037/0022-3514.77.2.337

31. Verhagen, H.J.: Norm autonomous agents. Ph.D. thesis, Stockholm Universitet (2000)

32. Watkins, C.J., Dayan, P.: Q-learning. Mach. Learn. **8**(3–4), 279–292 (1992). https://doi.org/10.1007/BF00992698

33. Winikoff, M., Sidorenko, G., Dignum, V., Dignum, F.: Why bad coffee? explaining BDI agent behaviour with valuings. Artif. Intell. **300**, 103554 (2021). https://doi.org/10.1016/j.artint.2021.103554

34. Woodgate, J., Ajmeri, N.: Macro ethics for governing equitable sociotechnical systems. In: Proceedings of the 21st International Conference on Autonomous Agents and Multiagent Systems (AAMAS), pp. 1824–1828. IFAAMAS, Online (2022). https://doi.org/10.5555/3535850.3536118, Blue Sky Ideas Track

Reasoning About Collective Action in Markov Logic: A Case Study from Classical Athens

Sriashalya Srivathsan[1]([⊠]), Stephen Cranefield[1]([⊠]), and Jeremy Pitt[2]

[1] University of Otago, Dunedin, New Zealand
ashal.srivathsan@postgrad.otago.ac.nz, stephen.cranefield@otago.ac.nz
[2] Imperial College London, London, UK
j.pitt@imperial.ac.uk

Abstract. Solving the collective action problem is to understand how people decide to act together for the common good when individual rationality would lead to non-cooperative selfish behaviour. Two important features that can foster collective action are achieving common knowledge about the problem faced and the existence of a shared cooperative ethos. Based on the work of Ober, who argued that the success of classical Athens was the result of its shared commitments, social values and specific procedural rules, we define a probabilistic model in Markov Logic of a specific prosecution against an Athenian trader who neglected to contribute to the city when it was in a crisis. In order to join together for a common good, our model focuses on a decision-making approach based on reasoning about common knowledge. For example, knowledge about the ethos of the court towards convicting traitors can be seen as common knowledge gained from public monuments recording these verdicts. We expect that our computational model of this case study can be generalised to other problems of reasoning about collective action based on common knowledge in future work.

Keywords: Common knowledge · Collective action · Markov Logic Networks

1 Introduction

Solving the collective action problem is to understand how people act together for the common good. Collectively reducing the emission of greenhouse gases [19] and managing common pool resources [17] are two examples of environmental collective actions. Solving collective action problems is important to overcome various social and environmental problems. Collective action requires communication, organisation, and incentives that motivate everyone to work together for the common good. Existing studies [17,18] introduce strategies and solutions to tackle these problems. While traditional solution concepts from game theory [14], such as the Nash equilibrium [9] suggest that collective action is irrational, Holzinger [10] discusses various solutions including norms, rules and sanctions. Besides common knowledge, expectations and credible commitment also motivates people to join together for collective action.

Political scientist Josiah Ober [16] discusses the role of common knowledge in making people join collective actions in classical Athens. He argues that Athens was socially, politically and militarily successful compared to rival states because of a superior ability to achieve shared commitments, shared social values and procedural rules

N. Ajmeri et al. (Eds.): COINE 2022, LNAI 13549, pp. 201–212, 2022.
https://doi.org/10.1007/978-3-031-20845-4_13

through common knowledge. In particular, a specific trial discussed by him has a lot of richness and information regarding the cooperation and social structure in terms of common knowledge. Therefore, we adopt this as a case study of the role of common knowledge in achieving collective action.

The trial was against an Athenian trader named *Leocrates*. It was alleged that he abandoned the city when it needed help to defend and reconstruct it after a battle had been lost with the Macedonians. *Lycurgus*, a famous Athenian politician, prosecuted this trial with the intention of convincing the jurors to convict *Leocrates* for the capital charge of treason. A record exists of the narrative *Lycurgus* gave to persuade jurors of the importance of convicting *Leocrates*.

The trial is an interesting case study in which we found the prosecutor's points convey the importance of common knowledge in fostering the collective goal of having a secure city and how the result of this trial will impact the security of the city. Therefore, we are interested in implementing a computational model using common knowledge to find how agents would make decisions based on a logical encoding of some of the arguments made by the prosecutor.

We consider several sources that lead to attaining common knowledge: the community acceptance of a collective goal through observation of an alignment cascade [22], measures of common knowledge about social attitudes to the collective goal through empirical observations, and observing states of affairs that satisfy four conditions identified by Lewis [13] as giving rise to common knowledge.

As Markov logic networks (MLNs) [5] express knowledge explicitly, and also help representing beliefs of a probabilistic nature, we use an MLN to model this trial. For example, a belief that a certain proportion of citizens are cooperative with city-wide goals is probabilistic in nature, based on an estimate of the percentage of cooperators.

The paper is structured as follows: The concept of common knowledge is discussed in Sect. 2, along with how it will be helpful to achieve a common goal. The discussion in Sect. 3 centers on points in terms of common knowledge made by *Lycurgus* during the trial of *Leocrates*. As the trial is modelled using a Markov Logic Network (MLN), Sect. 4 provides an overview of MLNs. A description of how this trial was modelled as an MLN is provided in detail in Sect. 5. Section 6 discusses how the model can be queried to inform the decision of a juror in the trial. Section 7 concludes the paper.

2   Common Knowledge

A range of studies discuss the importance of knowledge alignment in bringing people together. In fact, knowledge and action are intimately connected. In most situations, people act according to what they think. The term 'common knowledge' refers "knowledge of what other people know about other people's knowledge" [4]. According to Kuhlman et al., [12] "Successful coordination requires that people know each others' willingness to participate, and that this information is common knowledge among a sufficient number of people". This involves infinite information transmission levels which can be explained [13] as:

– I know something; you know something
– I know that you know; you know that I know

- I know that you know that I know
- You know that I know that you know; and so on ...

However, this infinite reflection is not how common knowledge is obtained in practice. Achieving common knowledge requires collective awareness and collective attention. Social coordination revolves around the achievement of common knowledge through group attention. From knowing where to find your partners, to communicating with them, to resolving public goods dilemmas, to following social norms, success in social interactions often depends on collective awareness [21].

The emergence of common knowledge occurs when people receive information simultaneously and publicly, when it becomes obvious that "we are attending" [20]. The places and events that make maximum eye contact [4] will create common knowledge. Transparent information provides no reason to doubt others' awareness of an object or event. It refers especially to the dissemination of information in public contexts (e.g., dinner tables, amphitheaters, stadiums, and town squares), or through public technologies (e.g., microphones, telephones, television, and social media) [21].

Ober [16] discusses how common knowledge was used in classical Athens to collect people for a common goal. Public rituals for honouring war heroes and monuments containing the list of traitors were a medium for spreading common knowledge that every citizen should act for the good of the city. Athenians used certain specific signs in temples to convey important messages to their citizens. Festivals were organized so that every citizen was forced to pass through them. The assumption was that if the signs were placed in public places, everyone will be able to see them.

During the construction of theaters and common halls, Athenians built circles facing inward. This allows people observe both speaker and the movement of other participants. By letting people see each other clearly or creating maximum eye contact they were better able to understand each other's opinions.

In Athens, People's Courts sat frequently, and the relatively long speeches of litigants provided excellent opportunities for sharing knowledge. Court was one of the places where collective knowledge was developed and used. The jury was drawn from the citizens. Citizens attended the court to observe the jurors' presentations during which they observed the responses of others, like facial expressions and exclamations. Prosecution points from the *Leocrates* trial argue for the importance of reaching collective action in terms of common knowledge.

Lewis [13] provided a game theoretic solution for coordination problems which considers the relation between common knowledge and mutual expectation. In explaining a choice of action, he says that the agent needs a reason to believe about what actions will be chosen by others. Then an equilibrium is sustained due to mutual expectations which come from common knowledge.

There are some properties that allow us to know when it is appropriate to recognize common knowledge based on a certain principles. Lewis separates the concepts of directly observable states of affairs and propositions that these states of affairs provide a reason to believe. This is modelled as an "indicates" relationship (a state of affairs indicates that a proposition holds). Lewis identified four properties that allow a state of affairs (s) to be recognised as a "reflexive common indicator" of a proposition (p), i.e. that observation of the state of affairs leads to common knowledge of the proposition.

The state of affairs should be self revealing and public, everyone should be able to infer p from observing s and every one should have reason to believe they share the same inductive standards and background information.

In the context of the trial that we model, Lewis's theory explains how common knowledge of past traitors and their convictions can be reached without explicit logical reasoning about infinitely nested knowledge operators. In addition, we consider another source of common knowledge noted by Ober: a cascade of actions by citizens to help rebuild the city's walls at a time of crisis, in response to a public decree to act collectively secure the city.

3   Points of *Lycurgus* During The Trial

During his time in Athens, *Lycurgus*, the prosecutor of the trial was a famous politician who performed many social services. He had successful past prosecutions of citizens who acted against security rules. During the trial of *Leocrates*, who was alleged to have abandoned the city, *Lycurgus's* speech focused on two main equilibria. The first one is a shared belief that is common knowledge among the citizens that everyone should cooperate to secure the city. As Athens' security was viewed as a common pool resource every citizen should play their part in ensuring it. Unless individuals give back to the common pool, it leads to the tragedy of the commons [8].

The second equilibrium is that jurors should penalize citizens who violate the first equilibrium through legal sanctions. As the city had been completely destroyed and lost territory after the war with the Macedonians. Athenian's cooperation was crucial during the period when *Leocrates* was alleged to have abandoned it. Other citizens of Athens committed themselves to rebuilding the city. For the common good to be achieved, there was a need for cooperation among citizens at the time. However, it was alleged that *Leocrates* had left the city by disobeying the generals and ignoring the shared interest of citizens of the city.

The above points are taken from *Lycurgus's* preserved speech [1,3]. We are interested in reconstructing the key arguments of *Lycurgus* as a case study in computational reasoning about common knowledge and collective action in terms of MLNs. In particular, the focus of our model is on the reasoning that must be performed by the jurors. They need to understand the effect that their decision about conviction will have on the maintenance of the citizens' cooperation with the group goal to keep the city secure.

4   Markov Logic Networks (MLNs)

Two important aspects of artificial intelligence (AI), expressing knowledge and uncertainty, can be handled with first-order logic (FOL) and probabilistic modeling, respectively. There are various approaches to combining probabilistic reasoning with explicit logical knowledge encoding such as probabilistic relational models [7], Bayesian logic programs [11], relational dependency networks [15].

Richardson and Domingos [5] proposed a logic framework Markov Logic Networks (MLNs). While a first-order logic (FOL) knowledge base contains formulas that can be seen as hard constraints on the possible worlds (assignments of truth values to ground atoms), in an MLN, each formula has an associated weight that reflects how strong a constraint it is. The higher the weight, the greater the difference in log probability between a world that satisfies the formula and one that does not, other things being equal. That allows to model the probabilistic nature of the formulas.

An MLN can be seen as a template to generate a Markov network (a type of undirected graphical model), given a finite set of constants, and this can be used to answer queries about the conditional and unconditional probabilities of specified ground formulas. An MLN contains a node for each possible ground atom, and has undirected edges connecting nodes that appear together in at least one grounding of a formula in the MLN. While MLNs are built from FOL formulas, inference is performed using the generated Markov network.

We are motivated to use an MLN for the following reasons. It allows explicit modelling of background knowledge and observed knowledge while presuming the full expressiveness of graphical models. The undirected nature of a Markov network means that the joint probability of ground atoms are defined without presuming ordered dependencies between them.

For example, Fig. 1 shows that the probability of a citizen cooperating with a group goal securing the city (coop(P, SC)) is interrelated with the probabilities of holding certain attitudes towards the group cooperation, common knowledge they have about the group goal and the attitude of the court towards punishing them (its ethos). This can be modelled by an undirected graphical model.

Formally, an MLN is given by a set L of pairs (F_i, w_i), where F_i is a formula in first-order logic and w_i is a real-valued weight. Given a finite domain of discourse (a set of constants) the ground Markov network generates a probability distribution over the set of possible worlds χ as follows,

$$P(\chi = x) = \frac{1}{Z} \exp \left(\sum_{i=1}^{|L|} w_i n_i(x) \right) \tag{1}$$

$Z = \sum_{x' \in \chi} exp(\sum_i w_i n_i(x'))$ is a normalisation constant and $n_i(x)$ denotes the number of groundings of F_i that are true in x.

Given a formula F, abbreviating the presentation of Jain [6], we define:

$$s(F) = \sum_{x \in \chi,\, x \models F} \exp \left(\sum_{i=1}^{|L|} w_i n_i(x) \right) \tag{2}$$

The outer sum is over possible worlds in which F is true and the exponentiated inner sum is the unnormalized probability of the possible world x. Using $s(F)$ we can calculate the probability of any ground formula F_1 given any other ground formula F_2 as

$$P(F_1|F_2) = \frac{s(F_1 \wedge F_2)}{s(F_2)} \tag{3}$$

5   An MLN Model of *Lycurgus's* Argument

In this section we present an MLN model of key aspects of *Lycurgus's* prosecution speech, which is shown in Listing 1. The model shows how a jury can decide whether to prosecute *Leocrates* using the following two conditional probability queries $Q1$ and $Q2$. These ask what is the likelihood of a random citizen *Polites* cooperating with a collective goal to secure the city when *Leocrates* is convicted and not convicted, respectively:

$$Q1 : \ P(cooperate(Polites, SecureCity) \mid convicted(Leocrates))$$
$$Q2 : P(cooperate(Polites, SecureCity) \mid \neg \ convicted(Leocrates))$$

There are two levels of collective action in this scenario: the citizens securing the city as a collective goal, and the jurors collectively agreeing to convict *Leocrates*. Our model currently includes only the first level. *Lycurgus* believes that there are two equilibrium conditions. Everyone should strive to secure the city as a common objective. That is the first equilibrium. The second equilibrium is for those who violate the first one to be punished. The jurors are responsible for maintaining the court's ethos of convicting traitors, thereby maintaining the equilibrium of people cooperating towards a common goal. It is specifically our concern that each juror can understand the prosecutor's arguments and realise that "if I convict *Leocrates*, I'm enhancing the collaboration among citizens; otherwise I'm undermining it".[1]

There is also a set of ground atoms accompanying Listing 1 representing firm knowledge about the domain. It states that the named citizens (other than *Polites*) are historic traitors. Among them, two (*Hipparchus* and *Callistrus*) of them were prosecuted and convicted while one (*Leocrates*) is prosecuted and waiting for the jurors' decision. To evaluate $Q1$, *Leocrates* is declared convicted, for $Q2$ he is not convicted. The details of traitors in these ground atoms can be found on monuments placed in public places where the list of traitors are carved and hence these ground atoms are common knowledge.

Listing 1 shows the structure of an MLN that represents the scenario, implemented using ProbCog[2] The listing uses nested function symbols, to represent a group goal as a complex term within a common knowledge modality. However, since ProbCog does not handle terms with nested function symbols our MLN uses a standard transformation [2] to eliminate these functional terms. For brevity we do not show the transformed version here.

Listing 1 starts with domain declarations that allow a set of constants to be associated with a named domain. Next, every predicate in the MLN is declared. A predicate declaration consists of the predicate name followed by a comma-separated list of the domain names of its arguments in brackets.

---

[1] We do not attempt to model any reasoning about whether a citizen prosecuted for treachery really is guilty. Instead we focus on the argument for conviction (assuming guilt) based on the upholding of social order. In fact, in the real scenario, *Leocrates* was not convicted, as evidence of his guilt was not convincing to the court.

[2] https://github.com/opcode81/ProbCog.

```
1
2   // Domain declarations
3   dom_citizen = {Polites, Leocrates, Hipparchus, Callistrus}
4   dom_institution = {Court}
5   dom_individual_ethos = {Ethos1, Ethos2}
6   dom_institutional_ethos = {Ethos3}
7   group = {Citizens}
8   goal = {SecureCity}
9
10  // Predicate declarations
11  individual_ethos(dom_citizen, dom_individual_ethos!)
12  institutional_ethos(dom_institution, dom_institutional_ethos!)
13  ck(group, goal)
14  group_goal(group, goal)
15  cooperate(dom_citizen, goal)
16  convicted(dom_citizen)
17  traitor(dom_citizen)
18  prosecuted(dom_citizen)
19  historic(dom_citizen)
20
21  // Background knowledge
22  ck(Citizens, group_goal(Citizens, SecureCity)).
23  ck(group, group_goal(group, goal)) => group_goal(group, goal).
24
25  cooperate(x, SecureCity) ^ !historic(x) =>
26      individual_ethos(x, Ethos1) v individual_ethos(x, Ethos2).
27
28  log(0.12) individual_ethos(Polites , Ethos1) ^
29            cooperate(Polites , SecureCity)
30  log(0.48) individual_ethos(Polites , Ethos2) ^
31            cooperate(Polites , SecureCity)
32
33  traitor(x) <=> (EXIST g (group_goal(Citizens, g) ^
34                           !cooperate(x,g)          )).
35
36  // Definitions
37  individual_ethos(x, Ethos1) <=>
38      ( !historic(x) ^
39        ck(Citizens, group_goal(Citizen, SecureCity))
40      =>
41        cooperate(x, SecureCity)).
42
43  individual_ethos(x, Ethos2) <=>
44      ( !historic(x) ^
45        ck(Citizens, group_goal(Citizen, SecureCity)) ^
46        institutional_ethos(Court, Ethos3)
47      =>
48        cooperate(x, SecureCity)).
49
50  institutional_ethos(Court, Ethos3) <=>
51      !(EXIST x (traitor(x) ^ prosecuted(x) ^ !convicted(x))).
```

Listing 1. MLN encoding of *Lycurgus's* arguments

We consider there to be a prototypical citizen named *Polites*. The Greek word *Polites* refers to a general citizen in Athens [25]. Our aim is to infer the probability of an arbitrary current citizen (*Polites*) cooperating with the shared goal to secure the city, without the known behaviour of a few past defectors having an undue influence on this inference. Given that *Polites* is a single constant representing a large number of citizens of Athens[3], the past traitors (including Leocrates, who is being prosecuted in absentia some time after leaving the city), are modelled as "historic" and the MLN clauses defining the current citizens' ethoses regarding cooperation with the goal explicitly exclude consideration of historic citizens.

Polites is observing the trial and he believes there is common knowledge of the existence of a group goal of the citizens to secure the safety of the city (e.g. by strengthening its defences). This is shown in line 22 of Listing 1. *Lycurgus* argues that this common knowledge comes about from a cascade [22] of action in cooperation with this goal when the city was in danger. Line 23 express a deduction that can be made from common knowledge. It declares "When there is common knowledge that a group has a goal, then the group has that goal".

The reasoning agent (a juror listening to *Lycurgus's* argument) needs to understand how the group goal affects the actions of the citizens. According to Tuomela [24], when members of a group are acting collectively in "we-mode", "one adopts the group's constitutive goals, values, norms, and standards-briefly its "ethos" ".[4] We assume that citizens may follow one of two possible ethoses in regards to securing the city (line 11 and lines 25 to 26). The ! in line 22 indicates a functional relationship: the indicated argument is uniquely defined given the other arguments of the predicate. These annotations in lines 11 and 12 means that an individual or institution can have at most one ethos.

Polites observes these two competing individual ethoses that citizens have regarding cooperation with the goal to secure the city. Ethos 1 (lines 37 to 41) is to unconditionally cooperate with a group goal. Ethos 2 (lines 43 to 48) is more selfishly to cooperate only if the court holds the ethos of convicting traitors.

Moreover, empirical knowledge about the proportions of cooperating agents in the city, and the proportions of agents holding Ethos 1 and 2 amongst those agents[5] is encoded using weights on the mutually exclusive joint probabilities in lines 28 to 31. *Polites* is capable of estimating the proportion of citizens who cooperate with the group goal, and who hold each ethos based on the background knowledge of current status of cooperation of the city. The background knowledge comes from the observation of public interactions (building walls, public oath), shared cultural information (honoring heroic warriors, celebrating war victories) and the present shared situation which all are matter of common knowledge. We assume that *Polites* has observed 60% cooperation with the group goal, a 20% incidence of Ethos 1 amongst cooperators, and an 80% holding of Ethos 2 amongst them. We assume that observations of these proportions is approximately the same across all citizens, and can be treated as common knowledge.

---

[3] MLN inference does not scale well [23], so explicitly modelling a large number of citizens is not feasible.

[4] According to Toumela [24] there is a mutual belief that, if a group has set of ethoses, all its members are collectively committed and accepted to that ethoses. Essentially this is common knowledge.

[5] Due to difficulties in expressing conditional probabilities in MLN clauses [6], this knowledge is expressed in terms of joint probabilities of cooperation and holding a certain ethos.

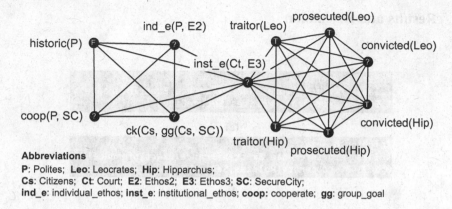

Abbreviations

P: Polites; **Leo**: Leocrates; **Hip**: Hipparchus;
Cs: Citizens; **Ct**: Court; **E2**: Ethos2; **E3**: Ethos3; **SC**: SecureCity;
ind_e: individual_ethos; **inst_e**: institutional_ethos; **coop**: cooperate; **gg**: group_goal

Fig. 1. Part of the Markov network generated from Listing 1

Ethos 3 is defined as "No traitor who is prosecuted will not be convicted" (lines 48 to 49)[6]. The weight of Ethos 3 is determined empirically based on historic common knowledge, which is expressed in the set of ground atoms. From public monuments, *Polites* knows about some past traitors (*Hipparchus, Callistrus*) who were prosecuted, and the outcomes of the trials. He can infer empirically how strongly the court has the ethos of convicting or acquitting traitors based on those decisions.

Lines 33, 34 define the term traitor: "A traitor is someone who doesn't cooperate with the group goal". This is also common knowledge which comes from the cultural background and shared knowledge that everyone knows what a traitor is.

All the clauses in Listing 1 come either from common knowledge, or are assumed to be common knowledge e.g., the observed proportion of cooperation and prevalence of Ethos 1 and 2. Some clauses refer to common knowledge explicitly. In other cases, the rules themselves are common knowledge. This is also common knowledge. As this MLN was constructed exclusively from common knowledge then the conclusions of reasoning with it are also common knowledge. If a juror believes that all this knowledge is common, then the conclusions reached by the MLN queries can also be considered common knowledge amongst the jurors, thus encouraging a consensus decision to convict or not.

Figure 1 shows an excerpt from the Markov network generated from the MLN and the chosen set of constants. The left hand side shows a grounding of the clause defining Ethos 2 (where x = Polites), while the right hand side is a partial depiction of the single grounding for the clause defining Ethos 3 (for brevity, only citizens *Leocrates* and *Hipparchus* are considered here). The nodes are annotated with F or T where their truth values are fixed by the set of ground atoms, and ? where the truth value is not fixed and may vary between possible worlds. The figure illustrates how the probability of *Polites* cooperating with the goal to secure the city is influenced by the probabilities of various other ground atoms.

---

[6] ProbCog provides an "exist" operator but not a "for all" one.

6   Results and Discussion

```
Infering queries
<class 'MLN.inference.ExactInference.ExactInference'>
1.000000  cooperate(Polites,SecureCity)
```

(a)

```
Infering queries
<class 'MLN.inference.ExactInference.ExactInference'>
0.107143  cooperate(Polites,SecureCity)
```

(b)

Fig. 2. Results obtained from ProbCog to compute queries $Q1$ and $Q2$ respectively

We are interested in finding the likelihood of *Polites* and thus the average citizen cooperating due to the common knowledge he/she received from the observation of the city. In particular, what is the probability that *Polites* will cooperate when *Leocrates* is convicted and when he is not? Using conditional probability queries, we can draw some conclusions as common knowledge, since all the input is associated with common knowledge. The result of convicting *Leocrates*, will be to reinforce knowledge of the court's ethos of punishing traitors, and thus to increase cooperation due to the greater probability of Ethos 2 holding. This will motivate a jury member to vote to convict *Leocrates* to uphold cooperation with the citizens' goal to keep the city secure.

Using the ProbCog tool with the exact inference mechanism, we obtained results of a random citizen's probability of cooperation (cooperate(*Polites*, *SecureCity*)) in both situations of conviction and non conviction of *Leocrates* (Fig. 2a and Fig. 2b respectively. When $Q1$ and $Q2$ are computed, in the case of the court convicting *Leocrates*, *Polites* will cooperate with probability 1.00 and 0.12 for when he is not convicted. The truth value for convicted (*Leocrates*) is defined differently for these two queries.

Given these predictions, a jury member can validate the argument of *Lycurgus* using this reasoning and as the conclusion comes from common knowledge he can be confident his opinion will align with that of other jurors.

7   Conclusion and Future Work

People act collectively for various reasons, and we are interested in knowing what makes them act as a group. Common knowledge plays an important role in bringing people together at the social level. We provided a computational model to show how cooperation will be achieved on the basis of common knowledge by investigating a specific trial of classical Athens. We used a Markov Logic Network (MLN) as it is capable of combining logical and probabilistic reasoning. Based on *Lycurgus's* argument we assume that the clauses in our MLN are common knowledge including ethoses, background knowledge about the term traitor, and proportion of cooperation.

Our future work will focus on building a simulation of this scenario in which common knowledge is created and assembled to form the MLN presented in this paper. This will happen in three scenes: (1) extracting common knowledge of the existence of the group goal from a public decree, followed by an observed cascade of action in cooperation with that goal; (2) observations of information about historic convictions of traitors on public monuments, which, due to a shared cultural and educational background can be seen as reflexive common indicators in Lewis's theory; and (3) empirical observations of the ethoses of the citizens towards the group goal. We will use notions such as salience and counts-as relationships between concrete and institutional events to determine which simulated events are candidates for common knowledge. Combining this simulation with MLN reasoning will allow us to show how *Lycurgus's* complex arguments about common knowledge an joint action can be realised in a computational agent.

Acknowledgements. This work was supported by the Marsden Fund Council from New Zealand Government funding, managed by Royal Society Te Apārangi.

References

1. Allen, D.S.: Changing the authoritative voice: Lycurgus "against Leocrates". Class. Antiq. **19**(1), 5–33 (2000)
2. Baumgartner, P., Fuchs, A., de Nivelle, H., Tinelli, C.: Computing finite models by reduction to function-free clause logic. J. Appl. Logic **7**(1), 58–74 (2009)
3. Burtt, J.O. (ed.): Minor attic orators. 2: Lycurgus. Dinarchus. Demades. Hyperides/with an English transl. by J. O. Burtt. No. 395 in The Loeb classical library, [u.a.] Heinemann, London, reprint edn. (1980)
4. Chwe, M.S.Y.: Rational Ritual: Culture, Coordination, and Common Knowledge. Princeton University Press, Princeton (2013)
5. Domingos, P., Kok, S., Lowd, D., Poon, H., Richardson, M., Singla, P.: Markov logic. In: De Raedt, L., Frasconi, P., Kersting, K., Muggleton, S. (eds.) Probabilistic Inductive Logic Programming. LNCS (LNAI), vol. 4911, pp. 92–117. Springer, Heidelberg (2008). https://doi.org/10.1007/978-3-540-78652-8_4
6. Jain, D.: Knowledge engineering with Markov logic networks: a review. Evol. Knowl. Theory Appl. **16**, 50–75 (2011)
7. Friedman, N., Getoor, L., Koller, D., Pfeffer, A.: Learning probabilistic relational models. IJCAI **99**, 1300–1309 (1999)
8. Hardin, G.: The tragedy of the commons. J. Nat. Res. Policy Res. **1**(3), 243–253 (2009)
9. Holt, C.A., Roth, A.E.: The Nash equilibrium: a perspective. Proc. Natl. Acad. Sci. **101**(12), 3999–4002 (2004)
10. Holzinger, K.: The Problems of Collective Action: A New Approach. SSRN 399140 (2003)
11. Kersting, K., De Raedt, L.: Towards combining inductive logic programming with Bayesian networks. In: Rouveirol, C., Sebag, M. (eds.) ILP 2001. LNCS (LNAI), vol. 2157, pp. 118–131. Springer, Heidelberg (2001). https://doi.org/10.1007/3-540-44797-0_10
12. Kuhlman, C.J., Ravi, S.S., Korkmaz, G., Vega-Redondo, F.: An agent-based model of common knowledge and collective action dynamics on social networks. In: 2020 Winter Simulation Conference (WSC), pp. 218–229 (2020)
13. Lewis, D.: Convention: A Philosophical Study. Harvard University Press, Cambridge (1969)

14. Leyton-Brown, K., Shoham, Y.: Essentials of game theory: a concise multidisciplinary introduction. Synth. Lect. Artif. Intell. Mach. Learn. **2**(1), 1–88 (2008)
15. Neville, J., Jensen, D.: Dependency networks for relational data. In: Fourth IEEE International Conference on Data Mining (ICDM 2004), pp. 170–177. IEEE (2004)
16. Ober, J.: Democracy and Knowledge: Innovation and Learning in Classical Athens. Princeton University Press, Princeton (2008). oCLC: ocn202545162
17. Ostrom, E.: Governing the commons: The evolution of institutions for collective action. The political economy of institutions and decisions. Cambridge University Press, Cambridge; New York (1990)
18. Reuben, E.: The evolution of theories of collective action. Ph.D. thesis, Tinbergen Institute (2003)
19. Sandler, T.: Collective Action: Theory and Applications. University of Michigan Press, Ann Arbor (1992)
20. Shteynberg, G.: Shared attention. Perspect. Psychol. Sci. **10**(5), 579–590 (2015)
21. Shteynberg, G., Hirsh, J.B., Bentley, R.A., Garthoff, J.: Shared worlds and shared minds: a theory of collective learning and a psychology of common knowledge. Psychol. Rev. **127**(5), 918 (2020)
22. Srivathsan, S., Cranefield, S., Pitt, J.: A bayesian model of information cascades. In: Theodorou, A., Nieves, J.C., De Vos, M. (eds.) Coordination, Organizations, Institutions, Norms, and Ethics for Governance of Multi-Agent Systems XIV. COINE 2021. LNCS, vol. 13239. Springer, Cham. (2022). https://doi.org/10.1007/978-3-031-16617-4_7
23. Sun, Z., Zhao, Y., Wei, Z., Zhang, W., Wang, J.: Scalable learning and inference in Markov logic networks. Int. J. Approx. Reas. **82**(C), 39–55 (2017). https://doi.org/10.1016/j.ijar.2016.12.003
24. Tuomela, R.: The Philosophy of Sociality: The Shared Point of View. Oxford University Press, Oxford (2007)
25. Wohl, V.: Rhetoric of the Athenian Citizen, pp. 162–177. Cambridge Companions to Literature, Cambridge University Press (2009). https://doi.org/10.1017/CCOL9780521860543.011

Design Heuristics for Ethical Online Institutions

Pablo Noriega[1] , Harko Verhagen[2] , Julian Padget[3(✉)] , and Mark d'Inverno[4]

[1] CSIC-IIIA, 08193 Bellaterra, Spain
[2] Stockholm University, 114 19 Stockholm, Sweden
[3] University of Bath, Bath BA2 7AY, UK
j.a.padget@bath.ac.uk
[4] Goldsmiths, University of London, London SE14 6NW, UK

Abstract. A major challenge in AI is designing autonomous systems that capture the values of stakeholders, and do so in such away that one can assess the extent to which that system's behaviour is aligned to those values. In this paper we discuss our response to this challenge that is both practical and built on clear principles. Specifically, we propose eleven heuristics to organise the process of making values operational in the design of particular class of AI systems called online institutions. These are governed systems of interacting communities of human and autonomous artificial agents.

Keywords: Online institutions · WIT design pattern · Conscientious design · Embedding values · Value alignment · Value-sensitive design

1 Introduction

In the Reith Lectures broadcast by the BBC at the end of 2021 [28], Stuart Russell spoke about the challenges Artificial Intelligence (AI) research has in ensuring that AI works for the benefit of human kind. There are several ways to address these challenges. One way is to "put ethics into AI"; and more precisely, focus on the challenge of the **value alignment problem** (VAP): "to build systems whose behaviour is provably aligned with human values". The VAP, in fact consists of two linked problems: how to *embed* human values into AIS and how to assess if, or to what degree, the behaviour of the AIS is *aligned* with those values.

We propose a principled and practical way of approaching the VAP, which we call *conscientious design*, that consists of: (i) *restricting the problem* to one particular type of Artificial Intelligence Systems (AIS) that we call online institutions (OIs); (ii) developing a *conceptual framework*—involving terminological distinctions, formal constructs and properties— that delimit the interpretation of the VAP;(iii) developing *methodological guidelines and heuristics* to guide the embedding of values in an online institution and assessing the OI's alignment with those values; (iv) developing *test cases* which provide both a source of inspiration for the conceptual framework and to evidence how our approach can be put into practice.

This paper is a contribution to component (ii) above. It contains some heuristics that serve to guide the process of making values operational for an OI. The heuristics are

N. Ajmeri et al. (Eds.): COINE 2022, LNAI 13549, pp. 213–230, 2022.
https://doi.org/10.1007/978-3-031-20845-4_14

intended to be as generic as possible in order to show what are the main practical issues involved in embedding values and assessing alignment. It is work in progress (rather than a completed design methodology) which builds on a decade long research effort investigating online institutions and a *conscientious design* approach for building them successfully (e.g., [34] and see for example references in [1,20,22]). In addition to that long lasting interest, we draw also from experience from a different application of the framework: policy sandboxes, where some of the concepts and constructs involved in the heuristics we present here were first devised [24,25].

Online institutions (OI) are a subclass of artificial intelligent systems. They are *hybrid multiagent systems* (that involve human and artificial participants), where all interactions are *regulated* (only those actions that comply with the OI's regulations can have any effect within that OI), are *online* (interactions consist of messages—or percepts—exchanged through the OI) and, finally, *situated* within a particular socio-technical-legal context [18]. Online institutions capture several intuitions of classical institutions: Searl's notion of separate "crude" and "institutional reality" [30]; North's characterisation of institutions as artificial constraints that articulate agent interactions [23]; Simon's thinking of institutions as an interface between a collective objective and the individual decision-making of participating agents [31]; and Ostrom's criteria for institutional persistence. Those similarities are shown as part of the WIT design pattern in Fig. 1a.

Our focus on online institutions is based on two observations: first, the specific features that distinguish them from other AIS provide the grounds for a principled approach to the VAP; second, plenty of deployed AIS which belong to the OI class and there will be more abundant in the future.

In addition to a precise characterisation of an OI, the main contributions to the conceptual framework of the CD approach are (i) the WIT design pattern, (ii) the (design) distinction between the isolated and the situated view of an OI; (iii) specifying three properties of OIs that one should aspire to achieve in their design: *cohesiveness* (that the three distinctive WIT aspects actually complement each other), *integrity* (that the OI is stable, not corruptible and works as intended) and *compatibility* (with the legal, technological and social constraints of the context where it is situated); and (iv) the proposal of three *conscientious design value categories*: thoroughness, mindfulness and responsibility. Needless to say, appropriate terminological distinctions and some specific constructs give substance to the three main contributions [18].

The main contribution of this paper is to show how each of these four concepts can be translated into methodological guidelines in the form of heuristics for the actual embedding of values. In order to achieve this, the next section provides an overview of our contributions to date. In Sect. 3 we describe a running example to illustrate the applicability of our heuristics. Sect. 4 presents the heuristics themselves and the paper ends with some closing remarks on what we have achieved and future work.

2 The Conscientious Design Story so Far

2.1 The WIT Design Pattern

The purpose of the $\mathcal{WIT}$ design pattern is to support the process of building online institutions (OIs). The most recent description [22] is a relatively high-level one intended for a non-specialist audience, while earlier iterations at previous COIN(E) Workshops [20] and other published research [18, 19, 34] are more technical, and chronicle the evolution of our ideas.

The first significant difference between earlier work, before [22], and the work in this paper is the use of the term *WIT Design Pattern* to refer to the range of concepts and approaches needed for the ethical design of OIs, where we draw on the principles put forward by Alexander [2, 3] to capture the idea of habitable *online* spaces that evolve to meet the changing needs and values of their inhabitants. This in turn draws on value-sensitive design (VSD) [8–10] which provides the basis for the role of human values in the design process of computational systems, and on Deming's underpinnings for Total Quality Management (TQM) [4] to account for the maintenance and evolution of the online space.

The second significant difference is our use of the term "online institution" (OI) instead of the previously used socio-cognitive technical systems or hybrid online systems. We next describe two distinct categories (or abstractions) of an OI as follows: (i) the *isolated OI* in Fig. 1a, which enables the design of an OI to be considered from three different but related perspectives: $\mathcal{W}$, the OI as seen from the world perspective; $\mathcal{I}$, the institutional or governance perspective of the OI and $\mathcal{T}$, the OI from its technological perspective; and (ii) the *situated OI* in Fig. 1b, where the isolated OI connects with the corresponding elements of the physical and social world to establish what "counts-as" [14] in both directions and to anchor the online institutions with its physical world counterparts.

For any isolated OI it is necessary to be able to demonstrate *cohesiveness*, which is to say the three views work as intended, and *integrity*, which means it is a persistent, well-behaved online system. In order to be fit for its purpose, the situated OI needs to be effective in the context of its use. Consequently, the OI has to be *compatible* with the technological, legal, social and economic requirements of its working environment.

2.2 Conscientious Design Value Categories (CD-VCs)

As part of the development of the WIT-DP framework we have developed the notion of *Conscientious Design value categories*: thoroughness, mindfulness, and responsibility. Here we summarise these to provide the reader with a sense of these below (the full definitions can be found in [22]):

- **Thoroughness**: this refers to conventional technological values that promote the technical quality of the system. It includes completeness and correctness of the specification and implementation, reliability and efficiency of the deployed system. Concepts such as robustness, resilience, accessibility, and security are all aspects of thoroughness.

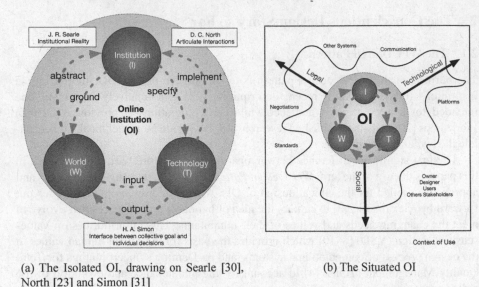

(a) The Isolated OI, drawing on Searle [30], North [23] and Simon [31]

(b) The Situated OI

Fig. 1. The views of an isolated online institution vs a situated online institution

- **Mindfulness**: is about engendering a wider awareness of the range of direct and indirect needs of, and impacts on, humans (both users and non-users) which is so often over-looked. Examples include data ownership, and the OIs accessibility and usability, and this category has much in common with Schwartz' "personal focus" values.
- **Responsibility**: addresses both the effects of the system on stakeholders and the context in which it is situated, as well as how indirect stakeholders and that context may affect internal stakeholders. Examples include liability and prestige, and are akin to the "social focus" values of Schwartz [29].

In our work on Ethically Aligned Design [22] we have shown how these CD value categories can be mapped onto different ethical AI value frameworks such as the initiatives from the EU [11] on Trustworthy AI and the IEEE guidelines for imbuing values in AIS [32]. As meta-analyses of the multitude of frameworks show [7,17], many have overlapping definitions and principles. However, the CD value categories have the advantage of supporting more than one way of looking at the principles included in these frameworks.

One final remark here concerns the stakeholders. Stakeholders are all those affected by, or those affecting, the system during both development and deployment. *Direct* stakeholders are those stakeholders who are responsible for the design and deployment, or are direct users of the OI. In practice, in every OI there are always three categories of direct stakeholders: owner, engineer and user and we will detail each of these in the next section. Those stakeholders who are affected by the system, but are not part of the decision-making and do not use the system directly, we call *indirect* stakeholders — as is the usual term in value sensitive design. The values of direct stakeholders need to be explicitly accounted for in the design and use of the OI.

In order to identify those values of direct stakeholders and make them operational, direct stakeholders can be separated in three different groups: *owner, engineer and user*. This separation reflects the distinctive objectives of direct stakeholders in every OI: the owner looks to deploy an OI that supports a collective endeavour "as well as possible", the users participates in the OI to achieve "as well as possible" their individual goals with whatever means are provided by the OI, and the engineer builds "as well as possible" an OI that satisfies "as well as possible" the owner and the user objectives. The point is that each "as well as possible" is guided by different values. Notice that since, in every OI, those distinctive objectives of each of the direct stakeholders are similar, the values that each of them holds are similar to some extent in every OI. See below, Sect. 4.2, Heuristic 4.

3   The Easyrider Online Institution

To support the understanding of the theoretical and practical concepts involved in the WIT-DP for ethical AIS, we introduce Easyrider, a rich enough toy example of an OI for buying and selling train tickets online. Are we mentioned in the last section the three categories of direct stakeholders are Owner, Engineer and Users and are detailed as follows.

1. Owner: refers to the individual or organisation that commissions and operates the OI. In this case the railway company is the Owner, because it commissions and operates the OI in order to sell tickets online through travel agencies.
2. Engineer: refers to the individual or organisation responsible for ensuring the requirements of the owner are satisfied in am effectively designed and deployed OI that supports intended usage.
3. User(s): refers to the users who will use the system and satisfy their goals by interacting with others. In Easyrider there are two categories of users: *passengers* (who are human agents) that use Easyrider to buy, and possibly return train tickets, and *travel agencies* (who are software agents) that buy tickets from the railway company to re-sell them to passengers.

In Easyrider, the indirect stakeholders would include the commerce and transit authorities that regulate the railway services, the banks and payment services that support purchases, phone companies and, to some extent, the population —and the environment— of those cities served by trains and affected by the travelling of people back and forth.

3.1   Goals and Values

The WIT DP approach to design we propose starts by identifying the ultimate objectives of stakeholders —the rationales for the creation, engineering, and use the particular OI. However, because we want to embed values in the OI we also need to make explicit the *terminal* (or intrinsic) values that motivate those objectives and those *instrumental* values that determine the means provided by the OI to reach those objectives [27].

Table 2 illustrates those three elements in Easyrider. For brevity, we only include the *ultimate goal* of the stakeholder groups, the key terminal values that guide those goals and the most prominent instrumental values that motivate the stakeholders' decisions and means to achieve those goals. Next to each "instrumental value" we indicate the type of CD category it belongs to (T for thoroughness, M for mindfulness, and R for responsibility). In the next section we build on these examples to illustrate how CD values can be embedded in Easyrider.

For example, the railway company who owns Easyrider develops an online ticketing service in order to sell enough seats to amortize capital it has invested in the train service, and it wants to achieve that objective guided by three terminal values: (i) a sense of good management of the company capital and its operation; (ii) the provision of a service through travel agencies that is profitable for these travel agencies which in turn leads to attracting both existing and new passengers to use the system; and (iii) an acknowledged positive impact because more persons travel in train instead of using less ecological means of transportation and also because a public infrastructure is better used.

Moreover, the specification of Easyrider should also reflect the railway company's criteria for instrumenting those terminal values. So, for instance, good management is achieved by a thorough implementation of management policies and practices; responsibly by achieving a healthy cash-flow. Alongside, the OI promotes an occupancy of wagons that provides that cash-flow without being uncomfortable for passengers; while enabling profitable margins to travel agencies.

We now move onto the issue of how to make values operational within our established framework for designing ethical OIs.

4   Making Values Operational

The proof of developing a value-imbued system is in the pudding of making values operational as well as choosing the values in order to be able to assess if the values are indeed enhanced or supported by the system. According to [26], there are three pre-requisites that need to be fulfilled to assess if certain values are embodied in an AI system: (i) values are addressed in the design of the system, i.e., there is no such thing as accidental value embedding;(ii) the AI system is seen as a sociotechnical system not an isolated technological artefact, i.e. it is situated; and (iii) the AI system is not ascribed any moral agency, differentiating it from human agents.

Since we want to embed values in a working system, we need to translate an intuitive understanding of values into precise constructs that can be specified as part of a system and then see whether or not they are supported by the working system. This is what we call the process of making values operational. Since this is a complex process the first thing to do is to make things manageable.

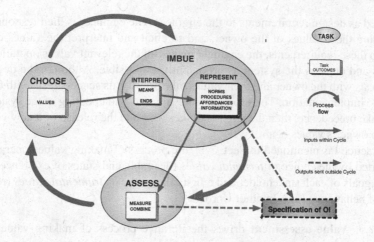

Fig. 2. The process for bringing values into the design of an OI

4.1   Three Heuristics for Structuring Value Operationalisation

The point of the heuristics for structuring value operationalisation is threefold: (i) to decompose the complex problem into subtasks, (ii) to facilitate the separation of design concerns and (iii) to put design priorities in focus. We propose three design heuristics for this purpose:

Heuristic 1. **Making values operational** is an iterative process.

Making values operational is a process of iterative approximation that converges to whatever is "just enough" for whichever stage the system has reached, from preliminary evaluation through to decommissioning. It also functions as the means to track the moving target of the changing needs and value preferences of the participants. As sketched in Fig. 2, the process starts with the choice of values and ends with a specification of an OI that is aligned with those values. The first task consists of choosing a *list of values* that are relevant for the OI. The task of the second stage is to make those values objectively measurable, for which we use a two step process: they are *interpreted* by linking them to concrete referents ("means" to support the value and "ends" that reflect its achievement) that may then be *represented* within the system in readiness for the next stage. The third stage consists in defining the *value assessment models* that establish (i) the precise ways in which one can tell whether a value is being attained and to what degree, and (ii) how to resolve value conflicts . The outcome of this process is to put the representation of the values and the assessment into the specification of the OI.

Heuristic 2. **Ethical design is a participatory effort** where all direct stakeholders have their say at different phases of the OI life-cycle.

The cycle of making values operational is active for the lifetime of the OI. However, the involvement of stakeholders is different in different phases of that life-cycle. The design of a value imbued process is started by the owner whose main goals and values are passed as design requirements to the engineer. The engineer is then responsible for interpreting these values of the owner, and to elicit and interpret the values of users. Based on these requirements, the engineer makes all the relevant values operational and specifies and deploys the system as proficiently as possible. Although the decision to deploy rests with the owner and their values take priority, its success rests with the users and in the implementation. Therefore, in the evaluation and updating of the system, user values take precedence, then the engineer takes over and the release of a new version is up to the owner's values again.

In practice (as mentioned in Sect. 3.1), the process of making values operational is kick-started by the choice of *terminal values* (desirable end-states of existence) for the ultimate goals of each stakeholder and a first take on the *instrumental values* (related to modes of behaviour) [27]. In other words:

Heuristic 3. **Value assessment** drives the iterative process of making values operational.

The rationale is that it is helpful to sketch which are the values that each stakeholder wants reflected in the OI and how stakeholder would assess whether the OI promotes or protects those values before starting the detailed process of imbuing values.

4.2   Heuristics for the Choice of Values

A first heuristic is based on the acknowledgement that the choice of values needs to take into account three frames of reference. First, the *application domain*, which determines goals and makes some instrumental values relevant and others less so. In Easyrider for example, values related to e-commerce and transportation become relevant, while those associated with, say, health services do not. Second, the *role of stakeholders* influences the choice of values. Stakeholders choose values that are relevant for the domain, however, regardless of the application domain, engineer values always reflect the goal of developing an OI that handles a particular collective activity , owner values always have to reflect the need of engaging users, and user values reflect their motivation and preference for choosing to engage in the OI. The third frame of reference that influences the choice of values is to profit form the fact that the *WIT design pattern* induces a natural separation of design concerns that remain valid throughout the OI life-cycle.

Regarding the use of the WIT design pattern, we argue that in order to embed the terminal and instrumental values of each stakeholder in the OI, one needs to address three main design requirements: (i) to enable collective interaction in a well-defined, limited part of cyber-physical reality; (ii) to set up the rules of the game so that the outcomes of those interactions are consistent with the values of the stakeholders; and (iii) to implement these rules in such a way that the actual online system runs according to those rules. The $\mathcal{WIT}$ pattern facilitates the analysis of those requirements by establishing **nine design contexts** where specific values are involved. These contexts are the six design concerns associated to the relationships between the $\mathcal{W} - \mathcal{I} - \mathcal{T}$ components of the isolated OI (Fig. 1a) and the three design concerns arising from the legal, technological, and social compatibility of the situated OI (Fig. 1b). Two points are worth mentioning: first, all CD, terminal, and instrumental value labels may be localised as more specific labels for each stakeholder in each of the nine contexts; second, not all the nine contexts are equally important for all stakeholders, hence one can rank the degree of involvement —in the participatory design process— of the three stakeholders for each context and each CD value class.

Table 1 illustrates value contextualisation for the OI engineer regardless of the OI domain. The top part gives an interpretation of the CD-value categories and the bottom part declares those contexts of the WIT design pattern where the engineer has the final word on the choice and interpretation of the contextualisation.

Heuristic 4. **Contextualisation:** Value choice depends on the domain of the OI, the actual stakeholder and the WIT-DP context where it is meant to be applied.

The second heuristic for choosing values suggests how to proceed in order to identify relevant values. The idea is quite straightforward: use the goals of the stakeholders to search for values and keep the CD value categories present to prevent overlooking a significant value.

Heuristic 5. **Value selection:** Define the *ultimate goals* of each direct stakeholder, then associate with each stakeholder the corresponding *terminal* and *instrumental* values and validate the selection of instrumental values with the *CD value-categories*.

In practice, each stakeholder is committed to an ultimate goal which ought to be legitimised by an ultimate or intrinsic value. However, that goal needs to be decomposed into means and ends that determine how the stakeholder may achieve its goal. In order to choose the particular means and ends that lead to achieving that ultimate goal the stakeholder will use its instrumental values[1]

The CD value categories serve a dual purpose, on one hand they are useful for labelling instrumental values (something that will be essential for value assessment and for the eventual termination of the operationalisation process); on the other hand, the intuitive understanding of the three categories (and the experience of using them in other OIs) is a practical way of validating that the instrumental values that have been chosen truly constitute a good coverage of each of the three main categories.

Table 2 is a partial contextualisation of the terminal and instrumental values of the owner and the users of Easyrider (the engineer's values are summarised in Table 1). In Table 2 we list only four instrumental values of the owner and users of Easyrider, and refine these with more specific values; some of which are underlined because they are used in Sects. 4.3 and 4.4, and in Table 3 to illustrate the interpretation and representation of value labels. Notice that each instrumental value is labelled with the CD value category it more naturally belongs to.[2]

---

[1] There are two ways of identifying ultimate and instrumental value labels. One is to ask the users to name them [15,33]; another is to draw from available value taxonomies like [12, 13,29]. Following the second path, we propose the CD value categories mentioned earlier: *thoroughness, mindfulness* and *responsibility* [20,22] that serve as intuitive catch-all labels that become more meaningful as they are applied to different design concerns as the design of the OI advances.

[2] Although individual passengers and travel agencies may have different value interpretations, the table stands for a consensus of what values to embed and how that is the result of the participatory design process.

Table 1. Engineer's value contextualisation (independent of OI domain). (1) The generic ultimate goal of an engineer is aligned with each of the CD-value categories, which are translated into intuitive descriptions of their most salient means and ends. (2) The engineer holds the ultimate responsibility for value imbuing in particular WIT pattern design contexts.

---

(1) Engineer's terminal and instrumental values

Engineer's ultimate goal: Design and build an OI proficiently

Thoroughness:
(i) Do the usual stuff to do a good job during the whole life-cycle of the system;
(ii) Adopt best practices and standards in the application domain;
(iii) Make the OI fit for the ultimate goals of direct stakeholders;
(iv) Validate cohesiveness and integrity

Mindfulness:
(i) Engineer all values of owner and users;
(ii) Be transparent about the quality and limits of the OI

Responsibility:
(i) Guarantee cohesiveness and integrity of the isolated OI;
(ii) Guarantee compatibility of the situated OI.

---

(2) Engineer's leadership in the WIT design pattern:
(i) Integrity of isolated OI;
(ii) Cohesiveness of isolated OI;
(iii) Technological compatibility of situated OI;
(iv) Priority design sub-contexts: specification (I→T), implementation (T→I) and user interface (W↔T')

Table 2. Ultimate goals and main instrumental values of the owner and users of the Easyrider OI. Each goal is associated with four instrumental values that guide its achievement. Those instrumental values are in turn partially refined into more specific values – labelled with their corresponding CD-categories – that will be imbued in the system. Underlined values are used in Table 3 and examples.

Railway company	Passengers	Travel agencies
Fill trains	*Buy train tickets*	*Profitable trading business*
Sound management	**Convenience**	**Profit**
adequate return on investment (M), balanced cash-flow (M), ...	flexibility (M), abundant offer (M), ease of use (M)	increase volume (M), increase margin (M), lower costs (M,R), ...
Proficient OI	**Restraint**	**Convenience**
trustworthiness, (R) effectiveness (M, R), impartiality (R), transparency (R), legal compliance (M,R), ...	lower fares (M), ...	easy to use (M), compatible with in-house practices and systems (M), reliable support (M), ...
Good customer relations	**Reliability**	**Reliability**
reliable support (R), accountability (R), privacy (R), ...	secure transactions (M), accountability (M), privacy (M), ...	transparent rules of operation (M), fair competition (M, R), secure transactions (M,R), ...
Good citizenship	**Pleasant travelling**	**Good citizenship**
support SDGs (R), corporate responsibility (R), prestige (M), ...	comfort (M), conviviality (M,T), ...	prestige (M), social recognition (R), ...

One last remark about the choice of values. Since the process of making values operational is gradual, the refinement of value labels is better served by the analysis of only the most salient stakeholder values in the first pass. One need only come back to this step of the operationalisation process when the value assessment process requires an improvement of the alignment of the OI to the stakeholders' values (see Heuristics 11).

4.3 Heuristics for Value Imbuing

Imbuing is a prerequisite for specification. Its objectives are to turn the *intuitive* understanding of a relevant value into an *objective* understanding that may be embedded into the OI. This task of imbuing values in a system involves two efforts: *interpretation* and *representation* of values. These two sub-processes are applied to each instrumental value label and while all stakeholders are involved, the stakeholder who chooses a given value leads the task.

1. Interpretation: Its purposes are to obtain an objective description of the the mechanisms and constraints that support (promote) or maintain (protect) each value, and an objective description of how one can eventually assess whether a value is in fact being protected or promoted. This can be articulated with two heuristics.

Heuristic 6. **Value interpretation (1)** is to articulate the meaning of a value as the *means* and *ends* that are most typical of it in a given context.

The leading stakeholder for a given value, with inputs from the other stakeholders, interprets it by looking at the concrete actions or objects that can afford its achievement and maintenance (the *means*) and identifying the states of affairs that show that the value is actually being promoted or protected (*ends*).

Once the means and ends are articulated, one needs to identify what the observable features of the states of affairs are involved in those means and ends in order to use them for measuring the attainment of a value and stating along those terms the degree of satisfaction of the different stakeholders. Consequently, this heuristic provides the essential elements for the definition of the value assessment models that we discuss in the next section.

Heuristic 7. **Value interpretation (2)** consists in associating with each value *observable features* involved in value means and ends, and discovering stakeholder priorities and thresholds of satisfaction.

2. Representation: From these means and ends, and their observable features, the engineer with input from the other stakeholders decides how to *represent* the instrumental values so that they can be implemented as part of the physical and governance model of the OI (or in the decision model of an artificial agent).

Heuristic 8. **Value representation** translates value interpretations into components of the abstract representation of the OI, that will be the basis for its specification.

Table 3. Imbuing of some instrumental values of Easyrider's owner and users. Each value is interpreted in these examples as one typical end that leads to the stakeholders' ultimate goals in alignment with the corresponding values, and some means that are conducive to the achievement of that end. These means and ends would be represented with some instruments that embody the means, in a way that one may objectively assess whether these values are satisfied or not in the deployed system.

	Passenger	Users and owner	Owner	Owner
Values	Flexibility	Accountability and transparency	Support SDGs	Adequate return on investment
Ends	Allow last-minute purchases, ...	proof of action, ...	promote the use of train to support SDG 7, 9, 13, ...	high occupancy of carriages
Means	Extend purchasing deadlines; install ticketing machines at station;	Reports of relevant transactions, ...	marketing campaigns, ...	attractive fares, ease of purchasing, marketing, ...
Representation	Norms and affordances	Procedures for issuing each report type	Banners and messages, poll	Procedure and physical action; add carriages when needed
Observable	Number of tickets sold close to departure; number of machine-issued tickets	List of reports of each type	Passenger and TA awareness of the good impact of trains	Occupancy level
Thresholds	more than 10% of total sales are late purchases	at least all legally required reports	increase of awareness and acknowledged motivation	between 60% and 80% occupied seats in a carriage

There are essentially three ways of translating value interpretations into value representations: as norms and standard procedures, as affordances, and as information for participants. Table 3 illustrates the interpretation and representation of some instrumental values included in Table 2).

1. Some values are represented directly as *norms* that promote, mandate, curtail, or discourage behaviour; or prescribe the consequences of institutional actions. For example, passengers' flexibility may be *interpreted* as allowing ticket changes, which may be *represented* with a norm that allows ticket purchase and devolution up to five minutes before departure.
   Sometimes a single norm is not enough and a value may have to be represented as a standard procedure. For instance, Easyrider may include protocols for issuing different reports. Such reports —say, tax-valid receipts for every final sale or a refusal to accept a devolution—, are *means* that support the *end* of having evidence to achieve the value of accountability and transparency for stakeholders.
2. A second way of going from interpretation to representation is through the introduction of new entities in the institutional reality that *afford* specific actions or outcomes that promote or protect a value like accountability. For example, passengers' value of travel flexibility may also be supported by allowing the possibility of purchasing and printing tickets in ticket dispensers at the station. In this case the physical model (of $\mathcal{W}$) would need to include ticket dispensers and their use would be regulated with norms that will be part of the "governance model" of Easyrider. In this example, the *affordance of using printed tickets* may require other devices in the station or aboard trains to validate tickets. The owner would have to decide whether the use of printed tickets is worth the extra regulations and the cost of dispensers, or not.
3. The third mode of representing values is as a set of facts, recommendations or arguments that are made available to users with the purpose of influencing

their decision-making. For example, the railway company's instrumental value support sustainable development goal (SDG) can be promoted through banners or messages that appear in the use of Easyrider or in marketing campaigns that make users aware of the beneficial impact of traveling by train (and eventually also increase the number of trips). The achievement of the value is observable, for example, through a customer satisfaction poll and its degree of satisfaction measured through the aggregate opinion users.

4.4   Heuristics for Value Assessment

We now turn our attention to the task of evaluating to what extent stakeholders values are reflected and met in the OI. The imbuing step that we proposed above entails three claims: (i) that —since ends are observable— the alignment of values can be "assessed" somehow (or *measured*); (ii) that stakeholders are capable of determining whether they are satisfied or not with the degree to which the system is aligned with the values they care about —since for each value interpretation, its satisfaction thresholds can be elicited from stakeholders; (iii) that the engineer is able to transcribe measuring and satisfaction into the specification of the OI. We make these claims operational with the construct of *value assessment models*. The value assessment model of a stakeholder *s* has three parts: a list of values, a way to measure each of those values, and a way to combine them.

Heuristic 9. **Value measurement** consists of mapping the observable outcomes that stand for the value and the thresholds expressed by the stakeholder on an ordered set that reflects the degree of satisfaction of the user with that value.

We mention two extreme possibilities of value measuring to illustrate this heuristic. As we saw in the previous section, the interpretation of a value commits to an observable feature that stands for the value and, ideally, to some bounds or thresholds that determine the degree to which the value is satisfied. one form of measuring values that allows for a crisp assessment assumes that the observable feature is an "indicator" (or a scale on a totally ordered set), boundaries determine thresholds that determine not only if the value in question is being satisfied or not but also to what degree.[3] For instance, in Easyrider, a travel agency recognises secure transactions as a mindfulness and responsibility value, which is being interpreted as "honouring deals". This instrumental value is interpreted, in particular, by guaranteeing that travel agencies pay all their dues to the railway company and to other travel agencies. The means the institution has implemented to maintain that value, are to require of travel agencies to post a bond that covers potential harm, and levy a fine for any mishap. The observable outcomes are the costs of the mishaps. The travel agency may use that representation of the value to measure secure transactions and also the satisfaction of its own value of lower costs by the sum of fines it pays over the year and prefer to pay no more than a fixed amount in a year.

---

[3] Ideally, the totally ordered set is mapped onto a convex function whose range goes from -1 (totally unsatisfied) to 1 (perfectly satisfied) and the mapping of thresholds define a region of "satisficing" scores.

A minimalistic way of measuring value satisfaction, on the other hand, may consists simply in mapping all the possible observable outcomes onto a finite set of proxy scores that are each labelled with a degree of satisfaction that reflect the boundaries defined in the interpretation of the value. For example, in Easyrider, the railway company wants to fill trains but not too much if it wants to keep passengers satisfied. The owner satisfaction depends not only on the number of unsold seats (few sold seats, not good; totally full trains, not good either), but also in how the empty seats are distributed in each carriage (few passengers but all stuck at the back, not good; groups of friends seated together, good). Satisfaction of passengers' comfort and conviviality as well as affecting the railway company's balanced cash-flow could be measured, for example with a pairwise preference combination of density vs seat configurations and the degree of satisfaction of each pair with a ranking, say, unacceptable, undesirable, satisfactory, very satisfactory. Even more radical, the value accountability may be interpreted as responsibility by the owner and in this case, if the same bonding mechanism is afforded, its fulfillment duly regulated and its enforcement strict – all these conditions achievable at implementation time – its assessment is *ex-ante* satisfactory.

The third component of the value assessment model is an aggregation function that combines the stakeholder's satisfaction with all and every value; and thus assess the extent to which the OI aligns with the combined set of stakeholder's values. The aggregation function should take into account the priorities and trade-offs between values and other features like their urgency, associated costs or expected evolution of the observable features involved with those values.

Heuristic 10. **An aggregation function** combines the level of satisfaction of several values into a single outcome that represents the aggregate satisfaction derived by the stakeholder from the combination of those values.[4]

A thorough discussion of aggregation functions is beyond the scope of this paper but one can get an idea with a simple version of the engineer's aggregation function. A top-down definition of the engineer's aggregation function may be to aggregate the degree of satisfaction of the engineer with each of its three CD values defined in Table 1, as follows: (i) Assessment of satisfaction of thoroughness and responsibility is essentially technical. The first will be the result of the aggregation of the degrees of satisfaction of the four thoroughness goals and by assessing that mindfulness, responsibility, integrity, cohesiveness and compatibility are dully validated. (ii) Likewise responsibility is assessed through the assessment of the (technical) soundness of integrity and compatibility of the OI. (iii) However, satisfaction of mindfulness requires that all the values of users and owner have been properly "engineered" (specified and implemented) but for that owner and users have to agree on the way their values are interpreted and represented. Thus engineer's mindfulness depends on users and owner agreeing that their own values of throroughness, mindfulness, and responsibility are satisfied with the observable features and thresholds that they agree upon.

---

[4] Note that to determine the alignment of an OI with a set of values, which is the ultimate purpose of making values operational, one needs a top level aggregation function that combines the degrees of satisfaction of all stakeholders.

This very last aggregation involving the satisfaction of the other stakeholders builds on the process of participatory design of the OI and on the assessment of each separate value in terms of the observable feature that stands for it (which is the same for every stakeholder). The way these detailed assessment are aggregated may be different for each stakeholder but in this case, the engineer has priority on some CD design contexts (part b in Table 1) and thus its aggregation function of non-priority context will be that of the other stakeholders but the engineer's may be more demanding for the values in its own priority contexts. The owner, as the stakeholder who is responsible for commissioning, deploying, updating and preserving the operation of the OI, has the last word.

Note that the purpose of the aggregation function is two-fold: first to commit to an encompassing measure of satisfaction that reflects value priorities and trade-offs for the stakeholder; second to determine if the alignment of the OI with the set of values is "good enough" for the stakeholder. Consequently, if the alignment is not good enough, the aggregation function and the value assessment model in general can be used to pinpoint those values that are not properly embedded in the OI. If a global assessment model is not satisfactory, a compromise can usually be reached by revising the aggregation function, simplifying value measurement, and relaxing satisfaction thresholds.

Heuristic 11. **Improvement of value alignment**. When a value alignment is not satisfactory, revise the steps of the operationalisation process backwards until stakeholders are satisfied.

The idea behind this heuristic is the following: from a bottom up perspective, each stakeholder chooses its own values, how to interpret them, and the observable features that are used to determine whether the value is being satisfied (and to what degree) (Heuristic 7). One underlying assumption of OIs is that there are observable features which are common to all stakeholders. However, not all stakeholders will hold the same values in general, and therefore not all observable features will be equally relevant for different stakeholders. This means that each stakeholder will combine and prioritize the observable features in different ways. This difference, is unproblematic unless a conflict of the interpretation and assessment of values among stakeholders arises. When this occurs, the conflict can be resolved by incorporating additional observable features (and the new required means to achieve them) that are relevant for the stakeholder who is unsatisfied with a specific interpretation of a value into means, ends and observable features.

From a top-down perspective, we can assume all stakeholders aggregate values in our three CD categories: thoroughness, mindfulness and responsibility. The aggregation function of each stakeholder is unlikely to be the same in general, and agreement, or some other form of reconciliation should take place, in order to the the OI to be aligned with each of its stakeholders values. This is unproblematic as long as the stakeholders agree on some trade-offs which may be reached if some stakeholders change the weighting of some values in the aggregation function, or choose to relax their levels of satisfaction with respect to certain values.

The final trade-off agreement may be reached by moving back and forth from the aggregation at different levels of value decomposition within each category.

5   Closing Remarks

In this paper we propose heuristics to make stakeholder values operational in online institutions. These heuristics belong to a larger task to provide general methodological guidelines for a principled approach to embedding values in AI systems. It seems clear to us that any such approach requires that values are made explicit, that their interpretation can be translated into a machine executable representation, and that their satisfaction can be objectively assessed. We claim that while these conditions are necessary, we do not impose any further requirements to value theory.

In the heuristics we propose, we remain neutral about the choice of formalisms used for representation and for the assessment of values. (Though we are considering using Z with its ability to capture both agent architectures, multi-agent systems and design methodologies [5,6,16].) However, we believe that for certain types of online institutions (and AIS in general) there are reasons to adopt specific interpretations of each value in terms of a means and ends decomposition that give grounds to more specific representation and assessment conventions, whilst recognising they might not necessarily be unique.

Whilst focus of this paper has been on heuristics for making values operational in governed multi-agent systems, we believe that heuristics could be similarly applied to the embedding and assessment of values in the design of individual autonomous agents. Nevertheless, there are specific aspects of the design process that would need to address the role of values in designing artificial agents' architectures and behaviour. For instance, for an artificial agent that is intended to behave in an ethically-consistent manner, the engineer may commit to some cognitive architecture that includes values as an explicit and necessary construct in their inference-based decision-making models, or make explicit use of value theories that explain ethical behaviour without assuming rational ethical reasoners [24].

We mention elsewhere [21] that one could apply the conscientious design approach to developing tools to prevent undesirable effects of existing third party software. The heuristics we propose in this paper can be used to determine whether the behaviours of a given system is aligned with any explicitly stated values. This leads us to the possibility of adding, to such existing systems, new functionality that ensure they behave with proper alignment with respect to any stated values. This is something we plan to address in future work. In addition, our intentions include developing our approach to support policy makers, evolving stronger good practices, and making use-cases readily available to facilitate uptake.

The process of making values operational that we discuss in this paper is at the core of the Value Alignment Problem, which concerns the embedding of values in artificial autonomous systems and assessing their alignment. However, our proposal can be placed in a wider perspective of developing a theory of value with a distinctive AI flavour. The value theory we foresee would be centered on the *interplay of governance, autonomy, and collective hybrid behaviour* and because artificial autonomous entities are involved, there are meta-ethical, normative ethics, and applied ethical problems that other theories of values do not address. In fact, unlike other theories of value, such an "artificial axiology" purports to embed ethical constructs into artefacts and assess ethical questions associated with them. The approach we envision shares with AI and other sciences of the artificial a peculiar mix of science and engineering; it would draw on constructs and methods from AI and other sciences of the artificial, and require a serious interdisciplinary effort.

Acknowledgements. D'Inverno thanks IIIA-CSIC Barcelona for hosting him during a research sabbatical and his host institution Goldsmiths, University of London for making that possible. Noriega's work is supported in part by the CIMBVAL project (Spanish government project #TIN2017-89758-R).

References

1. Aldewereld, H., Padget, J., Vasconcelos, W., Vázquez-Salceda, J., Sergeant, P., Staikopoulos, A.: Adaptable, organization-aware, service-oriented computing. IEEE Intell. Syst. **25**(4), 26–35 (2010). http://doi.ieeecomputersociety.org/10.1109/MIS.2010.93
2. Alexander, C.: A Pattern Language: Towns, Buildings, Construction. OUP, New York (1977)
3. Alexander, C.: The Timeless Way of Building, vol. 1. OUP, New York (1979)
4. Deming, W.E.: Quality, productivity, and competitive position. MIT Press (1982). https://en.wikipedia.org/wiki/Total_quality_management,   https://en.wikipedia.org/wiki/Kaizen, https://en.wikipedia.org/wiki/Eight_dimensions_of_quality
5. d'Inverno, M., Luck, M.: Development and application of a formal agent framework. In: First IEEE International Conference on Formal Engineering Methods, pp. 222–231 (1997). https://doi.org/10.1109/ICFEM.1997.630429
6. d'Inverno, M., Luck, M., Noriega, P., Rodriguez-Aguilar, J.A., Sierra, C.: Communicating open systems. Artif. Intell. **186**, 38–94 (2012). https://doi.org/10.1016/j.artint.2012.03.004
7. Fjeld, J., Achten, N., Hilligoss, H., Nagy, A., Srikumar, M.: Principled artificial intelligence: Mapping consensus in ethical and rights-based approaches to principles for AI. Technical Report 2020–1, Berkman Klein Center Research Publication (2020)
8. Friedman, B.: Value-sensitive design. Interactions **3**(6), 16–23 (1996)
9. Friedman, B.: The ethics of system design. In: Computers, Ethics and Society, pp. 55–63 (2003)
10. Friedman, B., Hendry, D.G., Borning, A.: A survey of value sensitive design methods. Found. Trends Hum.-Comput. Interact. **11**(2), 63–125 (2017)
11. High-Level Expert Group on Artificial Intelligence (AI HLEG): Ethics Guidelines for Trustworthy AI (2019). https://digital-strategy.ec.europa.eu/en/library/ethics-guidelines-trustworthy-ai
12. Hofstede, G., Hofstede, G.J., Minkov, M.: Cultures and Organizations - Software of the Mind: Intercultural Cooperation and its Importance for Survival. McGraw-Hill, New York (2010)
13. Inglehart, R.: Human beliefs and values: A cross-cultural sourcebook based on the 1999–2002 values surveys. Siglo XXI (2004)
14. Jones, A.J.I., Sergot, M.: A formal characterisation of institutionalised power. Logic J. IGPL **4**(3), 427–443 (1996)
15. Liscio, E., van der Meer, M., Siebert, L.C., Jonker, C.M., Mouter, N., Murukannaiah, P.K.: Axies: identifying and evaluating context-specific values. In: Proceedings of the 20th international conference on autonomous agents and MultiAgent systems, pp. 799–808. International Foundation for Autonomous Agents and Multiagent Systems (2021)
16. Luck, M., D'Inverno, M.: Structuring a Z specification to provide a formal framework for autonomous agent systems. In: Bowen, J.P., Hinchey, M.G. (eds.) ZUM 1995. LNCS, vol. 967, pp. 46–62. Springer, Heidelberg (1995). https://doi.org/10.1007/3-540-60271-2_112

17. Morley, J., Floridi, L., Kinsey, L., Elhalal, A.: From what to how: an initial review of publicly available ai ethics tools, methods and research to translate principles into practices. Science and Engineering Ethics **26**(4), 2141–2168 (2019). https://doi.org/10.1007/s11948-019-00165-5

18. Noriega, P., Padget, J., Verhagen, H.: Anchoring online institutions. In: Casanovas, P., Moreso, J.J. (eds.) Anchoring Institutions. Democracy and Regulations in a Global and Semi-automated World. Springer, Heidelberg (2022). in press

19. Noriega, P., Padget, J., Verhagen, H., d'Inverno, M.: Towards a framework for socio-cognitive technical systems. In: Ghose, A., Oren, N., Telang, P., Thangarajah, J. (eds.) COIN 2014. LNCS (LNAI), vol. 9372, pp. 164–181. Springer, Cham (2015). https://doi.org/10.1007/978-3-319-25420-3_11

20. Noriega, P., Sabater-Mir, J., Verhagen, H., Padget, J., d'Inverno, M.: Identifying affordances for modelling second-order emergent phenomena with the WIT framework. In: Autonomous Agents and Multiagent Systems - AAMAS 2017 Workshops, Visionary Papers, São Paulo, Brazil, 8–12 May 2017, Revised Selected Papers, pp. 208–227 (2017)

21. Noriega, P., Verhagen, H., d'Inverno, M., Padget, J.: A manifesto for conscientious design of hybrid online social systems. In: Cranefield, S., Mahmoud, S., Padget, J., Rocha, A.P. (eds.) COIN -2016. LNCS (LNAI), vol. 10315, pp. 60–78. Springer, Cham (2017). https://doi.org/10.1007/978-3-319-66595-5_4

22. Noriega, P., Verhagen, H., Padget, J., d'Inverno, M.: Ethical online AI systems through conscientious design. IEEE Internet Comput. **25**(6), 58–64 (2021)

23. North, D.: Institutions. Institutional Change and Economic Performance, CUP (1991)

24. Perello-Moragues, A., Noriega, P.: Using agent-based simulation to understand the role of values in policy-making. In: Verhagen, H., Borit, M., Bravo, G., Wijermans, N. (eds.) Advances in Social Simulation. SPC, pp. 355–369. Springer, Cham (2020). https://doi.org/10.1007/978-3-030-34127-5_35

25. Perello-Moragues, A., Noriega, P., Popartan, L.A., Poch, M.: On three ethical aspects involved in using agent-based social simulation for policy-making. In: Ahrweiler, P., Neumann, M. (eds.) ESSA 2019. SPC, pp. 415–427. Springer, Cham (2021). https://doi.org/10.1007/978-3-030-61503-1_40

26. van de Poel, I.: Embedding values in artificial intelligence (AI) systems. Minds Mach. **30**(3), 385–409 (2020)

27. Rokeach, M.: The Nature of Human Values. Free press (1973)

28. Russell, S.: Living with artificial intelligence (2021). https://www.bbc.co.uk/programmes/b00729d9/episodes/downloads

29. Schwartz, S.H.: An overview of the Schwartz theory of basic values. Online Read. Psychol. Cult. **2**(1), 11 (2012)

30. Searle, J.R.: The Construction of Social Reality. The Penguin Press, Allen Lane (1995)

31. Simon, H.A.: Models of Man: Social and Rational. Wiley, Hoboken (1957)

32. The IEEE Global Initiative on Ethics of Autonomous and Intelligent System: Ethically aligned design: A vision for prioritizing human well-being with autonomous and intelligent systems, first edition (2019). https://standards.ieee.org/content/dam/ieee-standards/standards/web/documents/other/ead1e.pdf

33. Umbrello, S., Van de Poel, I.: Mapping value sensitive design onto AI for social good principles. AI Ethics **1**(3), 283–296 (2021)

34. Verhagen, H., Noriega, P., d'Inverno, M.: Towards a design framework for controlled hybrid social games. In: Social Coordination: Principles, Artefacts and Theories, SOCIAL.PATH 2013 - AISB Convention 2013, pp. 83–87 (2013)

Author Index

Printed in the United States
by Baker & Taylor Publisher Services

Printed in the United States
by Baker & Taylor Publisher Services